SADOMASOCHISM
IN EVERYDAY LIFE

LYNN S. CHANCER

Sadomasochism in

Everyday Life:

THE DYNAMICS OF POWER

AND POWERLESSNESS

RUTGERS UNIVERSITY PRESS
NEW BRUNSWICK, NEW JERSEY

Library of Congress Cataloging-in-Publication Data

Chancer, Lynn S., 1954-
    Sadomasochism in everyday life :   the dynamics of power and
powerlessness / Lynn S. Chancer.
        p.   cm.
    Includes bibliographical references and index.
    ISBN 0-8135-1807-5—ISBN 0-8135-1808-3 (pbk.)
    1. Sadomasochism—United States.   2. Power (Social sciences)
3. Interpersonal relations.   I. Title.
HQ79.C43   1992
303.3—dc20   91-32362
                                                                   CIP

British Cataloging-in-Publication information available

CONTENTS

Acknowledgments   viii

Introduction Reflecting on a Set of Personal
and Political Criteria   1

PART ONE

Expanding the Scope of Sadomasochism

Chapter 1   Exploring Sadomasochism in the American
Context   15

Chapter 2   Defining a Basic Dynamic:
Parodoxes at the Heart of Sadomasochism   43

Chapter 3   Combining the Insights of Existentialism and
Psychoanalysis: Why Sadomasochism?   69

PART TWO

Sadomasochism in Its Social Settings

Chapter 4   Employing Chains of Command:
Sadomasochism and the Workplace   93

Chapter 5   Engendering Sadomasochism:
              Dominance, Subordination, and the Contaminated
              World of Patriarchy   125

Chapter 6   Creating Enemies in Everyday Life:
              Following the Example of Others   155

Chapter 7   A Theoretical Finale   187

Epilogue   215

Notes   223

Index   231

ACKNOWLEDGMENTS

This book germinated in the context of provocative discussions about sexuality within the feminist movement over the course of the 1980s. In addition, it grew out of numerous "personal" and "political" concerns dating back even earlier. Nonetheless, without the support of many friends and a number of professors at the Graduate Center of the City University of New York, the dissertation on which the book is based would not have been possible.

Stanley Aronowitz, the chair of my dissertation committee, has been a consistent source of inspiration and is a valued friend. His own vitality is infectious and intellectually challenging, and he contributed greatly to the fuller development of arguments proffered here. To the other members of my doctoral committee, especially Roslyn Bologh and Michael Brown, I also express appreciation for their extremely useful comments and suggestions. Taken together, they supplied more support than I expected to find in graduate school for a theoretical dissertation. Last, I also wish to thank Bogdan Denitch for urging me to come to the Graduate Center, and for facilitating a rather unique environment in the sociology department that legitimized unconventional projects of social, political, and cultural criticism.

David Forbes, Phyllis Jacobson, Isabel Pinedo, Jan Poppendieck, Ruth Sidel, Wendy Simonds, and Susanna Danuta Walters read the manuscript at various stages and provided much constructive criticism. Jennifer Hunt took the trouble to give me extensive advice from a psychoanalytic perspective on an earlier draft. I wish to thank Leslie Salzman for perusing chapters of the manuscript and for returning detailed remarks that allowed me to benefit from her precise and lawyerly mind. For comments on the chapter that deals with "enemy others," I am indebted to Phil Kasinitz, Jonathan Rieder, and Loic Wacquant. To Jon, too, I express appreciation for many interesting conversations and for his collegial generosity and encouragement over the course of completing this manuscript.

Much gratitude goes to Lila Karp both for editing the full manuscript and for extensive substantive suggestions. Long discussions with Lila sustained me through some difficult moments and gave me a measure of confidence that the arguments of this book may ring true to others. She and Renos Mandis also raised provocative questions with which I agree that a second book on this subject (if one were to ensue) would have to commence. Similarly, I extend both acknowledgment and admiration to Ellen Willis, a superb editor with whom I had the fortune of working while she was still at *The Village Voice*, for editorial assistance and general commentary.

To Bill DiFazio and Donna Gaines, thanks both for their warm friendship and for nurturing our shared belief in the need for ongoing intellectual and political community. I have also been involved in several feminist study groups that contributed important perspectives upon, and criticisms of, this work. Several groups of students at Hunter, Yale, and Barnard colleges (especially those in my feminist theory seminar last spring) have responded with lively discussion, questions, and comments to material presented in this work. I thank them all for the many joys I have experienced in teaching and learning from them.

Charlotte Sheedy provided an immediate and extremely encouraging response to this manuscript and gave much time and energy to it as my agent. Then as now, I appreciate her professionalism and the fact that I know she took on the work from a sense of conviction. Marlie Wasserman, editor-in-chief at Rutgers University Press, has been just as engaged and engaging. I am glad to have had the chance to work with so dynamic and enthusiastic an editor, and with an excellent press. Thanks should also go to Marilyn Campbell and Willa Speiser at Rutgers, and to Roberta Hughey for a fine copy editing job that went above and beyond the ordinary call of duty.

As the best friend I ever imagined and a remarkably beautiful human being, Annamaria Morales was with me even when she did not read the manuscript. Without her and Michael, I don't think I would have known in my heart and mind that alternatives to those sadomasochistic dynamics that are compulsive and destructive really can exist. And, to and for Michael, it would truly take another volume to describe the love and respect he has so steadfastly provided. There is no doubt in my mind that without him, this book would have been inconceivable. Finally, in peaceful memory of my parents, Annette and Marty, I am sorry that they are not here to see their daughter's first book and to realize what it meant to her. I would have liked to have made them proud, of themselves as well as of me.

SADOMASOCHISM
IN EVERYDAY LIFE

◆ ◆ INTRODUCTION ◆ ◆

Reflecting on a Set of Personal and Political Criteria

Ten years ago, I found myself deeply involved in two simultaneous love affairs that at the time I might have dubbed passionate or, in a more pessimistic moment, mildly destructive. I certainly would not have called them sadomasochistic, reserving that term, as do most people, primarily for sexual activity in which relations of dominance and subordination are enacted (even if veiled in privacy). In retrospect, however, I have slowly become convinced that those intimate relationships were neither as uncommon nor as different from sexual instances in which an inelastic ritual of dominance and subordination can also be played out as I once believed. My relationships exhibited the same structured, recurring features that can operate in many situations that are sadomasochistically oriented, whether the pattern appears in the well-publicized realm of sexuality or in other instances of everyday life, whether between a particular teacher and student, or a worker and boss, or in other highly charged encounters between parties caught in symbiotic enmeshments of power and powerlessness.

In this book I suggest that a distinctive dynamic between self and other that I call "sadomasochistic" does pervade each and all of these realms, reflecting deeply embedded aspects of our social and psychic experience far more widespread than is generally realized. Rather than sadomasochism being merely the property of individuals, our culture itself is deeply oriented in a sadomasochistic direction. We are living in a society sadomasochistic in that it bombards us with experiences of domination and subordination far more regularly than it exposes us to sensations and inklings of freedom and reciprocity.

Several caveats should be stated at the outset. The type of sadomasochistic relationship to which I allude is not simply synonymous with *any* interaction wherein power and powerlessness, dominance and subordination, are noticeably present. Clearly, a relationship between a student and teacher, or a given employer and employee, may be hierarchically organized—one person holding a position of relatively greater power, the other relatively powerless—and yet not be sadomasochistic in the sense of the term I will be exploring. It is not masochistic, for example, to want to stretch out and give oneself up to a sexual embrace or a vigorous massage, nor sadistic to bark at one's friends or intimates from time to time while omitting the niceties of polite social intercourse. Hierarchy and unequal power are necessary but not sufficient conditions for the ground on which a sadomasochistic dynamic may later develop. This distinction is important to bear in mind. Without it, we might overlook those aspects of exerting power and control (or letting oneself not exert them) within the world and over our lives that are positive and affirmative and that would necessarily occur in any event.

Nor does the sadomasochistic dynamic of this description necessarily equate with what straight or gay partners often call "top/bottom," role-playing, or "power/trust" S&M sexual activity, wherein the partners adopt passive and/or active positions as part of erotic pleasure, diversity, and consenting mutual self-exploration. In fact, practitioners of S/M sex sometimes see themselves as challenging and subverting sadomasochism in the more rigid and encompassing social sense to which this book refers.[1] As elaborated in chapter 1, theoretical precision requires recognizing that playing with sadomasochism is not identical with, even though it may deeply relate to, sadomasochism itself. And to consciously ape, enact, and mimic the desires for power and powerlessness bequeathed (at least in part) by a society shot through with controls in some cases may be paradoxically to rebel against that cultural universe, undermining a compulsive sadomasochism by bringing it to the surface and making it visible, public (as it were). It may be to admit openly characteristic patterns of behavior that a given social order, if indeed this order was of a sadomasochistic orientation, might prefer to keep hidden and unacknowledged.

No, the sadomasochistic dynamic referred to here is a very particular but common social relationship based on power and powerlessness, dominance and subordination, that by definition would have to conform to all of the following four interrelated criteria. First, an excessive attachment exists for both parties, extreme in that neither feels as though the other can be done without; dependence is of a symbiotic character in that both sadist and masochist feel a compulsive need for physical, but most critically for psychic, connection to the other. Second, interaction has a repetitive and ritualistic character in that the sadist is consistently drawn toward a position of control while the masochist is just as constantly in the persona of the more controlled. Their contact is not randomly shaped but repetitively structured, so that neither can assume or unassume their respective roles by an arbitrary or simple exertion of will.

For example, a white South African (male or female) who oppresses a black servant will not in general wish to switch positions any more than the man in the United States who batters his wife is likely suddenly to submit himself to being battered or than the boss is apt to want to become his or her own employee. And it may indeed be difficult for women sexually repressed as children to switch from a masochistic to sadistic position in their fantasies, just as the young investment banker accustomed to adopting a servile attitude toward the superior he wishes to impress may find it hard to assume a more commanding tone at will. That people in these multifaceted situations feel drawn, or have been drawn into, repeating lines and enacting parts that vary only with a certain mathematical regularity points suspiciously to the chance that something must have occurred earlier— in their exposure to social, to psychological, or perhaps to both types of influences—to predispose them, not necessarily of their own choosing, in one or the other direction. In other words, they may be legally coerced or socially sanctioned into a sadomasochistic dynamic in the present—by slavery, for instance, or by the structure of a job itself—or they may be party to circumstances that, though consensual at the moment, reflect rigid inequalities encountered in the past.

The third criteria presaging the presence of the dynamic is that at the same time sadomasochism has a regularized character, it is also a dialectical form of interaction, constantly changing and moving, in flux as the actions of the sadist bring about reactions on the part of the masochist and vice versa. Consequently, the static manner in which relationships between victims and victimizers are often described cannot capture the reality of sadomasochism's gyrations. As argued in chapters 2 and 3, both the insights of existentialism and those of psychoanalytic theory (not only object relations but more traditional Freudian and Reichian theory as well) can be used to show that each position has the potential for transformation into its opposite: the sadist has a constant potential for masochism, even if generally not realized or realizable by conscious intentionality; the masochist has an analogous potential for sadism. Each faces the possibility and perpetual risk of turning into the other, an observation that, if valid, has enormous ramifications for questions of how and whether personal and political changes are realizable in the form intended by their myriad architects. Persons who angrily break away from masochistic situations may find the original dynamic creeping in again through the back door, perhaps imperceptibly, when they note in horror their own sadism threatening to reiterate the old relationship—perhaps the former masochist is now sadistically blaming someone else for the suffering he or she has endured. Or a once powerful sadist, stripped by life of authority, may reproduce the masochist's resigned demeanor.

If one makes a logical extension of this third characteristic, the interesting possibility arises that sadomasochism may be a useful concept for understanding not only individual but group dynamics as well, for grasping simultaneously the personal and the political dimensions of change. The oppression of the colonized—the racially or territorially or sexually discriminated against—may smack of forcibly induced masochism that could conceivably turn sadistic if not caught and brought to conscious awareness during processes of revolutionary transformation and political protest. What happens when, say, a group formerly powerless and situated masochistically comes to power—will a transformation in both private and public relations evolve, or will old patterns continue to haunt the new in a seemingly altered, but formally identical, guise? A glance at the sweep of twentieth-century events should convince us that this dilemma is a critical one—perhaps even *the* critical one—and not solely theoretic and abstract. History seems to repeat itself in what could be called cycles of sadomasochism. In the Middle East, Arabs and Jews continue to vacillate between oppressed and oppressor roles. The history of Stalinism and recent rebellions from it could likewise be interpreted through this perspective: for instance, in Rumania, where the Ceaucescu government was recently called to task for its Stalinist injustices, ex-Communist officials of the regime face trial and possible execution (which may create a new set of resentments). The irony is, of course, that the Ceaucescu government itself arose in reaction to the terror of tsarism. Once masochistically situated, a group may become sadistic only to create a new class of masochists. Sadomasochism thus penetrates to the core of our social psychology, threatening to repeat itself until its underlying motivations are understood and begin to be consciously acknowledged.

But the fourth, last, and most central criterion for determining the presence or absence of the sadomasochistic dynamic is whether individuals (or groups) positioned masochistically face severe consequences should they question, talk about, or challenge the power of those individuals (or groups) who are structurally more powerful. Throughout this book, an analytical distinction is made between "limits" and "conditions." The former refers to the fact that it is virtually impossible to imagine a society in which restrictions and regulations do not exist at all, limiting freedom within some rational and mutually agreed upon guidelines. Therefore, in the aftermath of revolutions, limits are arguably unavoidable and must be set in self-defense against counterrevolutionary actions of groups seeking to halt the course of transformations and freedoms desired by majorities of people. But into this category would also fit more everyday situations such as that of teachers who place limits on students while not otherwise interacting in a sadomasochistic fashion; employers who likewise assign the duties of employees; parents who limit children, disciplining these young persons so they do not harm themselves or others; lovers who, though adoring, nonetheless have certain expectations of their beloveds; or practitioners of an S/M sex in which limits are set within a consensual framework. In a few of these cases such as those of the teachers or parents, ostensibly, limits are not exercised for the sake of power alone: rather, the goal may be to facilitate eventual transcendence of the hierarchical relationship as the less powerful party to it (the students, the children) progressively approaches a level of parity with the more powerful one. On the other hand, it is quite another matter for, say, a revolution to go through a predictable stage, a state of rage, at which time it is vengeance and not merely self-protection that begins to be sought. It is quite another matter for teachers or schools to punish young students who dare to question their authority (an extreme though telling example here is Beijing in 1989, when young Chinese students were arrested and in some cases killed for demonstrating in a way that displeased the Communist party hierarchy). It is something else again to be fired, or to face the threat of dismissal, if one objects to, protests, or tries to alter given workplace conditions, or if, as women often do, one faces discrimination or sexual harassment that makes one worry about promotion or about losing one's job. It is another thing to find that as a child, one's attempts to question or become angry at one's parents are repressed either through overt abuse or verbal or nonverbal messages; to discover one's lover becomes mean or exerts physical or emotional withdrawal, both intimidating in their effects, should one express some measure of dissatisfaction with, or autonomy from, a given relationship; to be in a sexual relationship in which the sadist refuses to stop, or beats and harms the masochist the more the latter protests, demonstrating an insidious drive for control. Such responses I dub "conditions," so as to signify the punishing and enraged repercussions that will almost always ensue should the persons(s) situated masochistically try to break from a symbiotic bond. Our sadomasochistic dynamic is in evidence if the question of whether the masochists must pay for their rebellion can only be answered in the affirmative.[2] Under those circumstances where "conditions" come to exist, sadomasochism begins to develop either on an individual/microcosmic or on a societal and more macrocosmic plane.

But perhaps the texture of this sadomasochism can be sketched more vividly in one of its variegated forms if I return to the relationships with which I began. In doing so, I hope to indicate the impossibility of separating myself from what I am describing, the writer from the written about: I am arguing that sadomasochism affects us both within and without, at once at the level of the personal and of the political, the microcosmic and the macrocosmic, the individually psychic and the collectively social. Looking back, my two college love affairs closely conformed to those four criteria of sadomasochism, but subtly, in a way that was barely perceptible to me at the time. Certainly they did not exemplify the usual, overtly physical connotations of sadomasochism. No reins were physically visible: they were figurative rather than literal, however experientially real. In other respects, however, the resemblance was striking.

At the time, I was madly in love with one young man who returned my affection inconsistently, with a certain aloofness and detachment. I was constantly insecure and uncertain about his feelings toward me. Though he insisted he loved me, I sensed our relationship to be eminently conditional. I seldom felt confident about whether he would greet me with warmth or with coldness; I felt any day, at any moment, my lover might reject me, judge me, find me wanting in some quality I could not guess beforehand. And, rather than diminishing his attractiveness, I believe in retrospect that the anxiety-ridden state with which he became associated was the dominant explanation of his particular appeal. I knew other men who were intelligent, who were interesting, who were interested in me. But it was only he with whom I was in love—that allegedly most mystical of states. His judgments were far more valuable than those of others because he alone called into question my feelings of self-worth, putting them into doubt by his coolness and by the uncertainty of his continuing affection. The others seemed to like me indiscriminately, to be content with me just as I was. He alone required that I be different, that I work for his approval; only he hinted that I was not good enough and that my existence could not be its own justification. Instead, calling forth a never-ending specter of possible rejection, disapproval, and pronouncements of diminished worthiness, he set up for me a true calling in the sense that Max Weber described for the restless and insatiable Protestant—the quest for a satisfaction that proves perpetually elusive.[3] I, too, had a quest, perhaps not altogether dissimilar from the one upon which those lonely Calvinists embarked. Whereas they pursued approval from God, I wanted it from my lover. Their security would be in heaven; I pursued mine on earth.

Like theirs, my salvation had its conditions: there were unstated though definite regulations, rules of the game I had to follow if my lover was not to reject me. It became necessary to anticipate his reactions, molding myself around the shape of his projected desires. Simone de Beauvoir wonderfully described the feeling in *The Second Sex*: I came to view myself indirectly rather than directly, through the eyes of the other instead of through my own. The obsession of that famous Proustian masochist, Charles Swann, himself madly in pursuit of the beautiful courtesan Odette, was painfully familiar. As discussed in chapter 3 with regard to the idea of thwarted mutual recognition acutely depicted by Jessica Benjamin in *The Bonds of Love*, no satisfaction seemed possible or forthcoming: the pursuit had no apparent meaning, no conceivable rationale, apart from itself.[4]

The second young man was infatuated with *me*. The roles somersaulted: if I played Swann to the first young man's Odette, I was simultaneously Odette to the second young man's Swann. I felt more secure, freer, safer in his company than I did with the first. That the second loved me was not perpetually in doubt, but neither did I deem his love valuable. The second man seemed to love me too much; I wondered what was wrong with him. His flaw was fatal, irredeemable. Out of a corner of my mind's eye, I watched in dismay as I became to the second what the first was to me. But where did I, narrating the story and perceiving both parts at once, fit into all of this, I remember asking myself. Surely I was in the masochistic role in the first relationship, but was I sadistic in the second? Eventually, the conclusion reached by other observers of sadomasochism became apparent to me as well: namely, that as long as I was capable of masochistic behavior, I also had a capacity—realized or not—for the sadistic. The two were inseparable, locked as though in a dance.

Indeed, I had a veritable interest in maintaining my relationship with the second man. It comforted me, better enabled me to take risks with the other—just as for spouses, the loyalty of a partner often renders extramarital pursuits mysterious by comparison. My interest held, regardless of whether the second man could obtain fulfillment of his quest within the structure of our dynamic. Certainly I represented as much a calling for him as the other did for me. Whether or not I chose to play a sadistic role, so long as I pursued the first man, I functioned to the second as sadistic symbol because I necessitated that he would have to pursue *me*. Like the paradoxical effects of suicide, my masochism could not separate its apparent directedness toward myself from its effect upon others. "Loving" the elusive other, I could never love the second man, yet he felt that if only he tried this, that, or the other tactic, perhaps. . . . The approval and vindication he and I sought were always maddeningly beyond reach, receding behind an infinite regress of quixotic advances. And in its multifaceted complexity, pieces of our sadomasochistic jigsaw puzzle fit into other sadomasochistic triangles. What of the person we knew who wanted the approval of the second man, he who had become elusive and potentially more valuable because of me? What of the person who might attract the first man by the challenge of her/his ambivalent lack of interest?

The puzzle can be given yet another twist. In my relationship with the first man, was my masochism really pure and uninfected by its opposite? Did the persistence of my pursuit (and, of course, that of the second young man's pursuit of me) indicate love or also hostility about dependency and about perceived delegitimation (the proverbial love-hate relationship)? Did we feel anger we would have directed toward them, toward the other, if a whole panoply of circumstances—social and psychic conditioning—had not habitually aimed it at ourselves? Certainly, as time went on, I had to resent the first man and the second had to resent me for the exaggerated authority each respectively represented. There was, therefore, always the seductive appeal of that opportunity to get back at the authority figure, the possibility of striking out in the same way the more conventionally political behavior of groups repeats itself sadomasochistically—an opportunity that, of course, might never become more than an ever-present potentiality. But if an opportunity to strike out at someone else (such as the second young man) did arise, would my resentment have been truly aimed at him (or his at me), and if not, at whom—or (as I hope to continue arguing in turning to a social critique) at *what*?

In effect, I am inquiring whether the Proustian Odette may have sensed that she, too, was loved only under certain very definite conditions—would Swann have loved and valued her if she were no longer elusive, if she gave him the approval and vindication he sought? And, if so, for how long? Perhaps we have been conditioned by social circumstances to fear the consequences of simply being human, of relaxing our vigilantly clenched minds and bodies that are posed and ready for judgment. Put slightly differently, did Odette perceive that if she stepped off her pedestal, she might cease to be Odette, having devised her own obsolescence only to have another Odette fashioned in her place? In a society where value seems to rise with unattainability, do we not feel compelled not only to fashion for others but also for ourselves elusive guises, until finally we are estranged from both?

This recounting of and reflection upon personal experience may appear to be a digression from the subject at hand—that is, from a closer inspection of the sadomasochistic dynamic, its characteristic features, its myriad incarnations. However, I will insist that personal experience is also the subject at hand, and that this example conforms to the four criteria of sadomasochism mentioned above just as thoroughly as would a more impersonal or typically sociological instance. In the chapters that follow my aim is to return to our sadomasochistic dynamic more systematically, to place it under closer inspection. This book is intended to be an exploration: an investigation into whether and how sadomasochism does affect more than just a few isolated persons, whether it is carved of both personal and political dimensions, and if indeed it does accurately refer to a persistent current in contemporary culture and social psychology.

The reader may wonder in all of this, why *sadomasochism*? Why use this particular concept rather than others to discuss relationships grounded in stubborn patterns of dominance and subordination? It is, after all, a loaded and quite controversial term. I would argue that the notion has several distinct theoretical advantages. First, unlike other descriptions, sadomasochism allows power to be understood in terms of an internally transformable dynamic: sadism and masochism are two sides of a similar coin, with all the already cited consequences. Second, in and of itself, sadomasochism is not an essentialistic concept. There is nothing about sadism or masochism that is intrinsically, inherently, or biologically bound to one group or another. Instead, sadomasochism refers to a ritualized pattern that in and of itself does not discriminate by race, class, sex, ethnicity, or sexual preference. Part of its complexity, as we shall see, is that a man can be a masochist as well as a sadist, a woman sadistic as well as masochistic (even though, of course, sadomasochism becomes gendered within a particular historical context); similarly, sadomasochism is not the exclusive property of straight or gay persons, or of a particular national minority, or of a caste.

Sadomasochism is conceptually useful, too, in providing an analytical link between relations of domination and subordination that run the gamut of the behavioral spectrum. Because of the traditional association of *sadomasochism* with sex, the term does not permit our most intimate relationships to be divorced from the workings of power in other arenas of social life. And, finally, even though the word *masochism* has been used very problematically (that is, in blaming the victim by accepting the simplistic definition of the masochist as taking pleasure in pain), it implies a dynamic in which the masochist has a choice to participate or not.[5] The idea of sadomasochism—and the open acknowledgment of one's own sadistic or masochistic inclinations—immediately suggests agents, existential subjects, who act out a dynamic that is not determined or static. Sadomasochism's own fluidity thus makes of the masochist's victimization not an inevitable, but an alterable, social fact. The experience of victimization is thus confronted straight on, noneuphemistically, so that change becomes an authentic possibility.

I have organized the book as follows. In chapter 1 I continue to place sadomasochism in a larger conceptual framework but start to focus on examples drawn specifically from the U.S. context. Since this is the culture with which I am most familiar, the majority of empirical examples used in the book as a whole refer to the U.S. experience. Chapter 1 also takes up the question of why there has been a resurgence of overt cultural interest in sadomasochism over the course of the 1980s and into the 1990s. Though focusing on the United

States, however, my hope is that my observations will be applicable to other mass societies as well, both capitalist and communist, wherein similarly structured experiences may be tending toward the production of similarly sadomasochistic social psychology.

In chapters 2 and 3, I describe with greater precision the characteristics and workings of the sadomasochistic dynamic toward which I have been pointing. Chapter 2 begins with a hypothetical example of a sexually sadomasochistic situation that exemplifies the definitional criteria of the dynamic: both sadist and masochist remain rigidly within the parameters of their respective roles; they are symbiotically interdependent; and the masochist has been forcibly restricted in such a way that challenging sadomasochistic intercourse (literally or figuratively) is, again, only possible under certain rules of the game that do not ever really allow the power of the sadist to be challenged. Given the constantly changing character of sadomasochism, how is an interaction between sadist and masochist most likely to play itself out? The purpose of chapter 2 is to cull paradigmatic traits of the sadomasochistic dynamic from a simple, basic, and potentially revealing instance. Here my approach is a predominantly phenomenological one, studying the way a form of human interaction appears on the surface to try to trace its internal logic.

In chapter 3, however, I elucidate my observations in chapter 2 through other explanatory frameworks. Beginning with Hegel's problem of recognition and Benjamin's restatement of it, I show that conclusions reached from existentially oriented premises are virtually identical to those that can be argued from within a more psychoanalytically oriented framework (again, in this chapter I draw on object relations theory as well as on more classical Freudian and Reichian insights). Ideally, by the end of part 1, a deeper definition of the sadomasochistic dynamic will have been reached. If several theoretical traditions employ different languages and conceptual frameworks to depict what appears to be at base a similar experiential reality, then our definition is that much stronger, one in which that much more confidence can be placed.

Once having defined the sadomasochistic dynamic, in part 2 I go on to see if, why, and how it might actually operate when we shift gears toward a more explicitly sociological framework. In chapters 4, 5, and 6, I concentrate on an analysis of three social examples—work, family (and other relationships of intimacy), and discriminatory phenomena in general—which, taken together, greatly affect the quality of most people's day-to-day lives. My approach is parallel in each of these segments. Initially, in each chapter I discuss whether the structure of these social institutions or experiences creates tendencies that accord on a *collective* level with the characteristics of sadomasochism adduced in the Introduction and chapters 1 and 2 on a more *individual* plane. In examining the ground on which a specifically *social sadomasochism* may be erected, I use theoretical perspectives drawn from feminist theory and from a number of sociological traditions including the Marxist and Weberian. In the latter portion of each chapter, I turn to empirical examples drawn from an extant literature on everyday life in the separate, yet interrelated, arenas of work, family, and discrimination. Last, the Epilogue is devoted to an overview of the theoretical argument I have tried to build throughout this book. The Epilogue frames questions about how a related work on this subject might develop from the point at which this one concludes.

Before proceeding, I stress that the word *tendency* is used here quite literally, for the structure of social institutions cannot once and for all determine the way we will react to life within the walls of our home, our school, or our workplaces. As George Herbert Mead described in *Mind, Self and Society*, we are constantly interpreting and symbolizing our social experiences back to ourselves; we act and re-act in ways surprising and multifaceted. Therefore, my analysis is of a poststructuralist bent insofar as sadomasochism does not have to develop, as though axiomatically, from the quite real social structural tendencies I will describe; whether or not it does so, and our responses to these tendencies, are affected by many cultural, social, and psychic factors that cannot be easily ascertained in advance. And, yet, to describe deeply rooted cultural textures—in this case, sadomasochistic orientations that may be embedded in the structure of contemporary societies themselves—nevertheless strikes me as a worthwhile endeavor. For the very process of naming such tendencies shapes and affects how consciously we react to them. At least, this is the assumption with which I begin.

PART ONE

Expanding the Scope of Sadomasochism

Exploring Sadomasochism in the American Context

Terrified by profound feelings of aloneness and fear in contemporary mass societies, human beings often seek to escape their isolation either by controlling others or having others exert control over them. So postulated philosopher and psychoanalyst Erich Fromm in 1941 as he and other intellectuals of a group that came to be known as the Frankfurt School sought, in desperation themselves, to understand the rise of fascism. The extreme form of totalitarianism they analyzed in German nazism died out. But what of the larger social, political, psychic, and sexual conditions that spawned the "authoritarian personality" sketched by another Frankfurt theorist, Theodor Adorno—were they buried in the same grave?[1] Or do relationships steeped in dominance and subordination continue to simultaneously oppress and seduce, albeit far less obviously, in an alienating, ultracommodified, and now ostensibly postmodern world? Do we turn, perhaps at some moments more hungrily than at others, to those strategies for relating to others that could be dubbed "sadistic" and "masochistic" because of pressures still socially generated, though now in less glaringly lethal form?

According to Fromm, sadistic and masochistic "character structure" can arise in large numbers of people in defense against modern society's failure to provide them a reliable sense of community and belonging.[2] As sociologists from Tonnies to Durkheim likewise contended in the late nineteenth century, the development of complex urban life brought individual freedoms at once liberating and burdensome compared with the more guaranteed securities of the close-knit, premodern world. Expected to be independent and self-sufficient, in reality the postindustrial individual was (and is) so belittled by feelings of insignificance, powerlessness, and anonymity that a need for others became (and becomes) paradoxically more acute. But this need for social security in the widest sense is neither acknowledged nor openly accepted as a collective responsibility. At least, however, via sadomasochism—either through dominating others or being dominated by them in a host of formal and informal ways—a strategy exists. One can create, and perhaps try to recreate, pleasurable feelings of vital linkages to, and symbiotic connections with, particular others and the outside world. Sadomasochism thus comes to permeate everyday life.

Nor is it especially remarkable that it would be sadomasochistic forms of interaction that are readily adoptable. As I will suggest, sadomasochism accords with the highly stratified and inequitable structures of social experience in modern life—patriarchy, capitalism, the bewildering layers of bureaucracy—to which we have become accustomed and habituated. Of course, this is not to suggest that sadomasochism did not exist prior to the particularly modern interpretation of it that Fromm propounds. In addition, it may be related to a variety of psychological and emotional factors that can preexist in individual cases. Nevertheless, as Fromm hypothesized in *Escape from Freedom,* the degree of "marked dependence on powers outside of themselves, on other people, or institutions, or nature," on "magic helpers . . . personified as God, as a principle, or as real persons such as one's parent, husband, wife, or superior," may be exacerbated and become particularly evident during historical periods when social anxieties are at their height.[3] Enter one explanation for the appeal of an authoritarian leader as the besieged pre-Weimar Republic began to disintegrate, or, for that matter, the appeal of strong leaders who take control of situations, while making peace or in waging war, even in the United States today.

But the critical question of whether this analysis is relevant to life in the United States in the early 1990s remains. Although the United

States is not a fascist state, the claim can still be made that the current era is one in which questions of insecurity and insignificance, as well as of dominance and subordination, take on an especially loaded meaning. For the first time, the United States has little choice but to begin acknowledging that it is not an unrivaled financial superpower but instead suffers from the ongoing specter of a depressed economy and a foreign debt so enormous as to be incomprehensible. The enormity of *perestroika* and of a disintegrated Soviet Union has robbed Americans of an external enemy and a cold war in which they can believe, and foreign-policy makers have had to acknowledge the significance of new historical actors and alliances—Germany and Japan, for instance—well on their way to dislodging the traditional U.S. hegemonies.

To some, the memory of Vietnam still mockingly demonstrates that invincibility can no more be taken for granted in the military sphere than in the economic. This suspicion lurked even as the United States invaded the Persian Gulf and attempted to take refuge in fresh nationalistic exhortation and the resuscitation of new bad guys. Meanwhile, the nice guy popularity of Ronald Reagan and the election of George Bush as his heir attest to a conservatism that is at least in part a desire to hold on to the traditional and, therefore, to the familiar and secure. Then, too, over the course of the last decade, a well-known study entitled *Habits of the Heart* implied the intensity of many Americans' longing for a sense of community and acceptance they simply do not obtain at work, for example, where job security is often in question and self-worth must continually be proved.[4] A sense of meaning, Bellah et al. argued, is lost, difficult to discover, or both, in a world where insecurities are experienced both personally and politically.

Regarding that supposedly more privatized realm of personal relations and the family, social workers and sociological researchers have produced alarming statistics on the scope of both domestic and other forms of violent crime, bombarding the mind with descriptions of rage turned outward into incidents of battering, rape, or child abuse of a decidedly sadomasochistic variety. Popular psychological literature is of late replete with references to "co-dependency" (a recent phrase redolent of the kind of symbiotic neediness Fromm equated with sadomasochism), whether a given author is describing alcoholism or drug abuse or "addictive" relationships with others. And, over the last few years, publishers have no doubt noted that prominent on the best-seller list have been self-help titles such as *Men Who Hate Women and the Women Who Love Them* and *Women Who Love Too Much*—books that counsel women to abandon destructive relationships and, by extension, to defy the frequently controlling behavior of men.

If there is any common denominator beneath the apparent diversity of these "social facts" (to borrow Émile Durkheim's sociological phrase), it may be that in each case some degree of connection to others is frantically sought. Perhaps last-ditch efforts are being made to grab for safety and a sense of fleeting control amidst the increasingly frightening reality of powerlessness. This may be occurring even if the price of that effort is the risky one of extreme dependence upon and guilt toward others and oneself, of destructive violence, or of never being able to relax a vigilant and domineering hold and watch over those others' lives.

From Fromm, then, can be borrowed a vision of sadomasochism as a social phenomenon inexplicable in terms that are merely individually oriented. If one wants to understand the genesis of sadism and masochism en masse, one surmises from his ideas, it is ludicrous to focus on people as though isolated from a larger historical context. This would be far too simple, a convenient and distracting diversion from the issue of whether social systems themselves tilt us habitually toward sadomasochism through their ideological premises and their ways of organizing daily experience. At the same time, this wider conception suggests that sadomasochism can and does manifest itself in a variety of social spheres and situations. In and of itself, a compulsive desire to control or be controlled is a generalized feeling, an amorphous and underlying state that permeates one's whole being and enacts itself in a panoply of different modes. Sadomasochistic interaction, then, may be a thread that subtly weaves its way through a number of otherwise dissimilar relationships in which we are frequently entwined: at the workplace, at school, in love, or with friends, family members, or significant or insignificant others to whom we are intimately related at home or in bed.

Yet, it is only this last context—sexuality—with which sadomasochism is most often associated, even if sex may be only the most obvious among the day-to-day encounters wherein desire, power, and powerlessness are experienced. But mention "sadomasochism" to most people and an underworld of pornographic scenery replete with black leather, whips, and chains springs almost immediately to mind. Sadomasochism frequently is taken to connote sexual and/or violent exchanges between two individuals—the sadist and masochist—who play out relationships of dominance and subordination in a language of explicit physicality. Generally consensual in the sexual realm, pleas-

ure and gratification ensue from the structured nature of their ren-
dezvous: for the sadist, from the experience of dominating; for the
masochist, from the experience of being dominated.

This association in common parlance tends to individualize S/M,
shifting attention away from questions of society's own possibly sadomasochistic characteristics and the other forms sadomasochism may
also embrace. And yet, given the origins of the term itself, the association is neither surprising nor coincidental. Freud borrowed the word
from Krafft-Ebing's classic work on sexuality, the 1898 *Psychopathia
Sexualis,* and proceeded to call sadism and masochism "component
parts" of the sexual instinct in his well-known *Three Essays on Sexuality.*[5]
(See chapter 3 for more detailed discussion of Freud's three separate
theorizations of sadism and masochism: two of these linked sadomasochism explicitly with sexuality, while the third—"moral masochism"—encompassed sadism's and masochism's tendency to take
nonsexual shapes, too.)

In turn, Krafft-Ebing was influenced by the description of sexual
and violent relationships in the writings of two aristocratically born
European novelists, the Marquis de Sade and Leopold von Sacher-
Masoch. From Sade's works (*Justine* or *The Hundred and Twenty Days at
Sodom*) came the notion of sexual pleasure resulting from the inflic-
tion or tolerance of pain, whereas Sacher-Masoch's *Venus in Furs* detailed erotic joy in being overwhelmed by another person more
powerful and authoritative than oneself. Based on clinical conclusions
similar to those reached by Freud, Krafft-Ebing believed sadism and
masochism to be part and parcel of the same underlying entity; moreover, the potential for taking pleasure in both positions always
seemed to exist within the same person. Consequently, Krafft-Ebing
coined a new type of sexual behavior, "sadomasochistic."[6]

Sadomasochism has connoted not only sex, but a type of sexual
activity that society has traditionally viewed as aberrant or deviant. As
did Krafft-Ebing (note the "psychopathology" in his title), Freud cate-
gorized sadomasochism as a sexual "perversion."[7] Over a century earlier, Sade's own writing had brought him into conflict with the state
and those bourgeois norms of sexuality that Freud—at his most sexist
and heterosexist moments—contributed to epitomizing and prescrib-
ing. As Angela Carter richly portrays in *The Sadeian Woman,* fear of
Sade's treatises with their depictions of a sexually violent imagination
caused Sade to spend most of his adult life in prison or asylums
(there, for "sexual dementia"), even though "nobody considered him
mad in everyday terms" or, for that matter, criminal.[8]

For many, the sexual whips-and-chains association traceable to the literature of Sade and Sacher-Masoch still smacks of the deviant and the taboo. There are disturbing signs that images of sadomasochistic sexual activity may still be encountering legal repression in the contemporary climate of cultural conservativism and of governmental restrictions encroaching on First Amendment liberties and sexual freedoms. In the United States, the photographs of Robert Mapplethorpe were appropriated by Cincinnati sheriffs and his shows censored for their allegedly harmful sexual content in 1990; sadomasochistic imagery figures openly in Mapplethorpe's work. Moreover, pressure from Jesse Helms and other conservative lawmakers in 1990 forced the National Endowment for the Arts (NEA) to withdraw grants awarded to four performance artists because of the sexually explicit nature of their work. A notorious clause in NEA contracts now demands that recipients guarantee they will not use grant money for "depictions of sadomasochism, homoeroticism, the sexual exploitation of children, or individuals engaged in sex acts which, when taken as a whole, do not have serious literary, artistic, political, or scientific merit."[9]

Yet, the very fact of governmental repression suggests that there has been a shift concerning visibility of sexual forms of sadomasochism, toward a far greater degree of public interest and acceptability over the last ten years. Even if one confines sadomasochism to its usual but limited association with sex and sexuality, as a phenomenon it appears to be more and more common—and undoubtedly an object of cultural fascination. Of late, sadomasochistic sex is more likely to be labeled "kinky" rather than "sick" by sophisticated cosmopolitan dwellers; and the term now circulates in casual conversation with more frequency and fewer stigmatized associations. Concomitantly, curiosity about overtly sexual sadomasochism appears to have spread beyond the old confines of pornography and prostitution into a more mainstream public presence.

The assertion that sadomasochistic sex figures more and more prominently in current U.S. practices and cultural imagery is not difficult to illustrate. As a subset of contemporary pornography, it is featured regularly and sometimes as a standard element of films, videos, and magazines; sadistic and/or masochistic practices are routinely demanded as part of the female or male prostitute's repertoire. While there is no way of knowing how often S/M takes place in people's homes, clubs devoted exclusively to sadomasochistic sexual activity exist in New York as well as in other urban centers. Outside the world of pornography, black leather and silver studs have taken on high fashion faddishness, co-opted from the avant garde punk and biker subculture. (Interestingly enough, similar apparel was frequently donned in the late 1920s cabaret culture of pre-Nazi, Weimar Republic days.)

Sadomasochism has moved into other spheres of mainstream popular culture as well. In the world of commercial Hollywood filmmaking, director David Lynch's 1986 *Blue Velvet* achieved quasi-cult popularity with its suggestion of sexually sadomasochistic eruptions in the heart of U.S. suburbia, and in 1987 the novel *9-1/2 Weeks* became a film starring respectable leads Kim Basinger and Mickey Rourke as lovers in a tempestuous sadomasochistic affair. More recently, one can cite Spanish director Pedro Almodovar's re-released *Tie Me Up, Tie Me Down, Wild Orchid* (filmed by the same director as *9-1/2 Weeks*), David Lynch's 1990 *Wild at Heart* (which, like most of his work, can be said to be fundamentally *about* sadomasochism in the cosmic sense conveyed by *Blue Velvet*), and Peter Greenaway's *The Cook, The Thief, The Wife and Her Lover*. Even Woody Allen's *Crimes and Misdemeanors* comically alludes to sexual sadomasochism when the sister of the befuddled filmmaker played by Allen tells him how she was tied up by her boyfriend. These are among those films that consciously represent or make reference to sexual sadomasochism as their subjects per se. If one were also to include those films in which sexual relationships not acknowledged to be sadomasochistic contain depictions of men acting abusively sadistic toward women (or vice versa, as in the tricky *Fatal Attraction*) in regard to sex, the list would be virtually endless. It would have to contain a vast number of films in the horror genre; erotic suspense thrillers of the Brian DePalma variety (in 1990, for instance, films like *Internal Affairs, Bad Influence,* or *Blue Steel*) in which women are almost always the objects of violence, brutality, and competition between men; and macho films of the Sylvester Stallone (*Rambo*) and Clint Eastwood variety.

On television, Calvin Klein commercials for Essence and Obsession exude an S/M texture, sometimes in color and sometimes in stark black and white, alluding subtly or not so subtly to the sexiness of power. Ads for Guess jeans often portray women adopting an implicitly sadomasochistic pose: as sociologist Ruth Sidel recently elaborated, Guess's magazine copy shows young women either mounting or leaning at the feet of young men who seem to be "calling the shots."[10] A massively viewed and cliché-ridden made-for-TV movie entitled *Favorite Son,* aired shortly before the November 1988 Bush-Dukakis election, satirized the frightening prospect of someone like Dan

Quayle suddenly catapulted into the presidency. The character of the barely disguised Quayle clone, played by Harry Hamlin, was presented as drenched in sadomasochism, on the one hand beating his wife and, on the other, himself whipped into sexual and political submission by a beautiful, domineering/dominatrix administrative aide. (Here, politics, gender, sex, and psychology all blended finally into a cherchez la femme theme.) In the TV arena, too, David Lynch made an appearance with his hit serial *Twin Peaks*, a Gothic postmodern soap opera meant to smell of sadomasochistic intrigue just as subtly but surely as do the Calvin Klein and George Marchiano Guess jeans commercials. Sexual sadomasochism has broken through the walls of high culture, too, as evidenced by recent dance and novel critics' commentaries on an S/M orientation in the arts, in literature, and in the images of photographers like Helmut Newton (in addition, of course, to Mapplethorpe).

Finally, the emergence of sexual sadomasochism into greater public visibility is also apparent within intellectual, academic, and feminist circles. In 1986, Barbara Ehrenreich entitled a book chapter about the effects on women of the much-vaunted sexual revolution "The Lust Frontier: From Tupperware to Sadomasochism," detailing a suburban Tupperware-style party at which the display of S/M paraphernalia was greeted not with surprise but with curiosity.[11] In Ehrenreich's view, S/M's new currency may be in part a by-product, for women as well as for men, of gains bequeathed by social movements originating in the sixties—most notably, the feminist and gay and lesbian rights' movements. One hopes that a long-term and sanguinary legacy of these movements has been greater respect for a range of sexual preferences, including sadomasochism. To be turned on by, but most importantly to be able to talk about, explore, and admit to being turned on by, sadomasochistically oriented wishes and fantasies may be indicative of a freer society in which a multiplicity of sexual rights and options have flowered and become relatively more available and tolerated.

At the same time, Ehrenreich is a cultural reporter sufficiently careful to note that sadomasochistic sexual practices have also been the subject of an intense and ongoing debate among feminists and intellectuals alike (both straight and gay, female and male). These "sexuality debates" (as many feminists have dubbed them) erupted into public controversy at a now much-cited academic conference on sexuality held at Barnard College in April 1982 wherein sadomasochism became a key issue. Shocked Barnard College administrators had censored a pre-conference brochure because of an image it contained of a razor blade placed between the spread-eagled legs of a woman. But the heart of the dispute was the claim of a West Coast lesbian group called SAMOIS (after the dominatrix in Pauline Reage's classic work on sexual sadomasochism, *The Story of O*) that they were just as entitled to representation on conference panels as were any other feminist participants. SAMOIS's members openly proclaimed the legitimacy of sadomasochism as a sexual practice in which they engaged and believed they had every right to engage.

The outcome was that the planners of the Barnard conference defended SAMOIS's right to participate on sexual libertarian grounds. Including Alice Echols, Carol Vance, and Ellen Willis, these feminists had organized the conference largely out of concern about whether "cultural feminist" attitudes had come to assume unquestioned predominance within the women's movement as a whole. Echols and others contended that cultural feminists, such as those involved with the group Women Against Pornography (WAP), often tended to associate women's sexuality with a pure and idealized vision, with an "erotica" (as distinct from the contaminated world of pornography WAP hoped to outlaw through local ordinances) from which disconcerting and misogynistic images of power and powerlessness would be absent. But what if, Echols and Willis persuasively argued, this view of women's sexuality had also resulted in the setting up of a feminist superego of "politically correct" sexual practices? What if it tended to intimidate those women whose experiences did not neatly correspond to this (for them) sanitized vision?[12] Women may have come to fear acknowledging pleasure they might find in heterosexuality, in pornography, or—as is most relevant here—in sadomasochistically oriented sexual practices, politically correct or not. By repressing the truth of some women's internal psychic realities, the feminist movement risked playing into yet another version of sexual repressiveness—a central component of the oppression against which feminists had rebelled in the first place.

That the complex issues raised at the sexuality conference are still being hotly contested today attests to interest in sadomasochism having surfaced conspicuously not only in mainstream cultural practices and imagery *but even in terms of academic discourses on and about itself.* Not only sadomasochism but analyses, mental representations of, and reflections upon sadomasochism have added to its public presence in contemporary America: this book, in fact, exemplifies and contributes to the very phenomenon I am describing. Interestingly enough, though, neither Ehrenreich in her popular sociological writing nor feminists at Barnard expressed much concern about developing a broader conception of sadomasochism. In contrast to a perspective like Fromm's, they, too, implicitly accepted our common linguistic tendency to ally sadomasochism predominantly with sex—perhaps sadomasochism's most glitteringly commercialized, most voyeuristically seductive, and certainly sexiest (figuratively as well as literally) incarnation.

Of course, I do imply neither that discussion of sexual sadomasochism is undeserving of a public place in its own right, nor that sexuality isn't a highly significant site of sadomasochistic desires. Focusing on sadomasochism as a broader phenomenon should not neutralize the specific characteristics of sexuality itself as a unique experience that involves both biological and social forces. At the same time, I do posit a theoretical danger in focusing so much attention on sexual S/M that a sadomasochistic *society* is able to escape through the back door, relatively unscathed and perhaps a bit grateful. Certainly, on the one hand, as the Barnard conference planners showed, it is unacceptably repressive to judge and attempt to control the explorations, fantasies, and desires of individuals interested in consensual S/M sex. (Such judgment is also ludicrous. Clearly implied in the proposition that we live in a sadomasochistic society is the idea that it would be startling if most of us did *not* experience forms of sadomasochistically oriented titillation, sexual or otherwise, at some point in our lives.) But on the other hand, it is just as troubling to thereby shirk from evaluating those more general sadistic and masochistic behaviors—sexual and nonsexual—we *would* wish to alter because they are not freely chosen and compulsive, those that relate to social experiences of a coercive character. After all, the ability to make judgments—to believe certain types of societies and ways of relating to others are better or worse than others—is fundamental to the very genesis of social movements. In a sense, this is their raison d'être, containing dreams of heightened freedoms and of possibilities for change. To forget these dreams threatens to negate the ideological power that fed those movements initially—including, of course, feminism.

The sadism of the imperialist, the racist, the xenophobe, the sexist, the homophobe; those persons who may take masked but real pleasure in abusing powers derived from their occupational situation— perhaps the boss, the prison guard, the cop, or the army sergeant, sometimes the teacher and the priest; the sadist who oppresses his or her lover, or child, or friend, in ways mental as well as physical, subtle as well as overt; or take the example of a masochist who finds herself or himself situated on the other side of any and all of these sadistic coins, often through no choice of her or his own, who tries to fight back from within the veiled and oft-indirect anger of a defensive powerlessness. As I will elaborate with regard to a Hegelian "problem of recognition" (see chap. 3), there are, and were, good reasons to criticize these myriad forms of sadomasochism judgmentally. But the above examples more closely resemble the characteristics of the *sadomasochistic dynamic* I began to define in my Introduction (and will continue to define in chapter 2) than they do the type of consensual S/M sexual activity described in depth by writers such as Pat Califia.[13] Ironically enough, by the Introduction's definition, S/M sex may in many cases not be terribly sadomasochistic at all (of course, in other instances it might—see the distinction made in chapter 2), based as it often can be on more or less equal power/trust relationships wherein the bottom (the presumed masochist) *can* question and challenge the power of the top (the presumed sadist), and where often it is the former and not the latter who is seen as calling the shots.

Indeed, S/M sex may mimic, mock, and appropriate to itself the sadomasochistic dynamic that is the subject of this work. The two need not be equivalent: the former may be a shadow of the latter, not the real thing. At the same time, S/M sex and the sadomasochistic dynamic of my description cannot be totally unrelated, either, any more than (in the terminology of French semioticians) a signifier can be severed entirely from what it signifies nor an image detached from the reality upon which it depends. Thus, it should be possible both to recognize the legitimacy of individuals' consensual pleasure in S/M play and fantasy, and to criticize the very real social structures that play partially reflects. It should also be possible to criticize certain types of relationships rather than others without having this judgment equate with suppression of individual freedoms. A judgment is in fact being made each time someone consciously engages in S/M sex and differentiates it from a rigid dominance-and-subordination interaction. Why make the distinction unless there is something being judged that one wishes to differentiate from? An analogous logical argument can be made about the relationship between rape as a masochistic fantasy frequently experienced by women who live in patriarchal societies, and rape itself: that women can, for a variety of reasons, be excited by a representation of a rape does not justify the sexist conclusion that they in any way wish to be raped in reality. One wants to indict the rape, not the fantasy—and certainly one does not want to let the rapist off the hook. The fantasy can allow women to take pleasure, subversively, from within a subordinate position that has traditionally repressed their sexuality and surrounded it with guilt and taboos. Nevertheless, the goal of altering the way in which sexist societies have been structured should not be lost, since that structure goes a long way toward explaining why those fantasies took a particular form in the first place. So, too, in a more generalized sense, should the culpability of sadomasochistic society as a whole not slip from sight.

Exactly what is it about society that we hope to change, and that we might be in danger of letting off the hook through a too narrow association of sadomasochism with its sexual manifestations? The ramifications of social modes of organization like patriarchy and capitalism for producing sadomasochistically oriented social psychologies in large numbers of people have yet to be analyzed. And, of course, these social structures may in part contribute to the genesis of sexual sadomasochism itself, and to its current appeal in contemporary life. Before turning to a brief discussion of capitalist social psychology, I will look at how patriarchy relates to the development of sadomasochistic dynamics in women and men and to the texture of their everyday relations, inside and outside the bedroom.

Meaning "law of the father," a patriarchal society is definable as one in which men consistently hold dominant positions of power. The scope of male dominance extends across the board, from apparatuses of state control like the military and the police, to the realms of economic, political, technological, and scientific knowledge (referred to by French theorist Michel Foucault as the "knowledge/power" axis), on through power exercised by men within hierarchically structured nuclear families. As feminist theorists have by now elaborated with extreme thoroughness, this system of social organization has traditionally confined women to the family and associated them with the private worlds of nature, domesticity, and emotionality because of their reproductive functions and their greater contact with biological processes.[14] Within the family, not only women's day-to-day activities but their sexuality, too, has undergone extreme restrictions and controls. Women's sexuality has been surrounded by guilt, by a coerced division between women who are pure and good (read: asexual and monogamous, women who reproduce legitimately within the bounds of marriage) and those who are bad and sexual. Little wonder, then, if fantasies of rape at one level represent a release—under duress—from feelings of guilt about sexuality and sexual pleasure.

And from all of this it has followed that, under patriarchy, the more powerful public spheres where men predominate have been considered superior and of more value than the private realms of domesticity, biology, and nature with which women have been linked. According to a well-known article by anthropologist Sherri Ortner, this valuation has been rationalized by the perception of nature itself as threatening and out of control: since women are associated with the world of biology, they, like nature, need taming and domination.[15] A host of secondary hierarchies ensues, rooted in the primary one promulgated along these lines of sexual politics: women come to be seen as the "second sex" of de Beauvoir's description, the passive relative to the active, the secondary relative to the primary, and the inessential relative to the essential. Correspondingly, elevated and supposedly greater social worth is accorded to masculinity, which comes to be equated with a nonemotive version of rationality, with externality and instrumentality. These ideological presuppositions may continue to hold sway in a patriarchal society even when and if women move into previously male-dominated positions of power. Thus, feminists take into account both ideology and the actual occupants of powerful positions in defining patriarchy.

It is not difficult to segue back to sadomasochism from this condensed yet evocative feminist analysis. Patriarchy creates a tendency for sadomasochism to become gendered, as women are socialized into a relatively more masochistic position, men into roles that are relatively more sadistic. (As I mentioned earlier, however, this is only a tendency: in and of itself, sadomasochism is not inherently gendered.) Both externally and internally, within and without the family, a sense of powerlessness is imbibed by women as the other side of the relatively greater sense of power bestowed on men. Moreover, as de Beauvoir elaborated in tracing a little girl's trajectory from adolescence to marriage and motherhood, women have been taught that their own route to power—to feelings of legitimacy, worth, and social gratification—lies along the path of winning some type of approval and sense of legitimacy from others, from men. Consequently, a feeling of more than average dependency on a male other is built into the feminine situation as women seek *human* recognition they have been denied within the patriarchal order. Paradoxically, then, deference to the other's power and ability to affect one's life may become the only means for forging a vicarious, if estranged, relationship to self. To undergo self-subordination may become habitual, ringing with the ambivalent comfort of the familiar and potentially rewardable. That women come to assume a relatively masochistic role in relationships and in love, then, may indicate just the reverse of masochism's usual signification—that is, the taking of pleasure in pain. Instead, a proclivity in women to assume a masochistic role more regularly than do men strikes me as a rather predictable, logical, and ultimately defensive outcome of any society organized patriarchally, of any situation that sunders human characteristics by gender, bestowing unequal worth on its divided parts.

The relationship of sadism to a socially conditioned masculinity can be similarly explained. Just as women confront relative powerlessness vis-à-vis men, so men become habituated to relative power and privilege vis-à-vis women. If theorists of patriarchy are correct, men come to believe in the inferiority of that feminine sphere with which feelings began to be associated. Or so it seems. When one delves deeper into the sadist's behavior (as I will try to do in the following chapter), the fact of patriarchal control over women may be seen to indicate something quite different from disdain for parts of life one truly devalues. Perhaps male dominance has been driven by insecurity about emotional experiences speciously melded to the feminine; although perceived as frightening and threatening, these experiences are nevertheless longed for and needed. Why control someone else and restrict their freedom unless one feels that holding onto that other is a necessity rather than a luxury?

Therefore, the tendency for men to assume a relatively more sadistic posture in relationships of intimacy and love likewise stems from divisions basic to societies organized around patriarchal principles. Perhaps, for both men and women, a foundation for sadomasochistic dynamics was laid when persons cast on either side of this gendered divide, constrained within masculine and feminine personalities, later attempt to clutch, cling, grasp, seize, or merge with the other. Perhaps they obsessively, compulsively, reach to repossess that part of themselves that has been coercively alienated. In the other, women may be reaching for a vicarious sense of self-confidence and independence, of ability to deal with the world at times in a matter-of-fact and instrumental way. Men may yearn for the ability to be expressive, intimate, vulnerable, and psychologically introspective about feelings conscious or unconscious, to tolerate uncertain and uncontrollable parts of life to which we are all subject.

One way of understanding the popularity of the how-to literature of the *Women Who Love Too Much* variety, and the commonality of the day-to-day relationships of love and intimacy that these books describe, is through the lens of this theoretical perspective on patriarchal structure. Of late, bookstores have devoted new subject sections to prolific outpourings of titles that include, in addition to the aforesaid best-seller, works like its sequel, *Letters from Women Who Love Too Much*, and *Men Who Hate Women and the Women Who Love Them*, *Love Addiction*, *Born to Please: Compliant Women/Controlling Men*, and *Why Can't Men Open Up?*[16] Usually written by therapists who use case studies drawn from their patients' experience, almost all these books discuss relationships destructive for and of the parties within them. They are primarily geared toward assumedly heterosexual women, offering step-by-step procedures for overcoming social conditioning that has inclined them toward a masochistic role in relationships where men act sadistically.

Books like Robin Norwood's *Women Who Love Too Much* and Susan Forward and Joan Torres's *Men Who Hate Women and the Women Who Love Them* typify the genre as a whole in that they do not usually label the repetitive patterns they describe "sadomasochistic." Norwood prefers to speak of "loving too much," while Forward and Torres employ "misogyny"[17]—understandably shrinking from the victim-blaming usages to which the term *masochism* has been put. Yet the distinction would appear to be a euphemistic one when the stories related by their patients are those of rigidly hierarchical inequalities between (dominating) men and (dominated) women that almost perfectly conform to the characteristics of dynamic sadomasochism. One finds recurring patterns of extreme dependency on the side of both partners, along with compulsively followed rituals of behavior and a clear understanding that the power of the "sadist" cannot be questioned without punishment or withdrawal of affection resulting for the "masochist." Women in Forward and Torres's book would indeed have to answer in the affirmative questions like "Does he assume the right to control how you live and behave? Does he yell, threaten, or withdraw into angry silence when you displease him? Do you walk on eggs, rehearsing what you will say so as not to set him off? Do you often feel confused, off-balance, or inadequate with him?"[18] Clearly, something that entails lived patterns of dominance and subordination is occurring in these intimate relationships between women and men, even when, or if, nothing particularly kinky is transpiring in the bedroom and the overt accoutrements of sexual sadomasochism are absent.

Yet, in not linking the relationships they describe to a more generalized sadomasochistic dynamic, these pop psychological writers repeat the fallacy of letting social structures off the hook by individu-alizing the same broadly based phenomena that narrow interpreters of S/M sex have tended to ignore. It is instructive that while therapists such as Norwood and Forward and Torres bemoan the common re-currence of the patterns they depict, their treatments are geared al-most exclusively toward altering only individual behavior (their books usually end with a five- to-twelve point psychological plan). But, if the problem's genesis also relates to the structure of patriarchal society itself, a far wider net would have to be cast. It would also be necessary to call attention to whether male domination of social institutions and the coercive powers of the state have ever been successfully dislodged, to examine whether or not the feminine realm of emotionality has risen in value and the masculine world of instrumentality fallen to an equivalent level. It would be necessary to look at the structures of everyday life in the family, sexual and nonsexual, to see whether women and men have actually come to live in greater equality. It would be necessary, in other words, to resuscitate a version of femi-nism that was oriented to the individual as well as to the collective, the psychic and the social, the political as well as the personal. All of which, of course, the popular literature fails to do.

The existence of patriarchy as a social system nevertheless cannot fully explain sadomasochism's currency in a recent and more histori-cal sense; after all, patriarchies have existed for thousands of years. Why the rising to the surface of sadomasochism now, especially when relations between the sexes have changed somewhat over the last twenty years, and the old patriarchal assumptions of separate spheres no longer do hold as stubbornly as before? It is clichéd knowledge that women have moved into the labor force in record numbers, while men's greater involvement with child rearing and domestic work is touted in multiple media, from home-oriented magazines that show men with a soft baby pressed to their cheeks to film variations upon the same theme. Shouldn't an effect of the feminist movement on U.S. society over the last several decades be to portend less sado-masochism rising to the surface rather than more, as the rigidity of patriarchal structures is under attack?

The most obvious explanation is that while gender segregation may have been altered officially in U.S. life, on a more profound and unof-ficial plane, the changes have been only superficial. Male domination of institutions of coercive power—technology, science, the military—does in fact persist, in the United States as elsewhere around the world. Women find themselves working, yet still in many cases worry to the point of obsession about personal appearance and attractiveness to the opposite sex—about weight watching, and aerobic classes to keep fit, and cosmetics, and achieving the right look. Beneath the surface, a nagging doubt may persist as to whether a fair bargain can be struck with only one party to the exchange present. Has the right to careers and greater economic independence been granted to women only at the price of loneliness, only at the cost of familial intimacies that were a prime fringe benefit of male companionship under the old system? As I have written elsewhere, depictions of gender roles in late 1980s films such as *Fatal Attraction* and *Baby Boom* have portrayed precisely this apparently punishing trade-off between high-powered achievement, on the one hand, and husbands and babies, on the other.[19] Moreover, the fact remains that greater economic independence was only granted to some women, anyway. The growth of a feminized poverty that differentially affects lower class and minority women, puts the lie to the thought that even in the economic sphere equality has been reached. That amidst these schizophrenic messages women may feel a heightened concern about holding on to men who themselves may now feel liberated from attachment would not have been hard to predict.

At the same time, and contradictorily, the influence of feminism has made women more aware than ever before that relationships based on extreme patterns of dominance and subordination are to be rebelled against: an oppressive situation is not accepted with 1950s-like resignation but inspires cognitive dissonance. The lure of the old, the call for courage in the new, suddenly mingle in a decidedly anxiety-producing fashion. The former makes its influence felt by feeding, maintaining, and perpetuating that earlier tendency toward masochism; the latter may force sadomasochism to the surface, to public attention, to the eye of publishers who have learned that books like *Women Who Love Too Much* strike a chord of mass recognition. And so I would see sadomasochism as a contemporary symbol of transition and struggle, an almost schizoid strategy of groping toward a historical compromise. It is a compromised form that affects men as well, many of whom feel themselves even more concerned and confused about losing women and the world of the feminine than they might have formerly, and thereby driven toward more controlling behavior, even greater fears of intimacy, or both. On the other hand, men may sense the ability to be even more cavalier and confident about women's nervousness in a situation of change. As a result, what has been called the modern push-pull relationship, explored in greater detail in my discussion of the family and gender relationships (see chapter 5), may take shape in the form of the sadomasochistic dynamic soon to be further outlined. It is as though we have been set adrift in an anomic world where Fromm's definition of sadomasochism as a defensive strategy for holding onto others doesn't seem all that farfetched.

The notion of sadomasochism as an historically compromised form can now be recycled to elucidate its recent sexual prominence in like manner. Confusion between the old and the new reigns here, too, as traditional sexual mores are reasserted and lent tragic ideological reinforcement by the advent of AIDS. The new conservativism has functioned as a dam, staving off a flood of social and cultural changes too overwhelming to be immediately absorbed, yet too firmly entrenched to be completely displaced. The net effect of this shift in attitudes may be to make sex again a repressed and scarce commodity, something worrisome and harder to approach with the carefree spirit of play. In one sense, increasing interest in S/M sex may correlate with social factors that have decreased sexual openness and freedom: in another, this interest lends credence to Ehrenreich's point about sexual diversity not going underground so easily once it has been let out of its Pandora's box. The existence of a community of both straight and gay persons who openly practice the top/bottom form of S/M mentioned earlier in the Introduction brings together old patterns of dominance and subordination and elements of rebellion, of willingness publicly to flaunt conscious pleasure in adopting sadistic and masochistic roles. Contradictory and compromised, symbiotic and desperate, yet perhaps the flashing neon of a rather wild and unpremeditated insurrection against something in the cultural air— sadomasochism does not seem out of place historically.

But patriarchy, including the traditional nuclear family with its restrictive notions of sexuality, comprises only one possible explanation for socially based experiences of domination and subordination. Sadomasochism, both as a constant undercurrent and more particularly within the climate of the 1980s, may be fertilized by processes that occur in other social institutions as well. Returning from gendered sadomasochism to my second example, one to which the entirety of chapter 4 is devoted, work relationships in the context of U.S. and other advanced capitalist societies may also foment feelings of excessive neediness and dependency on others. The psychological consequences of patriarchy and capitalism as differing social structures in this respect overlap, like concentric circles that share one important shaded area of intersection. In the case of patriarchy, a tendency toward sadistic exercising of power and masochistic experiencing of powerlessness has been bifurcated along the lines of gender, with each side symbiotically requiring services only the other can provide. In the case of capitalism, a similar fissure, with analogous emotional consequences, seems to unfold along class lines. Still other considerations underline the dissimilarity between these two forms of social organization, raising sadomasochism to yet another plane of complexity. When capitalism is introduced, it becomes obvious that male workers are frequently placed in a position more comparable to masochism than to sadism, while women are no longer entirely excluded from high-powered jobs that encourage domination rather than subordination as their habitual modus operandi. Turning to the workplace, consequently, is one of several ways to illustrate the notion that tendencies set into play by patriarchy are by no means determining: women are quite capable of acting sadistically for a variety of reasons and under differing sets of circumstances, while men are quite capable of adopting a range of masochistic behavior.

Just as it is would be ludicrous to discuss the concept of patriarchy without referring to developments in feminist theory, so the relationship between capitalist class structure and the cultural texture it generates at work points to ideas grounded in the Marxist tradition and in the writings of Marx himself. The class division between proletariat and bourgeoisie central to Marx's conceptualization of capitalism is simultaneously an interpersonal relationship steeped in experiences of extreme dominance and subordination. According to Marx, capitalists "appropriate" the surplus value produced by workers historically disenfranchised from ownership of land and forced to sell their labor in exchange for wages. A sense of powerlessness and dependency results for the worker forced to accept conditions of work set by the more authoritative capitalist, including what Marx called "subsistence" wages grossly unequal to the appropriated profit on which the capitalist is able to live luxuriously.

The capitalist's ability to impose his or her will is solidified and made all the more intimidating in being reinforced and supported by the coercive powers of the capitalist state. And so the worker confronts labor from a position of "alienation," estranged from a process over which he or she had once been able to exert a participatory and independent self-control; under capitalism, the labor process is experienced as though it were the sole prerogative, right, and belonging of an other. Simultaneously, the capitalist's desperate need for the worker, for the proletariat's labor that allows her or him to remain in a position of power, remains obscured.

Again, the possibility of a connection with sadomasochism is not difficult to elucidate—in particular, with the same type of sadomaso-chistic dynamic I defined in the Introduction and have argued can result from the characteristics of patriarchy. The external, objective relations of capitalism are hierarchical, imposed coercively, and, most relevant to S/M's potential development, characterized by extreme mutual dependency that takes different forms depending on whether one has been situated in the worker's or in the capitalist's position. Like the tendency set into motion by patriarchy between men and women, the relationship between worker and capitalist is also inclined in a highly symbiotic direction, creating a literally life-and-death situa-tion: the worker requires the job for his or her subsistence or the subsistence of his or her family; the capitalist requires the worker's labor and acquiescence to the "relations of production" in order to be able to subsist qua capitalist. As with women whose situation has been shaped by a patriarchal structure not of their own choosing, so the worker who has been placed in a masochistic situation learns to accept a subordinate role not because of any necessary pleasure in pain but defensively, and ultimately self-protectively. A final similarity lies in the worker's inability to challenge without fear of reprisal the hier-archical relationship in which he or she partakes.

As Marxist theory also implies, the habitual experiencing of subor-dination deeply affects a person's consciousness. Dependency is not only the product of an objective relationship in the external world but becomes subjective when the worker internalizes the idea that not only labor but the self that labors must be sold on the marketplace. Georg Lukacs, writing after Marx in *History and Class Consciousness*, implied that there was nothing accidental about volume 1 of *Capital* beginning with a discussion of commodification, nor with its proceed-ing quickly to differentiate the basic meaning of "use value" from "exchange value."[20] What distinguishes capitalism from all social sys-tems before it, asserted Lukacs in paraphrasing Marx, is that nothing any longer has value in and of itself: all relations, animate and inani-mate, become viewed as instrumental, commodities valued only inso-far as they are useful for *another* rather than for oneself, insofar as they become thinglike and exchangeable in market terms. "All that is solid melts into air," wrote Marshall Berman much more recently as he, too, quoted Marx's eloquent dismay at the pervasiveness of ex-change relations throughout all aspects of private and public life, through modernity and what we are now beginning to call post-modernity.

Although Marxist theory has quite aptly been taken to task for its lack of any developed social psychology, the consequences of com-modification and exchange value may be to create what I suspect is an implicit theory: namely, that what could be termed a *conditional psychology* correlates at the most individual and microcosmic levels of the mind and self with the more macrocosmic specifications of capitalism as a social system. Because capitalism makes the worker's ability to survive contingent not only upon his or her labor but on agreement to workplace conditions imposed from above without equal participation or consent, a worker's worth is never accepted and taken for granted simply because he or she exists and is a human being. Rather, value, worth, and legitimacy of self must constantly be earned, proved, sought, deserved. They are, as it were, conditional upon the approval of an other, in this case the capitalist, just as on that other plane of our social geometry, a woman may be conditioned by gender to look to a man for personal legitimacy. The average working person feels not only dependent but extremely dubious about his or her sense of worth, forever hoping to find a recognition that has been denied.

Nor have extreme feelings of dependency thus layered into social structure been ameliorated by labor's transformation from the blue-collar proletariat of Marx's nineteenth-century imagination, working generally in factories and heavy industry, to the more typical service sector employee of today, often employed in an office or storefront. If anything, the requirements of jobs within advanced capitalist settings may have expanded to include what sociologist Arlie Hochschild has dubbed "emotional labor" (see chapter 4): one must be willing to lend not only one's body to the capitalist work process but one's soul as well, the latter now drafted into the service of pleasing, and anticipating the needs of, the customer-or-client other. It is no wonder that Willie Loman in Arthur Miller's *Death of a Salesman*, or Jay Gatsby, the great Gatsby of F. Scott's Fitzgerald's creation, or the determined Clyde in Theodore Dreiser's *American Tragedy* take on such larger-than-life and socially symbolic significance within a decidedly American context. Like masochists, these characters are portrayed as excessively dependent upon and symbiotically tied to the judgments of others who, by contrast, are relatively empowered to bestow a sense of legitimacy on the self. The analogy to the proclivities of patriarchy is suggestive here yet again. As fictional representatives of the working class, a Loman or Gatsby each seek to recapture and win back a sense of self-importance that was somehow once coercively alienated, "appropriated," and through displacement made the possession of upper-class symbolic characters. Interestingly, in these literary references, men situated masochistically are compulsively driven to seek the approval of well-to-do *women*—in *The Great Gatsby*, the approval of Daisy, whose voice is "full of money"; in *An American Tragedy*, of a rich factory owner's daughter—who, at least in terms of class, have the figurative power that is a necessary if not sufficient condition for the sadistic role.

The net result is a disproportionate concern about, and sensitivity to, the opinions of authority figures: the social psychological ramifications under capitalism of an omnipotent orientation toward exchange value is that we evaluate everything, including ourselves, with greater regard to meaning for *them* than for us. How can we best sell ourselves, we wonder, best package ourselves in order to obtain a particular job? How do we rank on the meat market of sexual attractiveness as we fuss about particular cosmetics or deodorants or toothpastes or hair styles, or fret about similar considerations prior to an employment interview? According to this perspective, sex and work have been united, leveled by an encroaching sameness of commodification and the excessive compulsions and obsessions it has bred. Whether it is the approval of aloof lovers we wish to win (and all they may symbolize), or of our bosses, or of our teachers, something is terribly out of sync in the relative weight accorded self versus outside judge and jury.

Given a world in which there no longer seems to be much distinction between use and exchange values, chances are it will become habitual to think even of those *others* in terms of others, *their* value increasing if *they* are in demand. Consequently, it is not only that one feels personally commodified—one commodifies others in turn. As noted in chapter 1 regarding sadomasochism as an internally transformable dynamic wherein a potential for both positions coexists within the same person, so being commodified and commodifying, the defendant and prosecutor of personal value, is internally enmeshed within the Weltanschauung of capitalism I have been sketching. My friends and lovers may excite and impress me much more if they are wanted by others (a status of greater value that can then revert to me, increasing my own sense of worth). As an employer, I may be much more impressed by a candidate who is being wooed by other employers, that candidate's value suddenly rising in mocking testament to the subjective artificiality of the process as a whole and to the relative lack of usefulness I accord my own judgments. Indeed, my simply acting cool and aloof, someone relatively more sadistic in psychic orientation, may increase my appeal to others; or *their* acting in such a way may increase their appeal to me: in both cases, the perception is that one is more important because unavailable, scarcer in supply and therefore higher priced and in demand according to the rules of the marketplace.

Of course, none of this should be taken to imply that under some ideal social organization of the future, the opinions of others would suddenly cease to influence one's own. Such a vision would be horribly sterile, failing to admit some degree of inherent interdependency and connectedness between human beings. If one takes the perspective of symbolic interactionism, brilliantly elaborated in the theory of George Herbert Mead's *Mind, Self and Society,* then a dialectical give-and-take between self and other is so much a part of life as to be a sociological version of Kant's categorical imperative: it always occurs, whether recognized or not.

But what I am contending is that a fundamentally skewed imbalance between self and other has come into being in the overwhelmingly confusing and commodified world of the present, so that the self weakly mimics the inputs of the outer world, its ability to affect it innovatively and confidently in its own turn sadly diminished. The systematically repetitive character of this imbalance appears hardly accidental or eternal. Under other social conditions, perhaps the possibility would exist for a more mutual, back-and-forth and alternating play between one's *relatively* independent opinions and those influenced and depended upon from without. Contrary, then, to Christopher Lasch's well-known characterization of U.S. society as a "culture of narcissism," I see narcissism as itself symptomatic of a culture of sadomasochism and of obsessive concern about the opinions of *others.* The self has been rendered vulnerable and needy amidst social psychological pressures that create chronic self-doubts and insecurities that cannot ever be truly relieved.

And so there may indeed be a relationship between sadomasochism and capitalism as a social system that induces another hierarchical, now class-based, form of symbiotic overdependency. In structural terms, the position of the worker may condition him or her toward assuming a relatively more masochistic position, while the power of the capitalist tends toward relatively more sadistic treatment of the other.

On the other hand, another major characteristic of the modern advanced capitalist workplace is that it has become bureaucratized and stratified into multiple layers: it is no longer as easy or neat a task as it was at the beginning of the Industrial Revolution to classify occupations into one or the other of the two traditional Marxist classes of bourgeoisie and proletariat. A given employee will frequently be in the position of answering to a boss above and in charge of a group of workers below (for whom this employee has become the boss). This may be true, for example, for a bookkeeper in a middle management job or for an upper-level executive who must answer to the chair of the corporate board; true for the chief on a construction job, or for a professor in a college department who, although a figure of authority to students, still reacts out of great deference to the department chair (who in turn may respond meekly to a dean). It is true for the prison guard who, though possibly oppressed as a member of the working class or of a minority group, can still cull satisfaction from the power wielded over prisoners.

Like those of the sadist and masochist, the relationships of late capitalism are extremely complex. Because of these stratified boundaries, the worker and capitalist roles tend to merge and divide again until the line between bourgeoisie and proletariat just about vanishes, and the players are caught up in the same basic social psychology that unites the sadist and masochist in spite of their differences. Simultaneously, the dual modes of interaction implicit within the same job title function subtly in what Marx might have called "systemic perpetuation." Anger about workplace conditions that might otherwise be expressed directly to someone in a position of power above (thereby directly challenging that superior's authority) may regularly be channeled indirectly below, into satisfaction derived from controlling subordinates. This means that stratification compounds the effects of class in a complex and troubling manner.

It is not only workplace experiences that are stratified into layers of power and powerlessness, but racial, ethnic, and gender relations as well. Thus, as often noted, racism may comfort poor and working-class whites in their powerlessness; sexism and homophobia may substitute for the anger a poor white or a person of color may really feel; children may become the butt of their parents' social ire: in each case, discomfiture about one's own powerlessness is displaced into the satisfaction found in possessing some degree of greater power relative to others. If this line of reasoning is correct, then relationships in a bureaucratically stratified society resemble those of sadomasochism at least in this respect: as in sadomasochism, the possibility for the assumption of both a masochistic and sadistic position seems to coexist within the same person. As we have seen, in and of itself a sado-masochistic dynamic is neither static nor bound to sex, race, ethnicity, or, for that matter, class.

Having analyzed a very conditional and possibly sadomaso-chistically oriented social psychology, we should confront the question of S/M's visibility in the 1980s one last time. Returning to the historical canvas with which we began, perhaps one can now approach anew the question of why sadomasochism, broadly interpreted, would attract us more profoundly during moments of economic duress than in moments of relatively greater prosperity. Prosperity and a sense of social security and belonging are closely intertwined. If the structure of the capitalist workplace produces a set of relationships generally analogous to those that occur between the sadist and the masochist of my definition, then one would expect the dependency both parties experience to grow stronger when the stability of the worker's job or of the capitalist's rate of profit is called into question by the internal processes of the system. Nor does it seem logical that cultural styles can be entirely separated from the historical context in which they arise. Can it be entirely accidental that sadomasochistic imagery, practices, and fashions have appeared more prominently during the decade of the eighties than in the more prosperous sixties? At that time, counter-cultural taste ran toward the seemingly more egalitarian—toward unisex clothing and hair, for instance, toward free-form dance styles rather than following or being led by one's partner, toward a stress on sitting in circles, eschewing (certainly not consciously eroticizing) hier-archical modes of intercourse.

On the other hand, the nineties portends a continuation of enor-mous social and economic uncertainty amidst a new sense of scarcity. There are mind-boggling deficits, federally and locally, and fiscal crises regularly pepper the campaign speeches of political candidates at both levels. It's an era of plant closings, farm foreclosures, and homelessness that leaves nagging doubts as to whether we have really come that far from the nineteenth-century misery painted in Dicken-sian novels after all. It's a time of talk about recessions and avoidance of the word *depression*, when yuppie Wall Street analysts find them-selves suddenly unemployed in the aftermath of the biggest stock-market crash since 1929, just as insecure as those workers who are less bathed in status. It is hard to conceive of this culturally anomic situa-tion not exacerbating a sense of social symbiosis and dependency as jobs become dearer, insecurities run higher, and the capitalist has to tighten his or her economic belt. In this regard, a comparison between the eighties and the socioeconomic climate of the beleaguered and indebted pre-Nazi Weimar Republic in the twenties, with its own version of explicit whips and chains imagery and fashionable black leather, may not be so preposterous, however disturbing.

Nor is there reason to think that resulting urges toward greater control over others, or willingness to accept controls over oneself if necessary, would be confined only to the social realm of the workplace. If one feels insecure about one's job and economic prospects, intimacy achieved outside the office becomes that much more important, the home that much more an alleged haven in a heartless world. One who tries to escape through schooling may feel that much more concerned about the evaluations and judgments made by teachers and through grades. Feeling powerless, dependent, and possibly without a sense of communal belonging at one's job may heighten the need for symbiotic ties to one's partner in intimacy and love. The prospect of losing that partner and/or growing children becomes that much more frightening because with them, one at least has some measure of power and control.

Thus, social insecurities will no doubt affect the family as well where, as head of the household, for instance, one can be relatively more powerful. One may even be more likely to exercise such power sadistically, even violently, out of sheer desperation and fear of being alone, rejected, deserted. The woman who insecurely loves too much puts up with the demands of an equally if not more insecure man who loves too little or not at all, because of a sense of need and not knowing where else to go—a sense of no larger community to which she belongs. This increased dependency can in some cases affect the shape of sexual desire as well, increasing the passion and intensity of a drive to subsume oneself in or to absorb another. One may cling that much more to one's lover, for in some cases the gestures of sadomasochistic sex can be those of desperation—an erotic desperation—aimed at fusion with those parts of the self/other now desired in physical and bodily form. In addition, one may be loathe to experiment sexually outside the traditional nuclear family—to question that family, à la the social experimentation frequently associated with the sixties—for fear of losing what little security one already has.

And so we have come full circle to Fromm and his sense of sadomasochism as a strategy adopted to defend ourselves from socially rooted anxieties. From S/M in the sexual form with which it is so automatically associated, we have returned to a larger sense of dominance and subordination dynamics in society as a whole. My aim was to project the image onto a bigger screen, and in so doing, to at least make sadomasochism *conscious*. As practitioners of S/M sex sometimes say, if it is there, let it at least be brought to the surface and not kept invisible. In the process of conscious awareness, the dynamic itself paradoxically may be altered. It may lose some of its unconscious, and therefore its most insidious, power.

In this chapter, I have explored how various forms of social organization can affect the individual in historically specific contexts. For someone like Freud, however, sadomasochism can also be rooted in biology, in aggressive and passive instincts not particularly affected by our environment. Writing from quite another perspective, Jean-Paul Sartre, in his philosophical classic *Being and Nothingness*, conceived of sadomasochism as a response to mortality; he wrote of controlling and being controlled as two faces of a common strategy to escape fears generated by confrontation with death. Both thinkers, albeit in varying ways, thus envisioned sadomasochism in somewhat universal and transhistorical terms, as a phenomenon that there is no particular reason to expect will ever fully disappear or lose its appeal. And there are persuasive points to be made on this side of the theoretical fence. Perhaps, indeed, sadomasochism would reappear in a fully perfected and nonhierarchical society; perhaps our sexual lives would still feature an active component of fantasy in which we wished to experiment with power and powerlessness, would want to sometimes feel overwhelmed and at other moments to overwhelm. My argument, however, is that if this happened, ideally it would do so within an altered historical context, one in which sadomasochistic social psychology did not happen to coincide with sadomasochistic forms of social organization. It seems to me that if one can demonstrate systemic processes that suspiciously incline us toward sadomasochistic dynamics of the sort this book discusses, then the most we can say is that sadomasochism is an overdetermined phenomenon with many possible causes. My own perspective should by now be apparent, for while there are good and intelligent reasons to think that certain feelings and experiences belong in the category of the possibly inherent, are they not mediated, channeled, redirected through the visions born of our individual and collective, our psychological and social will?

In chapter 2, I return one more time to the world of sex in order to continue the process of elucidating the sadomasochistic dynamic discussed in the Introduction. Distinguishing consensual S/M sex from a sadomasochistic dynamic that could conceivably play itself out in the sexual arena as well, I further develop definitional traits that can then be used paradigmatically, and I go into greater depth about socialization processes at which I have only hinted.

And so, for now, let me begin again.

Defining a Basic Dynamic:
Paradoxes at the
Heart of Sadomasochism

Oddly enough, the best way to assess whether sadomasochism pervades U.S. culture outside the realm of sexuality is, I believe, to subject a sexual example of sadomasochism to closer scrutiny. That sadomasochism has been speciously restricted to its semiotic connection with sexuality does not, after all, exempt sexuality from its domain. Certainly, sexual interaction can, and often does, take the shape of the sadomasochistic dynamic I delineate. Teasing out the characteristics of a particular sexual situation based on rigidly defined roles of dominance and subordination should provide some insight into how this dynamic operates in other settings as well.

Grounding this definitional process in a sexual example is to catch sadomasochism at its most naked, revealed in a stark and obvious form; given the term's origins, the capacity of sadomasochism to be present in this sphere is obviously not in doubt. Analyzing an instance of sexual sadomasochism also renders inseparable the personal and political dimensions of life: on the one hand, sexuality is one of the most intimate and private activities in which we engage; on the other, it is remarkably public, touched deeply by the collective influences and pressures that assail us from other sides and sources. Sexuality, though, is not merely the reflection of weightier social forces to which it is easily or at all reducible. On the contrary, that which affects the body has its own specific features: the world of sexuality and the erotic melds that which is physically craved to that which is culturally channeled, conjoining the sophisticated to the primordial. Amidst the speculations of subsequent chapters, one would ideally wish to maintain a sense both of sexuality's sociality and of those aspects of it that relate to bodily and biologically based pleasures.

And so I begin with a hypothetical instance: a particular sadist has tied and bound a sexual partner so that the freedom of movement of this other—the masochist—has been decidedly limited or curtailed. The sadist is in a position of greater control: the masochist has been rendered relatively out of control. For the sadist to take pleasure in a resulting sexual interaction, the masochist can under no circumstances be unconditionally free; the masochist must not be able to express her or his will without restriction, lest the controlled situation be broken. How this control is expressed—whether through the mediation of a chain or a whip, or through handkerchiefs and ties used to fix the masochist's hands or legs—is of less interest for my purposes than the desire for some unequal restriction. Even more to the point, what are the existential ramifications of any act of sexual binding for defining a sadomasochistic dynamic? If sadomasochism is not static, how can the pleasure of the sadist and masochist be sustained over time? What are the tendencies implicit in sadomasochism as an ongoing process?

In this chapter, I proceed deductively, seeking implications of a given set of premises. But I will also show the above process in a less abstract way by weaving into my account illustrations from literary and popular cultural sources, especially from well-known novels about sadomasochism, among them *Venus in Furs* by Leopold von Sacher-Masoch and the Marquis de Sade's *Juliette*. In addition, I refer to more contemporary works: the *Story of O* by Pauline Reage (a 1954 French novel still frequently cited as a classic text on sadomasochism, which caused a good deal of controversy when released in the United States in the mid-sixties); Jenny Diski's 1986 *Nothing Natural*, published in Britain amid a similar spate of publicity, which concerns an independent young feminist who finds herself highly sexually aroused by a sadomasochistic affair; and Elizabeth McNeill's *9-1/2 Weeks*, an American novel (later adapted to film) and "true story" concerning a liaison similar to that in *Nothing Natural*. In the more recent novels, the masochist is generally a female, the sadist a male. Yet, taken as a group, these literary depictions are fascinating in revealing sadomasochism's complex capacity for internal transformability: Severin, the male narrator of *Venus in Furs*, casts himself as masochist to his prized Wanda's sadist; in *The Story of O*, in which O is sent to a dominatrix at SAMOIS, women are usually only in the masochistic position, and sadistically cast men flirt dangerously with their other side; ultimately, all of the above characters are shown as desirous of their opposite personae. I will use "she or he" to refer to the situation of the masochist (usually a she), and "he or she" to allude to the sadist (usually a he). This is simultaneously to emphasize sadomasochism's frequently gendered and socialized character, the topic of chapter 5 in its entirety, and to reiterate that these roles are not in any way biologically or essentially determined. As a dynamic, sadomasochism is not bound to any one gender, class, race, ethnicity, or sexual preference but takes shape only in specific contexts and under certain conditions.

Additionally, I draw upon these novels because each in its own way describes a *sadomasochistic dynamic*. There are several important respects in which the hypothetical instance about to be elaborated can be differentiated from the potentially more give-and-take instance of S/M sex alluded to in previous chapters. Neither the sadist nor the masochist in my paradigmatic case, nor the sadists and masochists represented in the referenced literature, begin as partners who have decided to explore playfully the assertive and submissive aspects of erotic desires within a *consciously* sadomasochistic modus vivendi. They do not found their interaction on mutual equality even as they adopt unequal roles in the sexual sphere. They do not see sex as one part of a relationship possibly quite egalitarian in other areas. Nor do they explicitly acknowledge, as partners often do who openly engage in consensual S/M sex, the masochist's power to call the shots by controlling whether sexual involvement continues or ceases at any given moment.

Rather, for the sadists and masochists of all of these accounts, the meaning of sexual power and powerlessness redounds much more fundamentally to the core of the involved persons' beings. Although their yearnings for experiences of domination and subordination are manifested in a sexual instance, they nonetheless *transcend the realm of sexuality per se*. Sex is not sought for its own sake, perhaps for variety and novelty, or for a merely libidinal satisfaction: instead, both sadist and masochist are searching for some kind of recognition and acknowledgment that goes beyond, and likely originated outside, the realm of the erotic—even as it somehow became married to it. Literary examples abound. In *Venus in Furs*, Wanda orders Severin to be her servant on trains, in public, in all aspects of their coexistence. O's stay at the chateau of Roissy, where she is taken by her lover René, is similarly holistic: in her masochistic persona, she is forced to be at the sadists' ever-present beck and call, while her ability to maintain outside facets of her life—her job, for one—is increasingly swallowed up in the dynamic. Sexual sadomasochism for the heroine of *9-1/2 Weeks* takes place only outside the hours of nine to five and is kept within the four walls of her sadistically oriented boyfriend's apartment: however, the rules require her to relinquish all control of her own feeding, dressing, and self-maintenance the moment she returns from a typical day at the office. Finally, Rachel in *Nothing Natural* has a life quite independent of her lover, Joshua, except that any interaction that should occur between them—in or outside the bedroom—must be initiated by him.

When deeply embroiled in sadomasochistic dynamics, the last notion in the world the sadist in these examples would wish to concede (as we shall see, the masochist tends to share these sentiments) is that the masochist is in any way his or her equal in power. Such an admission would deflate the endeavor, collapsing its larger ontological significance. The game of the sadist and masochist in a sexually sadomasochistic dynamic is much more serious than this, its rules far more calcified. The stakes are higher. And the dilemma both parties face is much more basic, corresponding to a longing the dynamic may or may not be able to fulfill. I commence with that dilemma as it confronts, first, the sadist.

The Sadist of the Sadomasochistic Dynamic

I assume a sadist who is sadistic insofar as he or she takes pleasure in ascending to a position of dominance. Consequently, the first defining trait of a sadomasochistic dynamic is the existence of a hierarchical structure from which any ongoing process will have to ensue. But the sadist who uses sadomasochistic sex as an arena in which to play out a script replete with ulterior motivations will not be content only with a situation of unequal roles. Instead, if it is domination the sadist really seeks, then the masochist must be rendered subordinate: inequality becomes a pretext for demonstrating superiority over the masochist who in contrast must be relatively inferiorized. The masochist, then, needs in some way to be put down or humiliated, made to grant the sadist's higher power—to state, perhaps, that she or he can't do without him or her, that this dependence is profound and (especially satisfying, titillating, to the sadist) enjoyed.

Of course, the degree to which humiliation of the masochist is sought may vary greatly, from those cases in which the sadist's need to demean is extreme and obvious, to those in which the sadist's will to power—figuratively speaking—is far less intense. Yet, the fact remains that not only control but the expression of contempt for and toward the masochist is required for and by the sadist. This seems clear both as a logical proposition and as a conclusion amply evident in each of the cited novels. In *Venus in Furs*, Wanda eventually finds pleasure in whipping the narrating Severin until she is finally beaten by her own sadistic lover; the 1,200-page *Juliette* is so filled with thrashings that the reader's mind starts to become boggled and rather inured to what is being described; the sadists of *The Story of O* are rarely content to separate sexual control from sexual punishment; and both *Nothing Natural* and *9-1/2 Weeks* entail regular smackings doled out by the sadist to the masochist.

That combinations and permutations of punishment appear with such regularity is worth querying, for why punish unless one wishes to demonstrate the badness and inferiority of another person? At one existential level, then, punishment manifests the sadist's quest for superiority through debasement of the masochist/other. (N.B.: The putting down of the masochist may take place verbally as well as physically. She or he may be called names—for women, "sluts," "whores," or "bitches," epithets that indeed are interspersed through the literature.) That such debasement takes place in a sexual manner ought not be ignored, either, for one of several rationales behind punishing the masochist in the first place may be that the sadist's bodily desires have been aroused. The specifically sexual import of sadism (as well as of masochism) may relate at least in part to sexual feelings that have been repressed, controlled, at once satisfied and denied. (As suggested in other chapters, a sexually repressive society would have to play some role in sculpting sexuality and desire into sadomasochistic shapes.)

But, to continue the argument, the sadist is only able to assert inequality and superiority from a structural position that bestows more freedom of movement on him or her than the masochist can claim. Having restricted the other, the sadist is filled with confidence and self-assurance that increases with the analogous diminution of these feelings in the masochist: his or her pleasure in power stems directly from the other's relative lack of it. But is the sadist of the sadomasochistic sexual dynamic really so self-assured? He or she certainly seems to be; after all, it is the sadist who is holding the reins or tying the knots. Yet, what is the underlying meaning of the sadist's desire and need to bind the masochist in the first place, the sadist's need to belittle the other in order to feel superior? For there can be no doubt, in this hypothetical sexual example, that the sadist required a masochist to bind. That the sadist's power is possible only relative to the masochist's lack of it implies the former's extreme need and dependence upon the latter. The sadist needs an inferior masochist to be perceived as relatively superior. Without a bound and degraded other, the sadist would cease to be as sadist, a label dependent quite literally on the corollary designation of a masochist. If we define *symbiosis* in a way akin to that term's usage in biology—that is, as one organism requiring another in order to survive—then indeed the sadist qua sadist is symbiotically connected to and in need of the masochist. The need is not biological but perceptual, deeply felt and experienced.

Therefore, the need to bind the masochistic other may be motivated by more than a yearning for self-definition and superiority. Curtailing the masochist's movements also reassures the sadist that the masochist will not go away, that she or he will not reject the sadist. This possibility was not safeguarded when the masochist was free and unbound. It is all too apparent that the dependence of the sadist on the masochist is so enormous, so intrinsic, that nothing can be left to chance. The very act of binding attests to this dependency, and provides another significant explanation for the pleasure experienced in physically restricting the other. The sadist's characteristic desire to shame and humiliate the masochist—to beat an O or a Severin—is more understandable, too, in terms of this dire need. One would hardly expect someone who requires an other this urgently to feel happy about his or her own dependency. A physically contemptuous act expresses the sadist's rage at vulnerability and desperate need of another person. At the same time, punishment aims quite frankly at control; it is an attempt to ensure that the other will know she or he is bad (and that some sort of vengeful consequences will ensue, as outlined in the Introduction) should any attempt be made to break from the symbiotic embrace. Extreme need is the common thread that links the sadist's desire for control to the desire to punish.

This analysis suggests a paradox that I suspect operates at sadism's very heart. *The sadist embodies precisely the opposite of what his or her situation on its face appears to imply.* To the world and to the masochist, the sadistic persona exudes confidence and self-assurance. The sadist seems to be independent, to strut through life often mocking and contemptuous of the masochist's alleged dependency. The sadist may fantasize orgasmically unlimited power in issuing commands (in this case, sexual) to which the masochist is expected to respond. However, a closer look reveals this appearance to be a lie, and extreme need to be the sadist's best-guarded secret from self and others. This is a critical difference between the structural position of the sadist and of the masochist. The situation of the masochist, as will shortly be apparent, leaves no choice about whether dependence on the sadist will be recognized: she or he is literally forced to make this admission. On the other hand, the sadist's denial of dependency suggests an even greater insecurity than that experienced by the masochist, a need that the sadist feels must on no account be acknowledged. (If dependency was not intensely frightening to the sadist, why not simply admit to it?) And so the sadomasochistic dynamic is characterized by an ideological myth of independence on the sadist's part when, in reality, the sadist is even more dependent upon the masochist than the masochist is upon the sadist.

Given the sadist's desire for control of the masochist on whom he or she paradoxically relies, one might conclude that a bound and compliant masochist would be the fulfillment of the sadist's sexual dreams. However, this conclusion assumes stasis—that time comes to a halt—and is thereby far too elementary. If a sexual situation is in fact to be ongoing, something must occur to keep it moving: once the masochist's freedom of movement has been restricted and brought under control, what then? How can the sadist's pleasure be renewed and perpetuated? If the process is not somehow rejuvenated, the sadist will feel dead and alone, stripped of an ongoing role in the world.

One option is that the sadist could head toward a new masochist. The novel and play *Les Liaisons Dangereuses* exemplifies this movement outside the realm of sexual sadomasochism, narrowly defined. The character of the viscomte prowls from one conquest to another: he is an archetypal Don Juan who seeks a new challenge after victory over one woman has been achieved and boredom has set in (read: the death of the process with which he identifies and by which he customarily defines himself). But should a different partner not be available, or continued pleasure be sought from only one person on whom the sadist's attention is momentarily fixed, some other solution must be found. At this point the desire to take and retake pleasure vis-à-vis the *same* masochist compels the sadist to present her or him with a set of tasks that have to be performed from within the latter's restricted situation.

Here, then, arises a second definitional paradox: the sadist, who seems so desirous of control, can now be anticipated to secretly crave *resistance* to, and challenges of, his or her own authority from the masochist. If the masochist resists, the sadist can then go on taking pleasure in asserting power anew, over and over, thus prolonging and sustaining the dynamic. One may thus expect the sadist not only to tolerate but to encourage, and to be excited by, role reversals in which the masochist dares their hierarchical positioning. By resisting, the masochist withdraws approval from the sadist and from the ongoing process of domination: at the moment of this challenge, the hierarchical order of their relationship is called into question. Toward the end of *Nothing Natural,* for instance, Rachel suddenly calls the sexually sadistic Joshua to inform him that their relationship no longer sufficiently satisfies her needs. This was indeed a bold move. In the context of the interactional rules they had established, only Joshua was empowered to initiate contact and make demands. But rather than Rachel's challenge resulting in the out-and-out rejection she fearfully anticipates, she is surprised by an interested silence on the other end of the phone. Joshua's response is to issue a new command, one which co-opts the daring of her initiative into a form that permits him both titillation and the maintenance of control: he coolly tells her to write a letter with her exact specifications, which he will then take under advisement.[1]

Nevertheless, the sadist can only tolerate the masochist's challenge if it is temporary and does not threaten the foundational structure of their game. After all, the sadist's need of the masochist is experienced as symbiotic. The sadist does not want the masochist to overthrow the system of control altogether by, so to speak, bursting her or his chains. On the other hand, loose chains are not only acceptable but desirable, allowing pleasure to be repeated. The masochist who fights back and resists can be expected to be a turn on, feeding the dynamic by giving the sadist a new obstacle to overcome. Still, because the sadist can never allow himself or herself to acknowledge the appeal of an uppity masochist (lest the desire to be controlled instead of controlling be revealed), the masochist in many cases must be punished for rebelling, however stimulating or desired it was in the process. Especially if the mutiny is perceived as a little too assertive, it provides yet another motivation for the clearly overdetermined importance of punishment to the sadist.

In both *The Story of O* and *9-1/2 Weeks*, the main female characters cast in the masochistic position initially refuse their respective sadists' demand to masturbate in front of them. (The request is an important one for the sadist, representing not only an assault upon the other's onanistic privacy and autonomy but also humiliation: the masochist is forced to publicize an act that in most sexually restrictive societies is seen as shameful. A point I will return to later is that a complex, dialectical effect of this coercion may be to give the masochist pleasure by neutralizing, sexual guilt by fiat. Sir Stephen's response to O's refusal is both to enter her (for him) passionately and to remark on the long road ahead before she learns proper obedience—a road whose length, of course, guarantees him, too, a place.[2] In *9-1/2 Weeks*, the sadistic lover is similarly at once aroused and infuriated by the masochist's assertion of will—a will that now has to be broken. In the movie version, the character of this (now stockbroker) sadist becomes excited when the masochistically cast woman refuses to crawl; they have passionate sex as she starts to walk out one day after refusing to lift her skirt and be spanked.

But it is also fascinating to speculate as to whether greater, and perhaps ultimate, pleasure for the sexual sadist would result from the very thing he or she ostensibly most dreads: the masochist revolting to the point where the masochistic role has been altogether transcended. In erotic fantasy, in the sadist's heart of hearts, does there lie the wish that the masochist switch roles and play the sadist so that, transformed, the other now brandishes the whip? Pleasure could then ensue from sheer relief at the sadist's secret having finally been discovered. At last, the sadist's real dependence could be acknowledged to a higher and stronger being. Again, relevant examples spring to mind in which the sadist becomes masochist not in relation to the already-labeled masochist, but in relation to a relatively more sadistic third party. As *Venus in Furs* progresses, Wanda becomes bored with the masochistic Severin whom she has so thoroughly come to control (as Jessica Benjamin writes, whom she has "consumed") and falls in love with a man perceived as superior and by whom she in turn is beaten.[3] Wanda the sadist is now transformed into Wanda the masochist. When Severin, the masochistic narrator, perceives this change in Wanda, he is angry and no longer respects her. By the novel's denouement, he is transformed from masochist into sadist, a sadist who dominates women: not all that surprisingly, the gendered order Wanda's sadistic character had disturbed is simultaneously reaffirmed. The allegedly sadistic René of *The Story of O* turns meekly masochistic in relation to the more powerful Sir Stephen; Sir Stephen, toward the end of the book, seeks to please another male character dubbed simply the Commander: in both cases, men are able to be masochistic only in relation to other men, the female O only an intermediary object of barter.

Note that these transformations do not occur randomly in this dynamic but with sadomasochistic regularity. Wanda is transformed into the masochist only when the sadomasochistic dynamic has begun to become boring and unsustainable for her as sadist. René takes O to Stephen as he becomes deadened by the dynamic in relation to her; Sir Stephen later does the same vis-à-vis the Commander. Or take Jean Genet's wonderful description of sadomasochistic turnabouts in his play *The Balcony*, in which lawyers and judges sadistic in their day-to-day lives unwind in a sexual underworld that allows them to be deliciously dominated. But even if masochistic at night, the lawyers and judges of Genet's vision remain sadistic during the day, reminding us that inversion is more likely a passing fantasy for the sadist. His or her desire for role reversal is not conscious, perceived not as dream but as nightmare. To acknowledge a secret desire for domination would mean that the sadist was no longer in control, an idea so alien to the sadist's usual sense of identity that it would undoubtedly feel frightening and overwhelming to the point of being associated with psychic, if not physical, death. The sadist's own resistance would thereby be enormous, even in the face of a deep yearning for a change in the power relations in which he or she partakes. The sadist is thus not really equipped to jettison the dynamic involving the original masochist, even as its future is threatened by boredom or extinction.

What if the masochist refuses nothing but resistance itself, if she or he does not fight back for whatever reasons and is resigned to and/or titillated by compliance? Given this eventuality, how can the sadist assure the continuation of the sadomasochistic dynamic? The sadist's only remaining option is to create resistance by bullying the masochist into greater and greater feats of submission. Tasks will be set for the masochist to undertake in a progressive sequence that makes it appear as though there is more the former could do if she or he truly loved the sadist. To create these tasks, the sadist must now use some imagination, must constantly innovate. The sadist will try hard and steadily to present the masochist with new challenges: will she or he (*The Story of O*) sleep with other men, touch herself, touch other women? Will she or he (*9-1/2 Weeks*) consent to be blindfolded, to dress as a man, to pose as a prostitute? In the film version of *9-1/2 Weeks*, the requested tasks move from less to more violent in a sequence that is depicted as though a dialectic progression. The character of the sadistic stockbroker casts about more and more desperately for more extreme ways of resuscitating the game each time it threatens to die out, as the older tasks become tired and routinized.

As one of the primary sadists in *The Story of O*, René has motives that are indeed multiple and overdetermined. By intimidating O into sleeping with his brother, not only does he wish to continue the sadomasochistic process but also to revitalize her attractiveness to him. In Benjamin's analysis of these characters in *The Bonds of Love*, she interprets René's desire to pair O with someone else, especially a more powerful alter ego figure like his brother, as a reflection of the fear that otherwise she would lose appeal for him, be somehow a less interesting figure for having become controlled.[4] Instead, René attempts to enliven the situation by introducing a third party, Sir Stephen. Through Stephen, whom René *cannot* control, O seems less controllable as well: René can then more successfully sustain his role as sadist, not consciously heeding his masochistic underside.

But is it O or Stephen René really wants? Again, I would contend that the particular gender or sexual identity of the desired party is less important than the structural position of a given party relative to the dynamic. René may be expressing the sadist's paradoxical, denied longing for the very opposite of what he or she is supposed to want. Thus, René may seek not total control over the masochist, but challenges possible only through interaction with someone else who is relatively free: enter, as Benjamin similarly observed, Sir Stephen, who is positioned so as to be relatively more independent and apparently less controllable than O in a patriarchal society that accords men greater power than women. Only Stephen, Benjamin writes, is free enough to bestow what she calls "recognition" upon René (a concept I explore in chapter 3).[5]

It does not take much imagination to recognize this pattern, too, in intimate, long-term relationships in which sadomasochistic sex need not play a prominent role or any role at all. For example, the married man who, on the one hand, consciously communicates to his wife the severe repercussions that will ensue should she take a lover may, on the other, exude increased interest when he perceives her as attractive to other men. The pattern can appear regardless of gender in any relationship, such as the one I experienced wherein a habitual partner's erotic value seems to increase with perception of the partner's value to others. Lila Karp and Renos Mandis spoke to a similar phenomenon when they noted the push-pull nature of many men's reactions to feminists in the early seventies.[6] Supposedly repulsed by feminist women, men pursued prolonged argumentation with them as though subliminally turned on by feminism's implicit threat to their traditional stronghold of power. Simply by being more assertively free, the feminist has the appeal of relative uncontrollability: she is more like a Sir Stephen, or the Commander, to the male sadomasochist.

In a sadomasochistic dynamic played out in the sexual arena, then, the crucial point is that the sadist is forced to be creative and is restricted by a process in which resistance must be sought or artificially induced. The sadist is driven by fear that the process, and his or her role within it, may wither and die. If one follows a dialectical logic, the sadist's innovations may lead to a fatal ending if he or she is inclined, or somehow forced, to dance through the dynamic with only one masochist. As each new demand from the sadist is progressively fulfilled, the next may be even more difficult and intense—if only because the older tasks have become as though obsolete, subjected to a routinized and bureaucratizing process. The sadist may grow more and more incensed at the inability to sustain pleasure indefinitely, while the masochist's physical ability for real or imagined resistance may wear thin.

Should the masochist become worn down, should she or he die either figuratively or literally, the sadist would be destroyed as well. (In this sense, when the sadist punishes the other, he or she is at the same time punishing himself or herself, engaging in an irrational pursuit.) Allegedly, the sadist takes pleasure in controlling the masochist and must continually innovate in order to keep the process moving and to perpetuate a sense of sadistic identity. But once the masochist has been negated, the dynamic comes to an abrupt halt. This can happen either literally through death, at the extreme end of the sadomasochistic continuum (in one ending of *The Story of O*, O asks Sir Stephen's permission to take her own life), or figuratively by the sadist having exerted so much control that the masochist retains no independent powers of resistance. Illustrating the second outcome, both Rachel in *Nothing Natural* and the young woman of *9-1/2 Weeks* exit the dynamic only when they have nervous breakdowns and their ability to respond has actually shut down.

It should be reemphasized that the dynamic I am describing is not a determined one. Given a sadist's and masochist's typical goal of sustaining a process, certain structural *tendencies* arise. Whether or not these tendencies are actually played out depends upon a host of factors that can intervene to offset and mediate their effect. The response of the masochist, for instance, will vary according to circumstances peculiar to the situation: is the sadist's ability to exert control affected or diluted by the masochist's job, by other friends, by family, by political engagements (at the group level, perhaps by the existence of a social movement), or by indeterminably unique traits of the masochist's own psyche? We will soon see that the sadomasochistic dynamic does not automatically produce—as though axiomatic, or by some law of nature—a weakened, dying masochist in response to the dialectically unfolding advances of the sadist's demands. Rather, the masochist may slowly become emboldened—exactly the opposite response. The more tyrannical the sadist becomes in *9-1/2 Weeks*, the more the young art dealer/masochist character begins to perceive the dynamic as self-destructive to her (in the film version, not in the novel). Her resistance becomes real, strengthened by the power she begins to discover as the sadist's dependence on her is slowly and ironically revealed. Eventually, she is sufficiently emboldened to leave the relationship altogether, a decision the sadist's increasing desperation gave her little choice but to make for her own survival. (Of course, a constellation of life circumstances allowed the young woman's responses to develop in this rather than another direction.)

Before turning to the masochist's situation in greater detail, I will summarize the argument I have been making by listing the characteristics of a sexual sadomasochistic dynamic deduced thus far from the sadist's dilemma. These characteristics may be generalizable to sadomasochistic dynamics wherever they occur:

1. *The establishment of a hierarchical division between self and other that rests on the attribution of superiority to the sadist and of inferiority to the masochist.* The sadist sets up an unequal relationship with the masochist in which the former is powerful and good, the latter powerless and bad. Although their sexual situation reveals that the sadist is deeply dependent upon the masochist, both accept the ideology that it is the sadist who is primary and the masochist secondary. But a deeper existential analysis

reveals that the sadist is symbiotically dependent upon the masochist and in fact *more* dependent on the masochist than is the masochist on him or her. Unable to admit this dependency, the sadist feels a need to punish the masochist to maintain control and connection to the other.

2. *Within this hierarchical order, the paradox arises that the sadist desires what I have called "resistance" within the sadomasochistic dynamic. Consequently, I contend that the sadist is characterized by a desire for noncompliance within an overall context, or mode, of compliance. Put slightly differently, the sadist wishes his or her authority to be challenged so that disapproval takes place in the mode or rules of the game of approval (of the sadist's authority).* One would have guessed that the sadist would be sexually satisfied by the achievement of control over a compliant masochist. However, pleasure in the assertion of power can continue only if resistance exists or is created by the sadist's progressive desperation. Consequently, the sadist's ideal is not total compliance but resistance within the confines of the masochist's chains.

3. *The coming into being of a process that requires the sadist to work at constant innovation. This process tends to be irrational in terms of its own goals, wearing down or encouraging the masochist toward rebellion.* If the masochist does not resist, the sadist will try to simulate obstacles by creating successive sexual tasks the masochist must perform to demonstrate loyalty. This process may wear down the masochist, literally as well as figuratively, as the sadist slowly eradicates the source of what once yielded pleasure via control—this source is the masochist's freedom. Another possible outcome, however, is that a masochist may resist and turn this dialectical process in the direction opposite that originally desired by the sadist. Rather than being worn down, the masochist becomes paradoxically stronger and more certain of the necessity of leaving until, at last, the sadist is rejected just as he or she once rejected the masochist.

For the sadist, the possible outcomes are in one sense equivalent. The dream of domination and control with which the sadist began, expressed sexually through the restriction of the other, remains unfulfilled as the dynamic unfolds. He or she may experience moments of satiety, but a restless anxiety will in all likelihood be haunting, tending to drive on the sadist's quest. A bound masochist who no longer resists represents a Pyrrhic victory for the sadist. Similarly, a masochist who has resisted to the point of rejecting the dynamic altogether has also slipped from the sadist's grasp. Both conclusions are unsatisfying within the confines of the sadist's customary role, leaving bewilderment, anger, and a frightening and paradoxical loneliness. Moreover, the sadist is no more able to acknowledge his or her dependency at the denouement of the process (if, indeed, it should come to an end) than at its beginning. It would appear that the sadist unwittingly dreams of being discovered—of being truly known and recognized by a more powerful being to whom he or she can admit neediness and the masochistic yearnings of character that the forced splitting of these personae has denied (read: René's desire for approval and recognition from Stephen; Wanda's from her sadistic lover). Again, for such recognition to occur, the other would have to be free, precisely what the sadist cannot tolerate qua sadist. He or she may thus move from one conquest to another, trying one creative innovation after the next, on and on for a short while or forever, never reaching the conclusion that the process is absurd on its own terms. For, colloquially speaking, the deluded sadist is barking up the wrong tree. But what about the masochist?

The Masochist's Analogous Dilemma

Sketching the characteristics of the masochist in a sexual sado-masochistic dynamic is unavoidably an exercise in mirror images, a flip of the coin. Physical restrictions demonstrate to the masochist the same unequal power perceived by the sadist. Not only do both sadist and masochist accept the position of differential power accorded the sadist in their hierarchical interaction, but they similarly operate within the context of the masochist's assumed relative inferiority. Just as the sadist wishes to control the other, the masochist hopes that the sadist will take charge. But what do these facts reveal about the masochist on an internal rather than an external level? What does it imply about O that she consents first to René's and then to Sir Stephen's sadistic demands?

That a particular masochist would consent to being restricted, or physically bound, suggests a belief that exertions of the sadist's will are more important than her or his own. Perhaps, due to past experiences of actual powerlessness, the masochist has not had an opportunity to exercise and develop any authority or sense of power in the world—including, of course, in sex—without guilt or fear of punishment. The masochist may experience an internal emptiness that propels the vicarious substitution of the sadist's will for self-assertion. It is the sadist who is accorded importance, who matters. By extension, the masochist accords little importance and value to herself or himself. One would expect the masochist's attitude toward self to be as contemptuous as the sadist's, who can hardly be expected to respect what the masochist has come to feel is so worthless. Self-abnegating, the masochist bows to the sadist, who gains disproportionate authority in comparison.

Consequently, it is not in theory difficult to comprehend why the masochist would be pleasurably aroused by feeling controlled rather than controlling. The masochist must be unequal and constrained, in some way bound, since she or he does not associate pleasure with the sexual assertions of this worthless self; she or he may feel guilt, as if pleasure is only allowable if the self is in some way punished. Here, the frequency in women of rape fantasies is explicable in terms of the feminine gender socialization producing a relatively greater tendency toward masochism. At least through a masochistic fantasy, pleasure can be permitted, if only because guilt has been neutralized by a situation in which the masochist is no longer responsible; and the masochist expiates the sin of pleasure through the simultaneous experience of punishment. As I argue in chapter 5, given double standards of sexuality for men and women in patriarchal societies, and their legacy of shame, guilt, and repression for women about their sexual feelings, it is not in any way remarkable that such fantasies among women would be common.

At this point, however, the situations of the masochist and the sadist begin to diverge because of their different positioning within the structure of the sexual dynamic. The masochist is exactly the opposite of the sadist insofar as she or he can have no illusions about having been rendered deeply dependent. René and Stephen walk confidently through Reage's sadomasochistically eroticized world, barking orders to O as though immune to the actual depth of their dependence on *her:* she, of course, harbors no such illusion, for why would she be obeying if she did not experience herself as needing their authority, as dependent (or forced to be dependent) upon their commands? This felt neediness compounds and recreates the masochist's contemptuous inner feelings. What is wrong with me, O must ask herself, that I cannot do without this other, that I am so desperately dependent that I consent to be overwhelmed by the demeaning sadist? The masochist, like the sadist, resents the sense of felt dependence upon the other. However, unable to openly admit this dependence, the sadist expresses resentment by blaming the masochist, taking it out on her or him through some demeaning behavior—violence, verbal abuse, or nonviolent sexual control. The masochist, on the other hand, expresses resentment by blaming the self, a reaction that can be given a more Freudian interpretation in reference to the expression of feelings of anger (see chapter 3). Whereas the sadist directs anger at the masochist, the masochist directs anger toward her- or himself.

But is the masochist truly as dependent as appearances suggest? Arguably not. I would contend that just as the sadist's best-kept secret from self and others is extreme dependency hidden behind a front of apparent independence and strength, the masochist's analogous secret is far greater relative strength and independence than she or he perceives, hidden behind a front of apparent and extreme dependency. This is the first paradox of the masochist in the sexual sadomasochistic dynamic, the exact correlate of that deduced to exist at the core of sadism. That O consents to be bound means that at some level, she is not afraid to acknowledge dependence upon and extreme need of the other. Logically, the masochist's ability to acknowlege dependence is possible only in someone for whom such an admission does not equate with death of the self, someone for whom the intimacy implied by neediness is not so threatening as to be avoided at all costs. On both these counts, oddly enough, the masochist appears to have an advantage over the sadist within the rules of their shifting game of power and powerlessness. Yet, for the masochist, this authority is precisely what she or he is loathe to admit: whereas the sadist cannot concede to needing the other, the masochist cannot concede to *not* needing the other.

This reasoning leads to the conclusion that the masochist has learned to hide this relatively greater strength, to act *as if* he or she is extremely weak and dependent. Perhaps such behavior was the only way the masochist was able to survive past experiences of oppression that was psychological, social, and/or political in scope. Masochism may have been in large part an effort to exert control from a powerless position. If so, then contrary to the now (it is to be hoped) discredited psychoanalytic equation of masochism with pleasure in pain, the masochist seeks not pain but pleasure. Unfortunately, she or he may have encountered obstacles in life that permitted the expression of pleasure only if linked to the experiencing of pain. The masochist must pay, must appear to be in the process of paying. But for now, let me bracket speculation about the social conditions and processes that contributed to the masochist's original predicament until chapter 4 and beyond. For whatever reason, the masochist in the sadomasochistic dynamic is constrained to hide such paradoxical strengths from the sadist and, more importantly, from self.

For that matter, the masochist does not wish to know that the sadist is more dependent than a first glance suggests, either. Such a realization would strip the sadist of the accoutrements of authority from which the masochist's sexual pleasure has habitually derived, undermining the masochist's ability to vicariously identify with the sadist's power. (An analogous example springs to mind from the world of work depicted in chapter 4: workers—perhaps the secretary, the administrative assistant, the beginning analyst—who closely identify with their boss may frequently react to that boss's demotion as though they have been demoted as well.)

Returning to our literary examples, *Venus in Furs*'s Severin most certainly does not wish to learn that Wanda simply wants to be human or, worse still, to indulge the masochistic side of her personality and have him dominate *her* for once. Indeed, the first half of the novel finds Wanda attempting on numerous occasions to tell Severin she does not really want to be the controlling party. If he will cease his pleas for domination, she says, she will marry him—supposedly the goal he holds most dear. He promptly changes the subject. When Joshua cries and loses control at one point in *Nothing Natural*, Rachel feels "scared, she didn't want him like this, and was relieved when at last his sobs died down and he lay quiet and asleep."[7] These are instances where the demands of the *masochist*, who has managed to cleverly hide that she or he, too, is exerting some power within the processes of the sadomasochistic dynamic, are controlling the dynamic as well. The sadist may feel as though there are potentially rejecting consequences for *him* or for *her*, also, should he or she step down from the sadistic role that the masochist may collude in creating, nurturing, or maintaining. One of the satisfactions of masochism for the masochist, then, may be the exercise of control over the sadist (who can be intuited to need her or him) within a mode of not seeming to exert control. Analogously, the sadist takes satisfaction in needing the masochist in a mode of seeming not to need her or him.

The masochist is thus interested in maintaining the sadist's image as a more independent, powerful, and superior being. This is again reminiscent of Proust's representation of the relationship between Charles Swann and Odette deCrecy (see the Introduction). Odette, of course, is that beautiful courtesan pursued by Swann, himself obsessively in love. As might Wanda in *Venus in Furs*, Odette may harbor the intelligent fear that if she were to become attainable, she might no longer interest Swann; Swann may be caught up in the ideology that her attractiveness depends upon her elusiveness, her apparently greater power and uncontrollability. So arises another case of an alleged masochist (Swann) exerting power over an alleged sadist (de-Crecy), although it is a power no more to be admitted than is the sadist's own powerlessness. If a given masochist were to reveal the ability to exert power that exists in the masochist's role (for indeed, she or he may have intuited the sadist's humiliatingly real dependence) she or he would no longer exist qua masochist. Revealed to be potentially *independent,* just as the sadist was revealed to be *dependent,* the masochist would face the anxiety and uncertainty she or he had attempted to avoid by turning to masochism in the first place. Once more, the complexities of sadomasochism are distinctly visible, a conundrum, as we are left wondering who is driving the dynamic forward: is it Swann or Odette, Severin or Wanda? And, if Swann and Severin, Swann and Severin as masochists or sadists? If Odette and Wanda, as sadists, or masochists . . . or both? Are the sadist and masochist, masochist and sadist, distinct from one another and yet, finally, as though one?

By this logic, one might even conclude that the analogue to the sadist's secret urge to become his or her masochistic counterpart (thereby owning up to the feelings of dependency forcibly repressed in the sadistic role) is the masochist's urge to become her or his sadistic opposite (thereby owning up to strivings for relative independence repressed in the masochistic role). For how could the masochist not be enraged at the powerlessness foisted upon her or him by the arrogant, cruel, demeaning, demanding, and altogether impossible sadist? How could the masochist not desire power of her or his own? Yet, the sadist's hold on the reins of power in the sexual dynamic means that such resentful feelings are for the most part directed inward. At the same time, in cases such as that of Severin or Swann, the masochist's angry feelings may also come out through small unacknowledged gestures, or through unwittingly hostile demands upon the sadist to *be* sadistic. (These gestures or demands may also represent a masochist's efforts to destroy the relationship from within; unable to openly admit to a desire that it end, she or he unconsciously acts in ways that subversively hasten the relationship's demise.) This, too, is not a simple case of masochism equaling pleasure in pain but represents again a thwarted effort at exerting power vis-à-vis the other. The fact remains that the only way the constrained masochist can have an effect on the sadist is through efforts to please by appearing to abnegate the self.

That Severin comes to a sadistic end is thus not in the least bit startling. At last, the narrator can express openly the depth of indignation he must have felt all along; he can exert his own newfound power to affect the sadist (now the masochist) who once oppressed him. The same phenomenon is portrayed in *The Story of O* when Anne, the dominatrix at SAMOIS, hands O a thonged whip and gives her the chance to assume the sadistic role by beating another young woman, Yvonne: "The first time, for the first minute, she had hesitated, and at Yvonne's first scream O had recoiled and cringed, but as soon as she had started in again and Yvonne's cries had echoed anew, she had been overwhelmed with a terrible feeling of pleasure, a feeling so intense that she had caught herself laughing in spite of herself, and she had found it almost impossible to restrain herself from striking Yvonne as hard as she could."[8] The literary universe of *The Story of O* reflects the polarized gendered world of patriarchy in that the un-admitted masochistic feelings of men (of René and Sir Stephen) are expressed toward other men, whereas O becomes sadistic only in rela-tion to another woman. And so the cycle has the potential to come full circle. The masochist who takes power, in fantasy or in reality, always faces the threat of repeating the dynamic—unless, of course, the mas-ochist can remember the experience of her or his own oppression and resist the temptation to sadistically satisfy old angers (however justifia-ble such rage might be) should an opportunity arise.

But within the sadomasochistic dynamic, longings for transforma-tion remain unfulfilled, the stuff only of fantasy and literary imagin-ings, as long as a particular masochist is so restricted that the opportunity for a turnabout never presents itself. This means that a given masochist's position may offer no possible escape to a sadistic or to a nonsadomasochistic position. Reality intervenes: it is not aston-ishing that Severin resumes a position of male authority by the con-clusion of *Venus in Furs*. Nor is the matter so simple even for the mas-ochist who has relatively greater freedom of movement in a particular setting. For just as the sadist profoundly dreads the consequences of abandoning an accustomed role and admitting feelings of depend-ency, so the masochist may be afraid to move outside the parameters of the masochistic role and admit strivings for more independence and power. As we have seen, the masochist qua masochist has per-ceived that her or his actual power must at all costs be hidden.

Taken to an extreme, then, one would expect the ultimate goal of the masochist constrained to play within the rules of masochism to be the state of being controlled by an allegedly superior sadist. But here, of course, the second paradox of the masochist emerges as readily as it did for the sadist, given a dynamic rather than a static approach.

How can pleasure be renewed for the masochist who is bound? How is satisfaction sustainable? Certainly, as with the sadist, the masochist can have many consecutive partners, moving from one sadist to another after each new sexual encounter has been exhausted. But how is it possible for the masochist to renew the process if she or he wishes to remain within, or to focus on, a relationship with the same sadist?

Resistance again suggests itself as a possible solution to the masochist's dilemma. In order to keep the sadomasochistic dynamic alive and moving, the masochist might do just what the sadist would most enjoy: resist from within the confines of her or his physical restrictions even if the sadist does not demand any such challenge. If the masochist does resist, the sadist's rejuvenated pleasure should also be her or his own: the masochist will feel controlled again when the sadist reasserts control. Yet, this second paradox of resistance, viewed from the masochist's rather than the sadist's standpoint, is that it accomplishes the very thing the masochist is supposedly attempting to avoid. Rather than being a movement of self-abnegation that bestows renewed power upon the sadist, such resistance may paradoxically become a movement of assertion that bestows a feeling of confidence upon the masochist. This is the mirror image of the masochist coming to realize that the sadist is dependent and the awareness is consequently just as problematical: the masochist's discovery of internal powers puts the lie to the masochist's identity qua masochist.

This failure of masochism to achieve its own goal may lead to the masochist's trying again, resisting *again*. But the more the masochist resists, the more provoked is the sadist in response and the more the masochist must resist anew, and so on in a process that points the masochist toward the dissolution rather than the perpetuation of the sadomasochistic dynamic. In this respect, I conceive the process as similar to the master-slave dialectic described by Hegel in his *Phenomenology of Spirit*. The more the masochist resists, the less the masochist is, and feels herself or himself to be, a masochist. The masochist begins to notice that the more self-assertion she or he exhibits, the more this strange creature—the sadist who is supposed to enjoy controlling—seems to be stimulated and controllable. The masochist, in other words, may discover the power she or he had formerly been compelled to subvert, a power that, as we have seen, has the potential to reverse the sadist's and masochist's positions. Imagination threatens to become reality as the masochist, all unknowing, comes to possess an inkling of the sadist's secret and intuits a possible source of control over him or her.

This process is illustrated quite well in *Nothing Natural* as we follow the course of Rachel's intelligent reflections on her sadomasochistic affair as it moves along in time. Early on, she ruminates that "the fatal flaw in sadomasochism, in dominance and submission plays, lies in the willingness of the victim. The last thing a sadist needs is a masochist; the one person who cannot rape a masochist is the chosen sadist. They can collude in the pretence that one is wholly dominant, the other submissive but . . . Rachel began to see that her willingness to be beaten and overwhelmed gave her, paradoxically, a power over Joshua." Little by little, she perceives that this power also encompasses the seeds of incipient rebellion. Joshua wanted to control not only her body but the rest of her life as well, so that "the part of her that lived from day to day and did not want to be at the beck and call of some man began to rage against it. Quietly." Eventually, Rachel's latent control over Joshua becomes more and more manifest as she begins to feel dead inside and to long for an emotional comfort her sexual interaction is not providing. She gets angrier and angrier until she confronts Joshua with her realization that "my pleasure is a necessary component of your own," and "she began to like the idea of getting a response from him and of making real the subterranean power she felt she had in the relationship."[9] When we reach the novel's denouement, Rachel has found a way to right their inequality, to express her anger, and to herself have become the party consciously in control.

But even this strategy may not be adopted by the masochist whose chains are sufficiently loose that resistance is actually possible. A given masochist, caught in playing out the masochistic persona, may sense the potential of resistance to destroy her or his identity as masochist. Another scenario then unfolds: either the masochist does not resist because resistance may not feel pleasurable as long as the individual preserves, or feels afraid of not preserving, the masochistic mode; or, even if the masochist feels driven to resist, she or he may be afraid of renouncing the dynamic altogether, swinging back and forth between forays into independence and frightened retreats. The pleasures derived from masochism may at such a point be confused and in conflict with themselves: on the one hand, pleasure is supposedly taken in subordination and the guilt it releases; on the other, the pleasure of gaining more and more control over the sadist threatens to dissolve the habitually comfortable role of the masochist qua masochist. Assuming the masochist does not or cannot rebel entirely, a stalemate is reached that can be broken only when the desperate sadist begins to initiate the set of tasks alluded to earlier. How far, he or she sadistically inquires, is the masochist willing to go? Whether suggested by the masochist or in response to demands initiated by the sadist, there is a tendency for the sadist to create progressively more extreme tasks for the masochist.

Even this move, however, only postpones the sadomasochistic dilemma and the tendency of masochism to fail at its own alleged goal of subordination to another. Let us imagine the masochist now playing out the set of tasks the sadist was forced to generate. The art dealer in *9-1/2 Weeks,* for example, gradually agrees to more extreme (sexual) demands made by her sadist; O moves from René to Sir Stephen when René cannot think of any other tasks she can fulfill in servicing him. Implicit in this interaction is the masochist's attempt to please the sadist by fulfilling his or her demands, thereby gaining approval. But isn't it disapproval that the masochist is supposedly seeking? Isn't the masochist the one trying to reinforce negative and contemptuous inner feelings rather than positive ones? Instead, here we find the masochist engaged in an ongoing process that seems to alternate, dialectically, the sadist's assertion of contempt for the masochist with moments during which the sadist's approval can be earned. In fact, it is *the very process of the masochist's performing acts to earn the sadist's approval that keeps the sadomasochistic process alive.* I would argue, therefore, that *approval in the mode of disapproval* is for the masochist the analogue to the sadist's *desire for disapproval* (or resistance, noncompliance) *in the mode of approval.* The sadist really wishes to be disapproved of, resisted, but can tolerate only expressions of disapproval within the parameters of a mode of interaction where he or she feels *in control:* the masochist, analogously, may truly wish to be approved of but has somehow learned to value expressions of approval only in a context where she or he is *out of control.* Each, then, tries to gain recognition of precisely that aspect of self—for the sadist, the ability to acknowledge dependence, for the masochist, the ability to acknowledge independence—that has been denied within the polarized sadomasochistic dynamic.

The importance of this point for understanding the masochist cannot be overemphasized: for the masochistic process to continue, approval must be a part of, and a moment within, the sadomasochistic dynamic. A sadist who was truly contemptuous of the masochist would not be in the relationship at all or would have murdered the masochist (of course, this indeed happens in the cases of horribly masochistic sadists), thus ending the process. In order for an ongoing dynamic to exist, however, the sadist has to demand something the masochist can and must do so that the sadist will be pleased. Why else be in the dynamic were it not in some way rewarding and pleasurable? But the moment it is acknowledged that the sadist experiences pleasure, one simultaneously admits that he or she can be pleased as well as displeased, *that there are some things more than others that the masochist can do in order to earn approval.* The sadist has standards, makes evaluations—as long as this is the case, there will be some things of which he or she approves as well as disapproves. If you really love me, the sadist exhorts, you will do or not do such and such—and so the game moves along.

By virtue of these demands, the masochist's situation in the sadomasochistic sexual dynamic I am describing tends toward the self-contradictory. Like the sadist, the masochist is engaged in a quixotic pursuit by seeking to have her or his existence approved of and legitimized by the same sadist whose very existence would be threatened by that approval's being bestowed. The masochist can never gain the approval and recognition from the sadist so fervently desired because the sadist is structurally incapable of bestowing it completely while remaining sadistic. The approval can only be bestowed conditionally, for the masochist cannot really be acknowledged to be free—just the acknowledgment that the masochist was unwittingly seeking. Yet, the masochist keeps searching, hoping, pursuing, looking outward toward the sadist for the approval and recognition she or he would so dearly love to feel from within.

The search is fruitless, time and time again, as the set of tasks through which the masochist pursues approval from the sadist leads her or him further away from the stated masochistic goal. In working at the tasks innovated by the sadist, the masochist may feel a sense of power contrary to conscious intention. This power of self-assertion stems directly from the logic of the sadomasochistic encounter. Because of the masochist's structural positioning, she or he is more likely to escape the dynamic because it is the masochist who gains power through working at the tasks the sadist merely demands, just as Hegel's master/slave dialectic depicts a slave who is empowered through labor. On the other hand, the masochist will not automatically escape from the sadomasochistic system. Rather, she or he will generally seek approval only in the mode of disapproval, within the rules of the game established with or by the sadist.

Still, no matter how earnestly the masochist tries to subordinate her or his will to that of the sadistic other and thereby to stay within the dynamic, the process ultimately fails. It fails for the masochist because, just as the sadist's dream was based on an unrealizable fantasy of absolute power, the masochist's dream of being completely controlled is impossible. Both goals are impossible and illogical even and especially within their own terms. The masochist can no more completely subordinate her- or himself to an other than the sadist can completely control someone else: the masochist can no more entirely escape evidence of her or his strength and independence than the sadist can wipe out every trace of his or her real dependency. What the sadist and the masochist have in common is their respective motivations for desiring a potential reversal of roles. But the masochist is one step ahead in that only the masochistic position within the dynamic creates a *tendency* toward escape as she or he paradoxically becomes stronger rather than weaker within the sadomasochistic dynamic. But will she or he in fact leave? Will the masochist renounce sadomasochism altogether or give in to the seductive temptation to repeat the dynamic? Because the outcome of the sadomasochistic dynamic depends on a complex set of historical, social, and psychological circumstances that pull its tendencies in unpredictable directions, ultimately, I would argue, the question is unanswerable.

3

Combining the Insights of Existentialism and Psychoanalysis: Why Sadomasochism?

"The problem of domination begins with the denial of dependency. No one can really extricate himself or herself from dependency on others, from the need for recognition," writes Jessica Benjamin in *Powers of Desire*.[1] Sadomasochism is fueled and motivated by a restless desire to somehow, in some way, procure recognition from an other. This conclusion is implicit in the logic of the earlier instance of a sado-masochistic sexual dynamic: the masochist is willing to subordinate herself or himself in order to be acknowledged as legitimate and worthy in the other's eyes; the sadist feels compelled to subjugate the other to maintain a much-needed tie. But versions of a related thesis have also been advanced within numerous writings of nineteenth- and twentieth-century philosophy, from Hegel's classic master-slave dialectic through the more existentially oriented thought of Jean-Paul Sartre and Georges Bataille to, most recently, the writings of Jessica

Benjamin (the last also influenced by both phenomenology and psychoanalysis). In *Death and Sensuality,* novelist and critic Bataille wrote that eroticism results from the yearning to transcend the boundaries of the isolated individual by merging passionately into a predifferentiated oneness. In sex, one is willing to risk even death to escape the self, as bodily pleasures become inextricably connected to this deep psychic longing, according to Benjamin. She specifies, as did Fromm, the social ramifications of psychological patterns, describing fantasies of erotic domination in terms of efforts to break from a stifling individualism—itself culturally maintained and enforced—into some connection with others.[2]

Yet, whether sadomasochism appears in sexuality or elsewhere, we have also intuited that it cannot resolve a basic human "problem of recognition" alluded to in one way or another by each of these philosophers. In this chapter I confront why both sadism and masochism in the broadest sense, sexually and nonsexually, fall short of attaining the apparent goal of providing a secure connection to an other. Following Benjamin's lead, I begin by stating this philosophical problem in existentialist language and then go on to show how psychoanalytic concepts—particularly of the object relations variety—can be used to describe the same underlying reality. In general, ideas culled from the post-Freudian object relations perspective provide greater insight into the workings of the dynamic explored here than did Freud's own explicit treatments of sadomasochism (reviewed later in the chapter). On the other hand, some of Freud's more general theories of sexual and aggressive drives, and his understanding of the unconscious, are critical as we turn to social sadomasochism, the subject of part 2.

The problem of recognition can be simplified and restated as follows. In order for life to thrive, the existentialist argument would go, human beings must feel acknowledged or recognized by others: if not recognized, they cannot possibly acknowledge and recognize themselves. How can "I" have any sense of identity unless there is someone who is "not-I" by comparison? Therefore, self-definition is possible only in relation to the definition of someone else (in simple mathematical form, "a" is conceivable as "a" only because it is *not* "b"). Without someone else legitimizing my existence by recognizing and acknowledging me, the unimaginable would occur: "I" as a separate person would have no meaning and would feel terrifyingly alone. I might experience emptiness so profound as to feel as though I no longer exist. In order to be, properly speaking, alive, an individual must thus relate and feel connected to others (and consequently to the social world) in such a way that brings recognition of both the self and the not-self, "me" and those who are "not-me." This connection is by no means of casual import: literally as well as figuratively, it may be experienced as a life-and-death matter.

But here a fundamental dilemma arises, for if I am dependent on those outside in order to experience any sense of independence within, how do I cope? What strategies are available to human beings in their interaction with others for obtaining the external acknowledgment so intrinsic to psychic well-being? Drawing again upon an existentialist-influenced perspective, it would appear that three major possibilities exist:

(a) The first strategy, or option, is to subordinate oneself to another person in exchange for the other's acknowledging, recognizing, and legitimizing one's existence. An extremely conditional strategy, this first plan assumes that the other will not recognize me unless I am willing to sacrifice myself in acts of direct or indirect subordination. I may feel that I am in such dire need of love and recognition that I am willing to pay this price, perceiving no other option to be available. Thus, I try to submerge myself in, or adopt the will of, another person, seeking union with that human being. This, of course, is the strategy that corresponds to the masochist's situation within the sadomasochistic dynamic. It is also the situation Hegel associated with the condition of the slave.

(b) The second strategy, or option, is to subordinate another person to oneself. I may feel as though I cannot be absolutely certain someone else will recognize, acknowledge, and legitimize my existence unless I demand that they serve me. I fear that left to their own devices, others may snub or reject me. Therefore, the only way I can feel secure about being recognized by persons I cannot control is to forcibly take away their freedom. This, of course, is the sadist's strategy and, at the same time, accords with the Hegelian "master." For Hegel, the master is so terrified at the idea of not being recognized that he or she is willing to fight to the death to achieve a victory of subjugation over the slave.[3]

However, in *The Bonds of Love*, Benjamin asserts that Hegel, Freud, and other thinkers steeped in Western intellectual traditions treated these first two options as though they were the only ones human beings turned to in order to solve the problem of recognition. For both Hegel and Freud, she suggests, the problem was framed in a Newtonian logic that would categorically assert "a is not b" without recognizing the unified field thereby implied. Thus, these theorists presumed a human nature intrinsically aggressive and requiring either/or choices—that is, that one person or the other must be subordinated if recognition is to ensue: "The I wants to prove itself at the expense of the other; it wants to think itself the only one; it abjures dependency. Since each self raises the same claim, the two must struggle to the death for recognition."[4]

(c) But a third option based on mutual recognition can nonetheless be posited, one more akin to a Buddhist koan than a Newtonian zero sum game. In this third strategy or option, recognition is based neither on the subordination of one's will to that of another person, nor upon the subordination of another person's will to one's own. Rather, recognition stems from mutual recognition by self and other that each is different from and yet independent of each other; at the same time, each is utterly dependent on the other. In this view, human beings are simultaneously both dependent on and, in other respects, independent of, an other; the other is at once independent of, and dependent upon, that person in turn. Paradox becomes not alien to, but part of, the human condition. In eroticism, the paradox can be magical: consciousness moves back and forth from a feeling of communion with someone else to a feeling of separateness.

Of these three possibilities, only the third seems to genuinely resolve the problem of recognition. If recognition entails nothing less than how life itself can be sustained, then the first two options tend to lead toward their own demise. "Metaphorically," writes Benjamin, "the sadomasochistic relationship [read: dynamic] tends toward deadness, numbness, the exhaustion of sensation . . . ironic because the relationship is first introduced to escape this numbness by pain, this encasement by violation."[5] This is so because recognition, to be authentic, must be granted by another person who in some way cannot be controlled by the self, who has a certain degree of actual autonomy. If another person is merely an extension of oneself, if I can control that other, then the very basis for a distinction between self and other dies and the self with it. Therefore, for recognition to occur, *the other and the self must be perceived as separable human beings.* In the psychological terminology of object relation theorists soon to be considered, self and other must not be *symbiotically connected.*

Of course, if one cannot control the person to whom one wishes to relate, then one is unavoidably vulnerable, having to recognize the independence of another human being upon whom one at the same time depends. I need this other, yet the other can conceivably abandon and reject me, scorn me, subject me to an unbearable insecurity. However, the saving grace and potential beauty of this third option is that the other is in exactly the same position of vulnerability. The person to whom I relate must also grant my independence, needing and depending upon me as well. If we can relate in such a way that we both acknowledge our simultaneous dependence and independence, then my resulting sense of security will be built on a more solid foundation. Then, and only then, will I know with certainty that the other acknowledged me freely, and that I did not control the other nor subordinate myself in order to feel legitimately human. Thus, uncertainty and the paradoxical character of mutual recognition are embraced rather than feared: paradoxical in and of itself, the ability to tolerate some degree of uncertainty between self and other bestows a stronger rather than a weaker sense of internal confidence as well as a genuine sense of recognition.

Put slightly differently, the first two strategies for interacting with and being recognized by others fail *precisely because their effect is to slowly erode any sense of tension between self and other.* In the either/or alternatives—either subordinating oneself to, or subordinating, the other—one has had to guarantee by fiat that the other upon whom one depends will not disappear. Clearly, the dominating or the dominated fear abandonment if they are not manipulating or consenting to be controlled. But if one has to be subordinate to the will of another in order to be recognized (the first option), how can the recognition that results be trusted? After all, it was not freely bestowed: again, in order to believe someone else has genuinely recognized me, I have had to deny my independence by donning a subordinate persona. Consequently, I do not really believe myself to have been accorded recognition at all. My efforts fail, for how can I be recognized by someone from whom I cannot be at some level independent (and who therefore cannot be at some level independent either)? The more I try to subordinate myself and feel truly legitimized, the more I feel frustrated. I engage in behavior that tries again and again to destroy the self so as to be subordinate, but I find myself never achieving the recognition I seek short of death. Only in death could I wipe out the physical fact, the biological actuality, that I am separate and cannot ever truly merge with an other.

The first strategy therefore accords with the dilemma of the masochist in the sadomasochistic dynamic of chapter 2 because it tends to be self-destructive rather than self-generative. The masochist is worn down, becoming wearier and wearier to no avail: she or he cannot merge and is therefore unsatisfied, forever yearning for some amorphous peace that is perpetually elusive. The masochist may have momentary highs, points at which the masochistic strategy appears to have worked and yielded some recognition from the sadistic other. But, in general, these moments are transient and fleeting, not pro-longable for the reasons that have been outlined. Therefore, to the extent that the sadomasochistic dynamic can be judged as a form of human interaction, the criterion for doing so would be in terms of its tendency to break down a constantly renewing and life-sustaining mutual tension between self and other.

The second strategy also fails to resolve the problem of recognition. Here, one seeks to be acknowledged by another human being by con-trolling the other, attempting to subordinate the other's will to one's own. But how can I truly feel recognized by a person I know I have enslaved and manipulated into providing some recognition of my self-importance and worth? The person adopting this second option can feel no more genuinely acknowledged than the person adopting the first; the former choice is the obverse of the latter. This second option accords with the situation of the sadist. The sadist does not and may never realize that in dominating the other to forcibly guarantee recognition, the other is slowly obliterated as someone who can pro-vide authentic feedback for the self. In taking away the freedom of the other, then, the basis of the sadist's feeling of being recognized and acknowledged by others is also removed. Viewed from this per-spective, the attraction of the sadist in chapter 2 to uncontrollable other(s)—the feminist's attractiveness to the sadist, Sir Stephen's to René, O's to women who fall in love with her—is easily explicable. Paradoxically, only someone the sadist has not forcibly restricted is capable of providing the sense of satisfaction he or she initially was seeking.

Common to the masochistic strategy adopted by the first person and the sadistic strategy adopted by the second is that each tries in different ways to resolve the problem of recognition vis-à-vis extreme symbiotic dependency. Neither masochist nor sadist exists in a rela-tionship with the other that allows simultaneous acknowledgment of independence and dependence; psychologically, each is attached to the other in such a way that either one's freedom or the other's needi-ness is too frightening to admit. So far, these existentially based con-clusions accord with the deductions reached about the sadomaso-chistic dynamic through the last chapter's hypothetical example. Yet, the motivations which underlie sadism and masochism can be ex-plored from still another angle. I switch now from an existentialist to a psychoanalytically oriented perspective, hoping that looking backward to the deeply felt emotions of childhood will continue to deepen our understanding of the sadomasochistic dynamic and its origins.

Symbiosis and Object Relations Theory

Object relations theorists argue that the character of one's first contact with others in childhood plays a formative role in fostering sadomasochistic propensities. Margaret Mahler, Suzanne Schad-Somers, Bernard Berliner, and Esther Menaker each sought to understand masochism from the perspective of the child's early relation to objects.[6] In contrast to Freud, who stressed sexual and aggressive drives and instincts and linked sadomasochism to conflicts deriving from the oedipal stage of development (see the next section of this chapter), object relations theorists conceptualized the pre-oedipal period as most central to the development of later sadomasochistic tendencies. (By pre-oedipal is meant birth through approximately ages four or five.) Conflicts originating in unresolved oedipal feelings are not entirely dismissed, but they do not hold the critical place they were accorded in Freud's ideas about the origins of sadomasochism.

Though not specifically focused on sadomasochism, the ideas of Margaret Mahler suggest psychological conditions under which a turn toward sadomasochistic dynamics may or may not take place. Benjamin, who cites Mahler in her own object relations-oriented explanation for the "bonds of love," criticizes Mahler's work for placing too much emphasis on "separation" as the proper goal of a human developmental process. For Benjamin, Mahler's theory contains the vestiges of the "intrapsychic" framework bequeathed by Hegel through Freud, continuing to envision the self as though in opposition to others. Benjamin's "intersubjective" theory conceives of individuals as evolving in relationship to and with others; the growing child/adult does not need recognition from others for purely instrumental reasons (that is, only for survival) but also takes lasting pleasure in the joys and discoveries of feeling connected to its social world.[7] In spite of this objection, Mahler's theory strikes me as potentially helpful in illuminating sadomasochism. Therefore, the account that follows represents an adaptation of Mahler's developmental model in a direction that makes its ideal outcome the intersubjective goal held out by Benjamin. This goal accords with the third existential option sketched above and would give equal consideration to both autonomy and relationship, dependence and independence, as human needs and psychic longings.

Based on her research into child psychoses, Mahler proposed several consecutive stages infants need to complete in order to feel satisfied about being both dependent upon, and independent from, others. According to Mahler, newborn children first enter a stage she calls "primary autism." At this point, the primary caretaker (in patriarchal societies, usually the mother) and child constitute a "monadic system," and little connection is sought with the outside world as the child sleeps, eats, and gradually comes alive. Next, she asserts, comes the "symbiotic" stage when the child is either breast-fed or given a bottle by the caretaker. In symbiosis, "the infant behaves and functions as though he and his mother were an omnipotent system—a dual unity within one common boundary."[8] The infant begins to differentiate painful from pleasurable sensations and to associate the latter with the parent. The significance of symbiosis is that it gives the child a feeling of security and connection to others as well as an ability to trust. Assuming that the child is satisfied in the stage of symbiosis, the "separation-individuation" phase follows. Separation refers to the child's emergence from the symbiotic bond with the primary caretaker, and individuation to the assumption of unique personal characteristics: both are intrinsic to the "hatching process" Mahler describes. She stresses that "hatching" has a psychological as well as a biological component. A child can perceive herself or himself as physically separate from the parent or caretaker, while psychologically feeling still symbiotically connected. Therefore, for authentic separation-individuation to take place, not only must the child experience a gradual and relative physical sense of autonomy but a sense of internal psychic autonomy as well; the child grows from experiencing the unity of symbiosis into a feeling of greater self-sufficiency. Separation-individuation is thereby just as crucial as symbiosis, for psychosis could result if both physical and psychological hatching fail to occur; the child would then be unable to distinguish itself from the outside environment, and be incapable of attending to its own bodily and mental needs.

Here, the theory takes a conceptually tricky turn because, as Mahler stresses, separation-individuation is only possible if primary autism and symbiosis have already been satisfactorily experienced. The child's separation can occur only relative to a solid connection with another having previously been formed. If symbiosis has not taken place or has been lived inadequately or partially, the infant will fear venturing out and asserting its separateness in unknown and uncertain surroundings. The familiar image comes to mind of infants who, in learning to walk, take one step forward and then glance behind to ascertain that their caretaker (their secure point of reference) has not vanished. The child reassures itself that exploring the world will not result in the loss of the secure ties already established. Granted that the child's environment was sufficiently secure that the autistic and symbiotic phases were comfortably achieved, Mahler writes that the consequent separation-individuation stage will itself be marked by four distinct subphases: (1) differentiation and the development of a body image (the child at this point begins to "look back"); (2) the practicing period in which, having ascertained the continued presence of the parent or caretaker, the child proceeds to test its locomotive skills, feeling more daring in its evolving confidence and temporarily forgetting about the other's whereabouts; (3) rapprochement, during which the child runs back to its parent, as if suddenly noticing that she or he had forgotten to check, and seeks reassurance that growth did not indeed produce loss; and (4) consolidation of individuality and the beginnings of emotional object constancy.[9]

Just as the ability to enter separation-individuation required the successful completion of symbiosis, so the child's ability to reach the fourth subphase within separation-individuation depends upon satisfactory experiencing of each prior phase. The third subphase, rapprochement, is especially loaded. The child who is symbiotically attached and beginning to separate finds a delicate and precarious situation. On the one hand, the child wishes to separate; on the other, the child needs to feel that separation is not achieved at the risk of losing security. In rapprochement, therefore, reassurance is sought that this price will not have to be paid: *the child asks for recognition, for approval of attempts to be at once a separate being and a being connected to others in the external world.* Should it be perceived that no such approval is forthcoming (if, for example, the parent or caretaker wishes the child to remain symbiotically connected for one reason or another), the child will most likely prefer to remain in this stage. The child knows that it can at least survive within the symbiotic bond and already has. To be left alone, however, should separating from the parent or caretaker result in the loss of approval, is a far more frightening possibility.

The stage is now set for making explicit a connection between Mahler's version of object relations theory, existentialism, and sadomasochism. Whether one refers to the psychoanalytically based concepts of symbiosis and separation-individuation or to the problem of recognition described in existential terminology, the conclusion reached is that human beings need a sense *both* of separateness and of connectedness to others. The masochist and the sadist, employing their respective strategies, feel they must deny one or the other of these needs. But the sadist is not aware of his or her own dependent desires any more than the masochist is aware of her or his independent strivings: both have been rendered as though unconscious.

Let us say—again adapting Mahler—that the ideal outcome of a child passing through symbiosis and the four subphases of separation-individuation would be a sense of simultaneous independence and dependence internalized as a taken-for-granted part of everyday life. If the child's environment has not allowed satisfaction of these needs, a tendency toward sadism or masochism may result. In this event, a turn toward either a sadistic or masochistic strategy to solve the problem of recognition would indicate a deeply felt desire for the reenactment of the drama of symbiosis and separation-individuation never satisfactorily experienced in childhood. Within the sadomasochistic dynamic, then, the sadist and masochist may be trying to produce a better outcome the second time around even as they couch this effort in the old patterns of behavior. This would explain why each moves toward the *opposite* role one would anticipate given their supposed personae as sadist or masochist.

Returning to the sadist, for example, his or her childhood may have in some way prevented a satisfactorily symbiotic relationship being formed with a caretaker. The child may have found that a nurturant bond was unavailable or, alternatively, may have been forced to "hatch" from it prematurely, before a sense of safety and security permitted outward exploration at its own pace. The second contingency was in fact developed by Nancy Chodorow in *The Reproduction of Mothering*, also written from the perspective of object relations theory. Chodorow argues that socialized masculinity originates in part from the little boy having been pushed prematurely out of a bond with his mother in the pre-oedipal stage: the mother "pushes out" the little boy because of the way in which she herself has been affected by gendered socialization.[10] Masculine socialization itself creates a tendency to adopt the sadistic role insofar as traditional masculinity demands that males repress emotionality and deny dependence upon others (see chapter 5). By extension, then, Chodorow's argument that the pre-oedipal boy has been pushed prematurely from a symbiotic connection would also apply to the pre-oedipal sadist. The child has evolved toward a sadistic pattern because of fright and anger that the need to depend upon an other has been repressed or denied.

Then, too, the behavioral patterns of the pre-oedipal child may evolve in a sadistic direction because the option for a masochistic pattern to develop does not exist. Suzanne Schad-Somers makes this point in a book specifically devoted to sadomasochism, also written from the object relations perspective.[11] She notes that masochism would only be possible for a child having difficulty extricating herself, or himself, *from a symbiotic bond in which she or he is already immersed.* Masochism, according to Schad-Somers, assumes a caretaker who provides conditions the child can fulfill in exchange for a sense of being recognized and loved. The child in a situation conducive to sadism, however, did not experience remaining in a symbiotic position as possible. Sadism, then, becomes a strategy to resuscitate the symbiosis from which the child feels ejected prematurely. The sadistic child's strategy (take the little boy of Chodorow's description, for instance) is to investigate, perhaps to test the environment so as to discover if something—a tantrum, perhaps, a child's version of a power play—will intimidate, manipulate, the caretaker into providing the much-craved contact. Initially, the child may have perceived the caretaker's withdrawal of symbiotic attention to be sadistic: now, in response, the child will attempt to place the other (the caretaker) in a masochistic position. Lest it seem preposterous that a small child can already be involved in sadomasochistic interaction, Alma Bond, a student of Mahler's whose research also involved clinical observation of parent and child relationships, wrote of sadomasochistic patterns in eighteen-month-old infants.[12] She details the story of a child named Hilary, whose feelings of rejection by her mother resulted in efforts at controlling first her parents and then Bond herself. When attempts at manipulation did not succeed, and Bond began to provide consistent attention, the sadistic behavior began to vanish. Like Hilary, the sadistic child is much too vulnerable to acknowledge how desperately the caretaker's love and attention are needed; perhaps the child has already had the traumatic experience of expressing vulnerability and a desire for love and of being met with rejection. Now the developing child tries to act cool and nonchalant, disinterested, oblivious to the profundity of his or her need. Instead of being denied attention and recognition (the vulnerable position of the victim), the child denies recognition of the other, hoping in this way that some recognition will be forthcoming in return.

Sadism, then, can be seen as an offensive strategy that can originate in a child's defensive reaction to the realization that emotional vulnerability and dependency were not acknowledged in a particular psychosocial environment. The sadistic child *seems to be independent when in fact he or she is still extremely dependent.* His or her bravado masks a psychological reality dramatically different from the front displayed to the world, just as the best-kept secret of the allegedly in-control sadist was the depth of his or her dependence on the masochist. This interpretation drawn through the psychoanalytic lens of object relations theory thus accords with, and provides yet another explanation for, similar observations reached via existentialist concepts and terminology.

What about the masochist? Implicit in object relations theory is that while the sadistic adult wishes to reincarnate symbiotic fulfillment denied in childhood, the person who develops masochistically is caught in a symbiotic vise. Relative to Mahler's categories, the masochistic child may not be able to separate and individuate if she or he senses that the caretaker does not wish the child to become too independent. (I will leave to later chapters the more sociological question of why parents might commonly fear losing their children as they depart for the outside world and so may discourage their offsprings' breaking a symbiotic connection with them.) The parent or caretaker may be apprehensive, may consciously or unconsciously signal to the child through conditional withdrawal of love and recognition that continued symbiotic attachment is desired. In distinguishing the masochist's childhood situation from that of the sadist, Schad-Somers mentions the masochist's "hope of redemption."[13] Unlike the sadistic child who may have been pushed prematurely from the symbiotic bond, the child developing in a masochistic direction feels that recognition will not be forthcoming if she or he dares venture away from a symbiotic tie with the parent/caretaker. Think here of this child in relation to Mahler's third subphase, rapprochement. After the child has honed its locomotive skills, freely exploring the world, it becomes frightened that the cost of asserting its own identity will be to lose the connection with others it also vitally requires: reassurance that this will not be the case is sought in rapprochement. In the case of the masochistic child, reassurance never comes. For the sadist, the symbiotic stage was at some point denied: for the masochist, it is rapprochement, since to allow the child too much independence threatens the caretaker's interest in maintaining the original union. Consequently, the child who evolves toward a masochistic pattern of interaction experiences biological "hatching," but not the crucial psychological analogue to which

Mahler referred. This child, in contrast to the child who learned to deal with the world sadistically, knows that she or he is excessively dependent upon the figure of the parent or caretaker. If gaining love and recognition desperately needed for survival requires the child to renounce normal strivings toward autonomy, so be it; she or he defends against the threat of overwhelming loss by remaining symbiotically connected, if need be, and renounces assertions of self.

The developing masochist and sadist diverge in another respect as well. In order to reach a point where both symbiosis and separation-individuation are possible (and where a sense of simultaneous connection and autonomy is experienced), the sadistic child must (1) resuscitate the symbiotic bond and (2) separate and individuate from this symbiosis. As Mahler describes, the separation-individuation subphases evolve naturally from a fulfilling symbiotic relationship. If, however, the sadistic child has been frustrated in his or her symbiosis, then it would seem he or she will have to first relive the symbiosis in order to leave it afterward. In other words, the sadistic child/adult would have to undergo a two-step process to break from the sadomasochistic dynamic. For the child who developed into a masochistically oriented adult, on the other hand, only one stage would have to be experienced. The masochistic child already exists in a symbiotic bond with the caretaker. The step she or he must take is to correct the already symbiotic bond to enter the separation-individuation subphases. This can explain the observation in chapter 2 that, paradoxically, the masochist seems to be less dependent than the sadist. In this developmental sense, the masochistic child may have greater resources of strength for having been allowed to acknowledge her or his dependent feelings. For the sadist to acknowledge dependence, of course, was far too frightening, leading to the conclusion that in terms of both psychoanalytic and existential concepts, the sadist may be the paradoxically weaker party to the dynamic.

Whether symbiotic needs inherited from childhood continue to haunt the adult in the shape of Benjamin's "fantasies of erotic domination" or come to be expressed in ongoing relationships with lovers or between colleagues—all are variations on the recurrent theme that again, somehow, in some way, the child once felt unable to be both separate from and connected to, independent from and dependent upon, others. The child who turns to sadism sees no strategy but controlling in order to stay connected to someone he or she desperately needs; the child developing masochistically sees no other strategy than to be controlled so as not to lose love and recognition. Both adults, both children that they once were, continue to desperately need the other who was once the powerful figure of a first love object. A passionate desire remains for this first recognized person, be it parent or caretaker, to recognize in return.

But why was that recognition not forthcoming? Are there identifiable social influences acting on large numbers of parents so that recognition of their children is only grudgingly bestowed? Perhaps the parent(s) experienced the world in such a way that symbiotic ties are difficult to relinquish. Perhaps insecurities experienced outside the family, such as no longer feeling tied to a larger social community (the thesis advanced by both Durkheim and Fromm), or feeling extremely powerless outside the home, lead to a desperate clinging to those intimates over whom they can exert some measure of control. Once again, I am inquiring into the possibility that symbiotic bonds are not merely a matter of individual psychology, not simply the result of particular personalities being excessively dependent themselves or uniquely prone toward the creation of excessive dependency in others. The possibility remains that social experiences within institutions of everyday life—work, school, the family—themselves reinforce excessive feelings of symbiotic dependency at a broader structural level. We will have to return to this sociological dimension to better understand how sadomasochistic tendencies are produced.

Before proceeding, however, it should be noted that we have dealt so far only with the object relations brand of psychoanalytic theorizing. Object relations theory has clarified the consequences of lack of mutual recognition in the pre-oedipal stage for how and whether sadomasochistic strategies for resolving the problem of recognition can develop. What happens in the oedipal stage? Do other psychoanalytic ideas help to explain why sadomasochism may take particularly sexual forms? Here, it is necessary to make a brief foray into Freud's ideas. Since object relations theory itself originated with Freud, I begin with his earlier concepts in order to get a longer view of the history of sadomasochism within the psychoanalytic tradition.

Freud's Three Theories of Sadomasochism

Within Freud's opus can be found three separate and sometimes contradictory explanations for the roots of sadomasochism. However, common to each of these theories was Freud's belief that sadism and masochism stemmed more from instrinsic drives—from aggressive and sexual feelings—than from the childhood relations to objects later psychoanalysts have emphasized.

Freud's first explanation of sadomasochism was propounded in the *Three Essays on the Theory of Sexuality* (1908), which described sadism and masochism as component parts of the sexual instinct that can take either an active (sadistic) or passive (masochistic) form. Nevertheless, Freud was careful to underline that sadism was the primary instinctual "aim" and masochism nothing but inverted sadism.[14] (This early belief was picked up at a much later date in a major work on masochism, Theodore Reik's 1941 *Masochism and Modern Man*, which concludes that hostile and controlling impulses are at the heart of masochism.) For Freud, sadism's primacy over the secondary phenomenon of masochism was apparent for several reasons. As a component part of the sexual instinct, Freud believed sadism could be explained by the element of aggressiveness or "instinct for mastery" that is particularly associated with the "second pre-genital phase" of the child's sadistic-anal organization. Freud tells us that "cruelty in general comes easily to the childish nature."[15] By granting or withholding feces from the eager parent, children can for the first time exercise control over external objects in relation to which they were hitherto helpless.

At this point, the explanation of sadism is not gender specific but rather thought of in active versus passive terms. If the child for some reason becomes fixated in the anal stage, sadism or masochism may come to dominate later sexual organization. In an earlier segment of the *Three Essays*, however, sadism becomes not only an active but a masculine component of the sexual instinct (by extension, of course, masochism becomes feminine, a gendered theme that was incorporated into Freud's later notion of "feminine masochism").[16] Thus, even within the same early work, Freud oscillates in his explanation of sadism's origins. Uniting these two suggestions, however, is his belief that sadism by definition refers to aggressive drives directed toward an external object. In this first theorization, then, sadism is seen as a primary drive relative to masochism.

Nevertheless, although insisting on sadism's causal primacy as an instinct consistent with the pleasure principle, Freud stresses in both the *Three Essays* and in *Instincts and Their Vicissitudes* that sadism and masochism are interchangeable. Masochism is sadism turned inward upon the self, but a masochist can also under certain conditions become once again sadistic or, of course, vice versa. Freud agreed with Krafft-Ebing's having linked Sade to Sacher-Masoch, and with the sentiment behind referring to a phenomenon not as sadistic or masochistic but as sadomasochistic:

> A person who feels pleasure in producing pain in someone else in a sexual relationship is also capable of enjoying as pleasure any pain which he may himself derive from sexual relations. A sadist is always at the same time a masochist, although the active or the passive aspect of the perversion may be the more strongly developed in him and represent his predominant sexual activity.[17]

The *Three Essays*, then, announces Freud's first explanation of sadomasochism's roots: he sees it as a biologically based manifestation of human aggressivity, a relic of a particularly conceived species heritage, that now takes on the aspect of a component of the sexual instinct. As such, it is associated with the anal stage, although it may be compounded later with a sexuality that also includes genital activity (which Freud, along with Ellis and Krafft-Ebing, referred to as "sexual perversion"). In this interpretation, sadomasochism originates as a pregenital, pre-oedipal problem that points toward a biologically based aggressive instinct in human beings.

On the other hand, Freud's second explanation hypothesizes that the seeds of adult sadomasochism are planted in the child's first oedipal encounter. The major text corresponding to this position is Freud's well-known essay "A Child is Being Beaten," in which he analyzes a common beating fantasy he had come to observe in both male and female patients.[18] Freud states that childhood beating fantasies recalled by his adult patients tended to have three layers of meaning, consecutively described by Freud: (1) a child, not the fantasizer, is being beaten by an unidentified party; (2) the fantasizing child, herself or himself, is now being beaten by a parent, usually the father (this stage is generally, though not always, unconscious and inserted through interpretation by Freud); and (3) a group of children are being beaten by an amorphous authority figure such as a teacher. Freud's explanation is that the child initially wants exclusive love and attention from its parents, desires that in the oedipal phase become sexualized. The child perceives that the possibility of these desires' gratification is impeded by other children, such as siblings, who come to compete for the parents' affection.

The first phase, then, takes a sadistic form with the child wishing the parent to beat the rival child. Its content is that the parent hates the other and loves only it. This fantasy is sexually satisfying to the child since, in punishing the interfering rival, it imagines the fulfillment of its own oedipal wishes. Yet, the child simultaneously feels tremendous guilt about this imagined fulfillment of its oedipal desires, leading to the second image, deemed by Freud the most significant, in which the child itself is beaten by the father. This beating fantasy contains aggressive feelings the child now aims at itself because it anticipates punishment for forbidden sexual desire. Thus, in this interpretation, which will be critically important within the Freudian tradition, adult sadomasochism is related to the repression of newly awakened sexual desire in childhood. The oedipal complex postulates that this desire will be most pronounced, as well as most forbidden, in relation to the all-important figures of parents. (For Freud, the child's sexual desires are assumed heterosexual, though he correlates a "negative" or "inverted" oedipal complex with homosexuality or lesbianism.) The child represses these desires and feels she or he will be punished for even entertaining them in fantasy.

On this question of gender, "A Child is Being Beaten" reveals some confusion. Freud is generally taken to presume heterosexuality in children. But then why would sexual gratification emanate for the little boy in the second fantasy from beatings by (presumably) the father? If in fact the child is gratified by its unconscious beating fantasy, Freud must fall back on the notion of polymorphous infantile sexuality, also promulgated in the *Three Essays*. Sexuality would have to be defined broadly as a variegated, rich, multidimensional flow of energy that merges with sensuality, in which case the child wants physical contact with love objects regardless of their gender. Freud, in that case, would implicitly admit to a sort of primordial bisexuality, a multisexuality, that is only later, presumably in the oedipal stage, channeled by social factors into a heterosexual outlet. And indeed, as Juliet Mitchell has argued, Freud at his most radical does admit just such a primordial bisexuality. This interpretation also provides substantiation for the claim I hold to throughout this work that sadomasochism refers to patterns of behavior (or, in Freud's case, conflicts related to the manifesting of instincts and drives) that are in no way essentially fixed by gender, though they obviously take on gendered forms. It is just as apparent that infantile polymorphous sexuality has already been channeled into heterosexual objects by the oedipal phase. This claim is explicit in "A Child is Being Beaten." But if Freud assumes heterosexuality, he finds himself in the absurd position of having theoretically explained only sadomasochism in little girls. This will be problematic for him as well as for us, since Freud has already stated (1) that the sadist is always at the same time a masochist, and vice versa, (2) that sadism is the province of little boys, and (3) that masochism is the province of little girls. Despite this considerable confusion, I nevertheless wish to give Freud the benefit of the doubt and to interpret the explanation of sadomasochism he offers in "A Child is Being Beaten" as referring to sexual feelings felt by children toward parental objects who are paradigmatic of an unresponsive other. This interpretation includes the recognition that in a patriarchal society where heterosexuality is hegemonic, society will attempt to channel these feelings toward the other-sexed parent, defining sexuality in a genital sense that makes one gender especially unavailable.

Therefore, guilt about the child's "oedipal feelings"—the child's burgeoning sense of sexual desires, feelings unique to the oedipal stage—is for Freud the underlying cause of the association now established in the child's mind between sexual gratification and aggression/pain, between sexual gratification and sadomasochism. Essentially, Freud's argument is that sadomasochism may result from sexual repression, a repression brought about by fear of punishment should the child acknowledge, let alone try to act upon, its sexual desires. Thus, weaving future possibilities suggested by this analysis, the child, later the adult, may wish to beat an other so as to attain forbidden excitement (the sexual sadist) or feel itself beaten (the sexual masochist). In either position, fantasized or enacted, the expression of sexual feelings is linked to the 'naughty' or taboo.

An important implication of this second interpretation is that it again conceives of sadomasochism as a defense. It is a way of maintaining the possibility of sexual desire by "paying" for it through the experience of guilt and the expectation of punishment (whether of oneself or others). In this respect, Freud's oedipal explanation accords with the object relations theorists' pre-oedipal approach: in both perspectives, sadism and masochism are compromised efforts at meeting ontological and sexual needs otherwise insatiable. However, Freud did not develop his analysis into a full-blown historical criticism of social institutions that are sexually repressive (such as, in many cases, the family). This task was taken up much more thoroughly by Wilhelm Reich in several of his works including *The Mass Psychology of Fascism,* a collection of essays entitled *Sex-Pol,* and *Character Structure.* In *Character Structure,* Reich also depicted masochism as a defense, defining "masochistic self-punishment as not the execution of the feared punishment but rather the execution of a milder, substitute punishment."[19] But Reich went much further than Freud in arguing that monogamous marriage and the traditional nuclear family require sexual repression. For Reich, then, masochistic sexual defenses in large numbers of people would result from the organization of the social world, and not from any innate biological predisposition within individuals.

Not only did Freud fail to draw a wider social conclusion from his sexual explanation, but his third theory of sadomasochism's roots reverted once more to instinct. In a 1924 essay entitled "The Economic Problem of Masochism," Freud reversed his earlier position. He now hypothesized that masochism was part of a death instinct and that it was the primary dimension.[20] As part of this death instinct (itself a controversial notion introduced by Freud in his 1920 essay *Beyond the Pleasure Principle*), masochism was initially self-directed before a portion of it became sadistic and turned toward an external object. In the same essay, Freud also spoke of "feminine" and "moral" masochism. For Freud, feminine masochism explained women's capacity to endure painful biological processes such as menstruation and childbirth. I return to the concept of "feminine masochism" in chapter 5.

But the more significant concept for this chapter is that of moral masochism. The introduction of moral masochism was the first sign in the Freudian opus that a sadomasochistic *character* needed to be explored in other than its explicitly sexual or instinctual incarnations. Until this juncture, Freud's explanations of sadomasochism reinforce the commonsensical association of sadomasochism with sex and the behavior of individuals. However, the moral masochistic type (which, like the others, Freud relates to the death instinct and masochism's new primacy) points beyond sexual manifestations to a wider meaning of sadomasochism. Moral masochism can be enacted in a variety of spheres other than the sexual. Yet, Freud carefully noted that while the ties to sexuality have been "loosened," the concept of moral masochism does not abandon sexuality altogether. In the last several pages of the essay, Freud speaks of the "unconscious guilt" that pervades moral masochism. The source of this unconscious guilt, he speculated, must be no less than the oedipus complex—and so the older, second explanation is reincorporated back into his theorizing about sadomasochism. The possibility of additional sources of guilt and anger in social life are not explored. Again, for Freud, moral masochism may take forms removed from the overtly sexual; it can explain, for example, a nonsexual but sadomasochistically tinged relationship between worker and boss, or teacher and student. But the originating cause of these forms will still be sexual, and more specifically, oedipal. "Conscience and morality have arisen through the overcoming, the desexualization, of the Oedipus complex," Freud wrote, "but through moral masochism, morality becomes sexualized once more, the Oedipus complex is revived and the way is opened for a regression from morality to the Oedipus complex."[21] Thus, the introduction of moral masochism into Freud's set of explanations did not encourage the consideration of historical and social factors as causes of sadomasochism *sui generis*. Rather, the tendency of these explanations, up until and including moral masochism, is to reinforce common associations between sadomasochism, sexuality, and aggression. They thereby focus attention away from the question of how sadomasochism might conceivably correlate with the structure of social institutions themselves.

However, this is exactly the issue with which part 2 begins. By now, I hope to have clarified the existence of a sadomasochistic dynamic with characteristics approximating my account in chapter 2 of a hypothetical sadist and masochist. This chapter delved more deeply into how one could explain these patterned traits, both phenomenologically (drawing upon the "problem of recognition") and psychoanalytically. Sadomasochism may be a defense, one that can manifest itself either in sexual or nonsexual forms, against insecurities that have very sociological dimensions. I now turn toward exploring the question of how, and if, sadomasochism operates in several social spheres of everyday life.

PART TWO

Sadomasochism in Its Social Settings

When the question of how and whether sadomasochism appears in other social settings is addressed, the assumption of a physically abstracted sadist-and-masochist dyad quickly breaks down: within the context of work or families, for example, the sadomasochistic dynamic stretches along a much more complicated continuum. In each of the three chapters that follow I attempt to extend the dynamic from the level of individuals onto a social canvas wider in scope. In chapter 4, entitled "Chains of Command: Sadomasochism and the Workplace," I take up the relationship between the dynamics of working within a capitalistic system and those of sadomasochism; chapter 5, "Engendering Sadomasochism: Dominance, Subordination, and the Contaminated World of Patriarchy," deals with the tendency of sadomasochism to adopt decidedly gendered forms; finally, in chapter 6, "Creating Enemies in Everyday Life: Following the Example of Others," I examine the dynamic's potential to facilitate the blaming of powerless others in societies divided, as is ours, by gender, class, race, and other forms of bias (such as that based on sexual preference).

In order to facilitate this shift, it seems to me that several concepts should be introduced for the special purpose of translating the individual sadist's and masochist's characteristics (already described existentially and psychoanalytically) into terms more suited to the complicated world of broader cultural interaction. The first is that of *dominant sadism* and *dominant masochism*, against which I will counterpose the experiencing of *subordinate sadism* and *subordinate masochism* to reflect my sense of sadomasochism as an internally transformable dynamic. It is here, perhaps most centrally, that the sadomasochistic dynamic has the potential to describe relationships of dominance and subordination layered into society in complex shapes. The same person who is masochistic in a situation where she or he is powerless may take comfort in the ability to exert power over someone else in a situation that has accorded her or him relatively greater power: the corollary proposition, of course, is that the same person who is sadistic in a situation where he or she holds power may act quite masochistically when confronted by someone relative to whom he or she feels powerless. In the sexual example of two people, however, only the dominant form of interaction was analyzed and made explicit.

Dominant sadism and *dominant masochism*, consequently, refer to the primary mode of interaction through which a person has come to relate to the world. This is the posture of which one is more or less conscious, if conscious of either (which is often, obviously, not the case); it is the mode of behavior most perceived by others in describing another person in terms of sadism or masochism. In my college relationships, I perceived myself to be predominantly masochistic, and indeed I was; masochism had generally informed my habitual responses in dealing with others; I could not have imitated the sadistic young man at will, so that the subordinate posture was not one intentionally adopted. But, though masochistic in the dominant form of interaction, the effect of my treatment of the second young man (consciously or unconsciously) was subordinately sadistic. Other examples can be taken from the literary examples of sexually sadomasochistic dynamics cited earlier. Wanda's subordinate masochism is enacted in relation to the stronger lover she encounters at the same time that she is predominantly sadistic toward Severin; O still "loves" Sir Stephen in a predominantly masochistic mode even when she is beating Yvonne in a subordinately sadistic moment. Thus, the concept is a relative one, dependent on time and place: obviously, in relation to Yvonne's perceptions, O may seem to be predominantly sadistic, her masochism at that moment being relatively subordinate.

Similarly, as in my discussion in chapter 5 of love and the family, an abusing husband may be a dominant sadist toward his wife and act within a mode of subordinate masochism toward his boss—the more powerful party now—at work. Or, given the coercive mandates of the traditionally patriarchal family, perhaps a particular woman cast masochistically in relation to a husband finds herself exerting far too much control over the lives of her children. The white worker powerless on the job may vent racist, homophobic, or anti-Semitic feelings on a steady basis, perhaps displacing dissatisfactions subordinately onto others he or she sees as possible scapegoats, as even more powerless. Thus, power exercised in the subordinate mode can be viewed as an effort to compensate for anger at powerlessness experienced in the dominant position. While the dominant masochist or sadist embroiled in the vicissitudes of this form of sadomasochistic interaction may be totally unaware of the subordination dimension, the reality of "acting out" the latter is an inescapable potential in a world where the structures of power make it difficult or impossible to express dissatisfaction and anger at the person or party who is actually generating such responses.

The effect of these layered situations may be to render ambiguous whether a given individual is predominantly sadistic or masochistic, giving the sadomasochistic conundrum a further twist in the social scenarios that are the subject of part 2. Is, say, a male middle manager (who may be powerful in relation to a female secretary but powerless in relation to his male or female boss) a dominant sadist, dominant masochist, or both? It seems to me that this person shifts back and forth within the sadomasochistic dynamic as a whole: he may relate to the secretary as dominant sadist, with the potential for subordinate masochism toward the male or female boss lying dormant within him; toward the more powerful boss, his dominant behavior is masochistic, while the potential for subordinate sadism persists only in latent, subtextual form.

While I grant that dominant versus subordinate roles can be more clear-cut in some cases than in others, the fact of dependency—whether or not acknowledged—is common to any and all of these sadomasochistic combinations. This leads to the second concept that will be relevant throughout part 2. On an individual level, both sadist and masochist can be said to be symbiotically dependent upon the other. But how does it come to pass that large numbers of people seek symbiotically tinged connections with others in the first place? For example, it may not simply be parents who are to "blame," who are responsible for inclining children/adults in the direction of a masochistic or sadistic psychology (though, to be precise, in another and simultaneous sense, individuals also have the ability to act—they possess some degree of autonomous agency—and therefore some degree of responsibility). But parents have themselves been conditioned toward excessive dependency by social structures and situations—the experiencing of chronic economic insecurity, for example, or the yoke of gendered expectations—they did not elect independently.

From time to time, then, I will make use of the term *social symbiosis* in the ensuing chapters. *Social symbiosis* is meant to suggest that the structure of social institutions themselves, and the customary experiences they engender (literally and figuratively), may make us excessively dependent upon them. These experiences have the effect of fostering the imbalanced sense of others' judgments and evaluations being more important than our own, a result of the differential power of others in society to affect our self-evaluations and feelings of self-worth. For example, it is not at all surprising that extreme dependence on intimate partners and family members will be common in societies where these persons are the main (and often the only) source of community and connection to others we possess. Similarly, if extremely concerned about job security, we may come to experience a kind of symbiotic dependency at the workplace as normal. These specifically social experiences may then have as insidious an effect as childhood factors (and have affected our childhoods, more or less directly), perhaps predisposing us to sadomasochistic tendencies within an excessively and socially symbiotic culture. With these addenda in mind, I continue.

4

Employing Chains of Command: Sadomasochism and the Workplace

Nagging worries about suddenly being fired, vague insecurities experienced when the promotion or demotion of co-workers shifts their status relative to one's own, a panoply of emotions from little pleasures to rage stirred when bossing, or being bossed by, a colleague or an associate or an office manager who has a great deal of power to affect one's daily existence . . . on the face of it, such sentiments would seem to have nothing to do with the dynamics of sadomasochism. The world of labor appears too far removed, and much too impersonal, to be touched by patterns usually identified with relationships involving the sexual desires and psychological longings of individuals.

Yet, it is hardly likely that these two universes—the one apparently public, the other private—can be so neatly sundered in day-to-day life. How could the huge numbers of hours most people spend laboring in offices, or in factories, or behind store counters not deeply affect feelings toward self and others, both at the work site and after leaving it? (Logically, this observation can also be reversed: one would expect feelings of, say, self-esteem or hatred generated within the

intimate world of the family to affect expectations from, and responses to, work.) Therefore, the central question raised in this chapter is not whether working in the context of the contemporary
American capitalist workplace influences the social psychology of
large numbers of persons, but how it comes to do so. Specifically, do
the structure, implicit rules, and imperatives of work under capitalism
produce and reproduce dynamics of sadomasochism parallel to those
found in intimate relationships?

That capitalism as a social system operates on sadomasochistic principles (as its social psychological analogue, a framework it both con-
structs and is constructed by) seems less than far-fetched when some
of capitalism's fundamental premises are unearthed, even superficially. For wage earners, the vast majority of those under its aegis,
capitalism has inextricably tied work to survival; one has no choice but
to labor in order to meet basic subsistence needs. Yet, although a job is
requisite to the sustenance of life, its provision is not taken to be a
simple human right. Under capitalism, the likelihood of ongoing
work is contingent on a variety of factors over which most individuals
have little and often no control. Whether, for instance, one happens
to find oneself equipped with the right qualifications and living in a
place where jobs in one's field happen to be available (that is, being in
the right place at the right time); whether one has happened to become too old to be perceived as marketable; whether cyclical recessions have happened to result in persons' being employed one moment,
laid off the next (or, if not laid off, living in more or less chronic, more
or less repressed, states of anxiety about this eventuality).

Reflecting on the interrelated criteria outlined in the Introduction,
it would appear that a definitional sine qua non of capitalism, just as
of the sadomasochistic dynamic, is that most who labor within its parameters are rendered excessively and symbiotically dependent. In
this case, however, it is a social rather than a merely individual or
psychologized form of symbiosis that has been created by the structure of capitalism (a) making human survival conditional upon laboring, eliding two potentially separable exigencies, (b) then proceeding
to make labor available only conditionally, never guaranteed and secure, so that, finally, (c) survival itself becomes conditional and bathed
in uncertainty. If symbiotic need equates with the perception that one
cannot live without someone else or something else (in this case, literally, without a livelihood), a more dependence-inducing form of social organization than capitalism would be difficult to imagine.

Its endemic manufacturing of insecurity brings capitalism into conformity with another of those interrelated criteria that I contend characterize the sadomasochistic dynamic. For it is not only macro-economic considerations that result in job security being constantly contingent but also the demands and standards of performance imposed by those in charge at particular workplaces. A given person may feel that at her or his particular job, the supervisor is totally unreasonable, overly exacting, and arbitrary; or that changes in pay, hours, or rules of workplace operation have been imposed unfairly from above. Perhaps she or he believes corrupt and/or unethical decisions are being enacted from on high at the governmental agency, company, corporation, factory, or store where he or she works. More subtly and insidiously, the person may constantly fret as to whether he or she is doing a good enough job and how her or his job performance is being evaluated. Since the overwhelming majority of the U.S. work force remains unorganized (as of 1990, only approximately 16 percent of workers were organized into unions, a figure that reflects a decrease from earlier highs of 21–25 percent), grievance procedures to protect workers should they protest, question, or challenge demonstrable inequities are more the exception than the rule.[1] Consequently, feelings of dependency are compounded and reinforced by the realization that one can be fired if one makes too much trouble, rocks the boat, or simply complains—a reality that cannot but have influenced the low unionization figures just cited. "If you don't like it, leave, find another job," one knows one can be told, and there isn't much that can be done about it.

Excessive dependencies experienced at the workplace are often compounded by the presence of gendered inequalities. A woman may be afraid to report overt discrimination or sexual harassment that she has experienced. In a *New York Times* article (22 October 1991) summarizing findings on sexual harassment, it was noted that only 3 percent of women in these cases ever bring formal complaints. According to one study based on 2,000 women working at large state universities, women do not report harassment "because they feared they would not be believed, that they would suffer retaliation, would be labeled as troublemakers, or would lose their jobs." Such concerns are more common than rare and suggest why, in the highly publicized case of law professor Anita Hill, she may have feared bringing immediate charges against Supreme Court Justice Clarence Thomas while he was her supervisor. Sexual harassment thus exemplifies a gendered component of workplaces where power differentials have created a sadomasochistically charged environment.

On this social psychological plane, capitalist imperatives bequeath a chasm of fear that gapes beneath the surface of the working person's consciousness: Will I be thrown out of work? What will I do? What will my family do? How will I live? No other job is assured should one be dismissed, so that submission to authority becomes both habitual and an act of survival, sociologically speaking, to be expected. Nor is the chronic character of such insecurities in any way limited to semi-skilled or unskilled laborers, to the classic factory or blue-collar worker of Marx's now outdated description. As the recession of 1990 continues, more and more young urban professionals, from Wall Street analysts and bankers to lawyers, are being laid off and faced with uncertain futures. Moreover, defiance of the corporate/governmental/capitalistic powers that be can often take on individual dimensions, becoming acts of deviant and courageous souls, solitary badges of courage that could impose martyrdom on willing or unwilling saints. Like the repercussions meted out by the sadist, capitalism threatens to make one pay for rebellion by throwing the rebel out into the cold. (This image is given even more potency by the large numbers of homeless and unemployed persons who are visible in large cities as the apparent other, the underside or underclass of the employed person's position: even when one attempts to deny that the other could be transformed into oneself, the spectre is nonetheless haunting). As a system, consequently, capitalism is based on the setting of conditions rather than the possibility of limits to which I alluded in the Introduction.

An extreme form of this conditional logic is exemplified in the illegal form of structured enterprise we call organized crime. In one sense, all organized crime is identical regardless of the type of crime (gambling, racketeering, drug dealing, prostitution, or so-called legal operations), the ethnic background of a particular organized crime formation, or its occurrence in a capitalist or noncapitalist context. In all of these variations, the thematic consistency of organized crime's power resides in its willingness to kill those who refuse to comply with its dictates, or those who try to break from its grip. In this clear-cut instance, there can be little doubt that organized crime is structured around exactly the type of sadomasochistic modus operandi established in our definitional criteria. Organized crime presents the ultimate ultimatum—"if you don't go along with this system, you're dead"—in an extreme and immediate form: its iconography is unmistakable. Yet, implied within less extreme and more everyday situations of work under capitalism (legally and extralegally) may be a related, albeit chronic and far more veiled, threat. For just as focusing only on the starkness of sexually sadomasochistic dynamics can obscure those subtler manifestations of dominance and subordination that run the gamut of social life, so our cultural fascination with the extremities and horrors of organized crime and gangsters may blind us to the fears for our lives we feel on a much more ongoing and daily basis. The crux of these fears is that if we do not conform, we will not survive.

By now, I mean to have established only that positing a relationship between capitalist and sadomasochistic dynamics—namely, that both may be characterized by a similar underlying structure—may not be such an absurd idea after all. But the argument deserves more thorough exploration. One way to proceed may be to examine not only how capitalism conforms to the criteria presented in chapter 1, but how the analogy fares when confronted by the characteristic traits of a sadomasochistic dynamic adduced in chapter 3. It will be recalled that three uniquely defining traits of sadomasochism emerged. Sadomasochism was seen as resting upon: (1) a hierarchy of power and powerlessness, physical and/or psychic inequality that takes differing forms for sadist and masochist, and that involves one party assuming a superior position relative to the alleged inferiority of the other; (2) a tendency for both parties to desire the opposite of what one would expect in order to keep their dynamic alive and moving (the sadist seeking disapproval and resistance in the mode of approval, the masochist yearning for approval, power, and independence, if only within the rules of the game); and (3) the irrationality of the dynamic in terms of achieving both parties' alleged goals. Do these characteristics, too, play themselves out amidst people's experience of work in the context of U.S. capitalism? Are they fomented not only by the structure of capitalism but by divisions and stratifications of modern bureaucracies as well?

Hierarchy, Dependency, and the Promulgation of Superior Versus Inferior Roles

While working for several years as a legal secretary in one of the largest corporate law firms in New York City, I perceived a high degree of dependency between secretaries and attorneys. To date, most secretaries at the firm are women, the lawyers predominantly men (statistically speaking, however, women lawyers are more common than male secretaries). While in general one secretary worked for two attorneys, a sign of status for the higher-ranked partner was to have *his* (or, as in four or five cases, *her*) own secretary. Language itself, then, provided a clue to the texture of this employed/employer relationship, for what did it imply to the secretary to hear the attorney refer to his or her secretary as if a possession one controls, to hear the attorney boast, "I'll have *my* secretary bring this to you or get on the phone"? Being asked to serve coffee to the boss's clients or to perform personal tasks for him or her were not simply job functions but also demonstrations of the attorney's status; the boss/secretary relationship reflected considerations of power as much as efficiency. If one of the secretary's unspoken job functions was to endow the boss/attorney with greater predominance and status, she would certainly feel less powerful and less important by comparison. In the firm where I worked, a quasi-caste system had quietly but rigidly carved a chasm between lawyers and the secretarial staff. While it might be acceptable for lawyers to have affairs with secretaries, for instance, such actions as living with them, marrying them, or introducing them socially to other attorneys were in general frowned upon. Little wonder, then, if the secretary came to be dependent on the attorney not only for the specifying of tasks to be done but for the provision of a vicarious sense of self-importance undermined by the relative powerlessness implicit in her or his own situation.

However powerless and dependent a secretary might come to feel in relation to an attorney, the structure of this corporately organized firm did bestow relative status and power upon the secretary in contrast with people further down the chain of command such as Xerox operators, mail room workers, and messengers. The partner's secretary felt superior to the secretary of a mere associate. Here, a potential for subordinate sadism may exist (though not, of course, necessarily be enacted) for persons like the secretary cast in positions that structurally might tend to produce dominant masochism. Nor were these simultaneous dual roles confined to secretaries, being built in just as solidly to the attorneys' own daily lives.

Attorneys were divided along the axes of relative power and powerlessness according to whether they were associates or partners. As in most large law firms, the majority of attorneys were younger associates whose goal was partnership, a reward attainable only after seven years and only for one in every six or seven candidates. Thus, the associates also found themselves in positions of extreme dependency, sharing more with secretaries than they might care to admit, yet compensated for this sobering similarity by their relatively higher status. The secretary looked to her or his boss for approval and legitimation, since the boss had the power to continue or discontinue her or his livelihood as well as to reject her or his work. This behavior was not particularly different from that of the associate trying to please the partner. The corporate rung might vary, but anxieties were invoked everywhere along the ladder: a secretary worries about whether she or he has done a good enough typing job or presented a sufficiently pleasant front to the world on the attorney's behalf: an associate frets as to whether the partner will like the brief he or she has written. Will the partner think I'm sharp and hardworking enough, the associate wonders, or that I am a good enough team player (terminology borrowed typically from the world of sports)?

At a most fundamental level, then, the associate, like the secretary, is structurally dependent on his or her relative superiors: like the secretary, the associate seeks approval, legitimation, the sense of fitting in, and is surrounded by the uncomfortable reality that the partner's opinions and judgments count far more than his or her own. It is the partner who controls and has extraordinary significance in determining the associate's future fate: the partner's gestures and tone of voice may be nervously scanned for shades of approval or disapproval, just as the associate's own voice may be laden with extreme significance for the secretary dependent upon him or her. Within this framework, is the associate a dominant sadist or dominant masochist? Relative to the secretary, he or she may be a dominant sadist (with a potential for subordinate masochism in relation to the partner); relative to the partner, he or she may be a dominant masochist (with a potential for subordinate sadism, now in relation to the secretary). Based on this analysis, all the characters on stage—from the partner to the associate to the partner's secretary to the associate's secretary all the way through to Xerox operator and messenger boy—are enmeshed within the same psychosocial structure.

I am suggesting that the structure of modern bureaucracies, which Max Weber described as featuring fixed chains of command and rationalized rules and regulations, may itself contribute to producing a sadomasochistic orientation. Should this thesis have any validity, then cultures steeped in bureaucracy are potentially implicated—if, that is, they are organized in such a way that questioning or challenging those rules and regulations results in extreme reprisal. Again, in and of itself, the existence of hierarchy within bureaucratic structures need not suggest the presence of sadomasochistic dynamics. But when bureaucracy is combined with capitalist social structure in such a way that hierarchies are unquestionable, I would argue that then the potential for sadomasochism arises. (This allows for communist societies based on bureaucratic collectivism to also be analyzed through this framework.)

Clearly, U.S. capitalism has developed along the lines of multiplying bureaucratization in the Weberian sense. In his book on labor organization, Richard Edwards portrays the phenomenon of job stratification as one of the most significant transformations in the twentieth-century workplace. At the Polaroid Corporation, a case study Edwards cites, 9,000 employees were classified for purposes of regulations and benefits into 6,397 workers covered by the provisions of the Fair Labor Standards Act and paid on an hourly basis and 3,016 "exempt" employees who were salaried. Within this division were 18 job families, 300 job titles, and 14 pay grades, a system that resulted in 2,100 "individual slots" for the 6,397 hourly workers.[2] According to Edwards, this type of stratification plays a role in facilitating "bureaucratic control" because it internally divides the workplace and reinforces this division in terms of supposedly objective laws. I would translate this explanation into social psychological terminology by claiming that the deeper effectiveness of bureaucratic control is to tie the worker into an infinitely regressing sadomasochistic structure. Not only within the law firm I described but also in the Polaroid example of Edwards's depiction, a given employee is frequently situated so as to be both bossed and boss. The worker who is subordinate to one unit head and perhaps redefined with a new title in another capacity may have a few subordinates of her or his own. (The secretarial job has itself undergone recent stratification, dividing those who do straight secretarial work from the more euphemistically entitled "administrative assistants" featured in job descriptions and advertisements.) If one feels upset at the dependent and controlled position in which one has been placed from above, this anger can be rechanneled (subordinately) by way of one's ability to exercise some control below. Unhappiness is thereby dissipated, resulting in the perpetuation and constant recycling of a rather efficient sadomasochistic (social psychological) system.

But this discussion of dual roles within bureaucracy does not negate the persistence of predominantly sadistic and masochistic positions, either at work or elsewhere. It is still the case that, overall, many workers are relatively more powerless than powerful with regard to control of the rules and regulations of the workplace, even if they may sometimes have the opportunity to compare themselves favorably with, or to instruct, workers below them. In this general sense, most bosses are also still relatively more powerful than powerless, even if from time to time they must answer to a higher up board chair.

At this juncture, Marx's analysis of capitalism supplements Weber's analysis of bureaucracy. Marx's theory suggests an analogy between, on the one hand, the position of a dominant sadist and a capitalist and, on the other, the position of a dominant masochist and a worker. The class relations of capitalism described by Marx—the division between capitalist and worker, bourgeois and proletarian—seem to accord with the first deduced characteristic of sadomasochistic interaction in also being a hierarchical relationship based upon inequality. The capitalist's power is only possible in contrast with the relative powerlessness of the worker, just as the sadist's was possible only relative to the disempowerment of the masochist. Like the sadist, the capitalist of Marx's account is completely dependent upon workers' labor in order to exist qua capitalist. Continuing the analogy further, the capitalist cannot, any more than could the sadist, admit this dependency, trying at all costs to either hide or deny or overcome this reality. Consequently, the capitalist of Marx's description uses ideological tactics to encourage the worker's perception of the system in which both are embroiled as eternal and unchangeable. Capitalists fear that were workers to intuit their own pivotal role in the day-to-day functioning of the capitalistic dynamic, to sense (interpolating from Marx's terminology) that it is their own labor that makes capitalism possible, the system's self-perpetuation might be in danger. As a result, capitalists seek to control workers, to keep them dependent so that the capitalists' own dependency is mystified.

Do capitalists, like sadists, also promulgate hierarchical judgments about their relative superiority in contrast to allegedly dependent, inferiorized workers? According to Barbara Garson's ethnographic account of workplace conditions in factories across the country, *All the Livelong Day*, the position of structural dependency in which workers find themselves brings with it feelings of deep self-doubt and inferiority. "People are treated like children at work," she writes. "They can be moved, they can be scolded, they can be punished by being made to stand next to a pole and of course they can be fired . . . one is constantly reminded, 'You're little; we're big'."[3] She found that while factory workplaces varied greatly according to the degree to which workers were isolated from one another or organized, an infantilizing control was uniformly present behind a given employer's more or less paternal practices. Garson interviewed a large number of people in a nonunionized ping pong factory where workers could not talk with one another freely, take breaks, or even use bathroom facilities without permission from repressive supervisors.[4]

At a Helena Rubinstein lip gloss factory where workers were organized, Garson approvingly describes a very different job experience resulting from a female-led union fight that produced rotating jobs, high wages, and good maternity leave benefits. Yet, even at Helena Rubenstein, workers who provided collective support for one another still found themselves cast by the employer into a reactive position, responding to terms and conditions of employment the employer had dictated. This reality was painfully apparent with regard to the introduction of "speed up," or, as one woman put it, the machines' peculiar habit of "accidentally" increasing the rate at which make-up bottles came down the line. Even the union had no control over the speed of the line, having been forced to recognize in its bargaining agreement that "the employer shall have the exclusive control and supervision of its operations, and the union agrees not to interfere with any of the employer's rights and prerogatives."[5] Setting the rules was still predominantly in the capitalists' hands.

Several reasons can be cited to explain how workplace inequality leads to feelings of inferiority on the part of the worker relative to the capitalist who is perforce accorded greater significance and worth. There is the obvious structural powerlessness of workers, eloquently decried in much of Marx's writing as built into a situation in which people cannot exercise control over their lives. But the object relations perspective referred to in chapter 3 fits in here as well. A strong sense of power and self-actualization can only emerge with its own exercise; psychologically speaking, a sense of simultaneous dependence and independence only develops when the child can strike out on its own without fear of losing connections to others and the human community. If the child is not able to strike out on its own, however, chances are it will feel negatively toward the self which has been forced to remain in a situation of excessive dependency. Unfortunately, the structural situation of the factory workers Garson describes permits no possibility of exercising simultaneous independence and dependence: striking out, literally and figuratively, may indeed result in loss, as argued above. The hundreds of workers she interviewed were well aware that failure to follow the company's specifications would not be met with tolerance or understanding. Workers knew they could, and probably would, be fired and replaced if they failed to play the game as it was given. In Freudian terms, a second reason for negative internal feelings is the inability to direct anger outward at the capitalist/other. Too often, workers feel that there is no place to direct anger except inward, at the self that feels inferior and is consequently more likely to accept the conditions of psychic and social dependency.

Of course, though the factory worker was Marx's classic proletarian, most people who work are no longer employed within factories. It is by now a cliché to note the twentieth-century changes in the composition of labor that have led to an increasing number of jobs in the service sector. More and more persons are employed in white-collar jobs and clerical occupations, working in offices or stores physically and organizationally distinct from the traditional blue-collar factory and manufacturing workplace of Marx's description. In his oft-cited account of these changes, Harry Braverman noted that "service workers," which he defined as including persons employed in cleaning, food, health, personal (airline flight attendants, welfare service workers, barbers, child care personnel), and protective services (police, fire fighters, etc.) had grown as a factor of nine since 1970, whereas employment as a whole had less than tripled. The growth in clerical jobs is just as striking, as is its feminization: in 1900, 200,000 women were clerical workers (three-fourths of the clerical jobs were held by men); by 1970, the figure had risen to 10,000,000 (three-fourths of all clerical jobs, those held by men dropping to a mere one fourth).[6] Do these developments make of Marx's classically alienated factory workers a group that, in the minority of all workers, experiences the combination of attributed inferiority and extreme dependency associated with the first characteristic of sadomasochism? Or does the situation of service workers create an analogous effect?

In *The Managed Heart*, sociologist Arlie Hochschild implies that excessive dependency for certain service workers may characterize not only the *relationship* between employee and employed at a particular job, but *the character of the work itself*. She notes that in 1983, less than 8 percent of workers were employed on assembly lines whereas the number of people engaged in "emotional labor" had grown to approximately one third of the workplace and one half of all working women. By Hochschild's definition, emotional labor involves the suppression of one's own feelings in order to produce a particular state of mind in an other. Using airline flight attendants as an example, Hochschild writes that they are trained to place the satisfaction of passengers above their own emotional gratification at all times. Passengers, they are taught, wish the attendant to smile, to reflect pleasantness and contentment. If a passenger should happen to anger the attendant by obnoxious behavior, she or he (though male flight attendants are still rare) is advised to "think about the *other* person and why they're so upset, [then] you've taken attention off of yourself and your own frustration. And you won't feel so angry."[7] One should not respond as one actually feels. The labor itself demands that the feelings and needs of the other be prioritized over one's own, a demand similarly placed by the sadist of the sadomasochistic dynamic upon the masochist. It is as though jobs based on emotional labor are not content to control body and mind but insist on reaching out to grab the soul as well. Though studying flight attendants in particular, Hochschild contends that her analysis holds true for a broad range of occupations: it would certainly apply to the secretary's predicament as I and others experienced it. One passage is worth quoting at length, as Hochschild describes

> the secretary who creates a cheerful office that announces her company as "friendly and dependable" and her boss as "up-and-coming," the waitress or waiter who creates an "atmosphere of pleasant dining," the tour guide or hotel receptionist who makes us feel welcome, the social worker whose look of solicitous concern makes the client feel cared for, the salesman who creates a sense of protective outreach but even-handed warmth—all of them must confront in some way or another the requirements of emotional labor.[8]

Another important example of emotional labor is cited by sociologist Judith Rollins in her excellent book *Between Women: Domestics and Their Employees.* In this case, labor does not take place within a public capitalistic workplace but is far more privatized. Not only is a class relationship involved between employer and employee, but also a gendered interaction between two women of different races. According to Rollins's description, this relation is frequently sadomasochistically tinged, by this book's definition, involving forms of "emotional labor" that give the employee little choice but excessive dependency. Here, the usually white female employer may herself be cast in a role of subordinate masochism toward her white male husband (in relation to whom she is relatively powerless) at the same time that she acts out predominant sadism in relation to the usually black female employee. As an employer, she often demands that rituals of deference be followed. As Rollins writes about a change in her own behavior while working as a domestic, "She [the employer] did not question the change; my behavior now expressed my belief in my inferiority in relation to her and thus my acceptance of her superiority in relation to me. Her desire for that confirmation from me was apparently strong enough to erase from her memory the contradiction of my previous behavior."[9] But Rollins also notes that the supposedly "inferior" domestic, allegedly cast in the dependent position, is nonetheless astutely aware of the rules of the dynamic in which she has been asked to engage. The domestic makes her own quite independent judgments about her employer, often rebelling inside and exerting much more control over the situation than the employer ever recognizes.

Hochschild's analysis of "emotional labor" might be relevant even to people working in positions supposedly more prestigious, whose jobs require and are desired for their ability to yield large salaries, bonuses, or commissions. In this respect, the law firm example is apt insofar as the young associate eager to please the boss knows only too well that it is not just his or her mind and attention the superior judges: subtler cultural indicators (how cool the associate is under pressure, how well he or she is able to make jokes and exchange social niceties) are also being constantly assessed out of a corner of the partner's eye. Michael Lewis, who worked as a Wall Street bond salesman at Salomon Brothers after graduating from Princeton, depicts the conditioning of the entering class trainees as an exercise in humiliation, an initiation through what Goffman called "rituals of subordination." (Rollins also cites these Goffmanian rituals.) In his commercially successful 1989 book *Liar's Poker*, Lewis recalls the immersion of trainees in the process of attempting to become "good players": "Life as a Salomon trainee was like being beaten up every day by the neighborhood bully," with little positive reinforcement and a constant sense of having to "wriggle and squirm." (In a *New York Times* book review of Donald Trump's *Surviving at the Top*, Lewis explicitly describes some of Trump's day-to-day business practices—practices not altogether different from those he must have encountered at Salomon Brothers—as "sadomasochistic.")[10]

Whether referring to factory, service, or domestic workers, or to modern young urban professionals, then, a symbiotic situation can arise that is again analogous at the social level to the individual psychic symbiosis with which sadomasochism has already been associated. For the employed persons we have looked at—whether factory workers, secretaries, flight attendants, domestic employees, law associates, or investment bank trainees—questioning the rules and regulations of the workplace is often difficult or impossible, for challenging the boss's authority may be tantamount to committing job suicide. The person who works may thus commonly feel (or be asked to feel) a socially generated obsession with whether or not she or he is acceptably pleasing to others, whether or not to her- or himself. This perspective informed the incisive beginning of Woody Allen's film *Zelig*, in which Allen portrayed a man who rises to fame because he is able to instantly become what others wish him to be. To the extent Zelig, or the character of Willie Loman in Arthur Miller's play *Death of a Salesman*, really does strike a chord that runs deep in American culture, his dilemma resembles that of the person who has been situated sadomasochistically. Many workers, like the masochist, find themselves subject to chains of command that induce extreme dependency and a tendency toward the experience of oneself as inferior relative to an allegedly superior authority. Thus, interpolation from this first criterion of sadomasochism points toward an association between bureaucratic and capitalistic work structures and the creation of social symbiosis. Social symbiosis, in turn, is intimately connected with the dynamic form of interaction under study.

The Paradoxes of Disapproval within the Mode of Approval and Approval within the Mode of Disapproval

Let us return to the sadist whose most cherished alleged goal was the achievement of a perfect control over the masochist, and yet whom we deduced at a deeper level actually to require resistance within the boundaries of the sadomasochistic dynamic. Does the boss referred to above, or for that matter the capitalist, demonstrate an analogously paradoxical disposition? Does he or she reach a point of contentment, or is he or she, like the sadist, perpetually restless? Here I would like to return a second time to Marx's and Weber's writings, searching for insight into the capitalist's inner state. Capitalism, wrote Marx, is a dynamic process in which the capitalist is constantly in flux, always in search of new markets to invest accumulated profits. But *why* is the capitalist so driven toward continued accumulation? Marx's answer was that he or she is egged on by competition with other capital-ists who are constantly innovating, forever inventing more efficient technology to capture a larger share of the market. In other words, the capitalist must continually reinvest accumulated profits *in order to survive*; in this one sense, the capitalist is like the worker in being trapped in a set of systemic imperatives not of his or her immediate making. At first the distinction between masochism and sadism may here be erased as well. Still, what about the capitalist who begins the process with which other capitalists must later compete?

Though Marxist theory did not provide a ready response to this query, Weber's *Protestant Ethic and the Spirit of Capitalism* located the motivating force of the burgeoning capitalist in the Protestant's obses-sion with winning religious salvation from God. As Weber noted, most early capitalists were indeed Protestant. If this is so, then the burgeoning capitalist Protestant has characteristics resembling those of the prototypical *masochist;* he searches for the approval of an exter-nal other (God) that can never come in this lifetime but only, it is hoped, in death. Weber's Protestant may therefore be characterized by both the dominant and subordinate roles within a system compar-able to the sadomasochistic dynamic. Dominantly masochistic in rela-tion to God, he is subordinately sadistic in relation to the human beings who become instrumental in this pursuit. Thus, the Weberian capitalist drove workers on in a chase toward greater and greater profits for reinvestment. Of course, it is only this subordinate sadism toward workers—based upon the masochist's anger that arises from an impossible and therefore frustrating pursuit—that will ever be vis-ible because only it takes place on the material plane. The impossible approval from God sought by the capitalistic Protestant of Weber's description was just that, impossible within *this* life.

As Weber himself prognosticated, however, the modern capitalist has no scruples about God, for only vestiges of this original Protestantism remain. Why, then, is the modern capitalist never con-tent? Is this discontent simply a product of greed (a theory of innate human nature that Marx, and most Marxists, would be forced to re-ject)? Or is it a product of the material scarcity that, as alluded to above, initially forced capitalists to constantly compete with one an-other? In both existential and psychological terms, perhaps the cap-italist could not be satisfied *even if there was no competition from other capitalists*— a lone capitalist would nonetheless start the ball rolling. It is an empirical and theoretical truism that a capitalist is motivated by

the desire for profit, for reinvestment, by a seemingly limitless acquis-
itiveness. Less obvious and theorized is the psychological and existential question of why? What lies beneath the surface of the
capitalist's observable acts—what is his, or in still rare cases her, social
psychology?

It is hard to argue with the proposition that quests for profit,
money, and wealth are not only about money, wealth, and profit but
also symbolize a desire for power. This desire for power can itself be
interpreted as indicative of a yearning for complete control. And it
might be taken as symbolic of a longing to somehow escape death,
that most inescapable reminder to human beings of their final inability to avoid being limited, vulnerable, and restricted by certain givens
of life. In reality, there is no human power that is not delimited by
considerations of the body's frailty, or of the environment's ability to
wreak vengeance if we attempt to dominate it too brutally, or of
others whose wants and wills contradict our own desires. Independence and power can go only so far before they encounter these concrete reminders of a seemingly unavoidable dependence and
powerlessness—*before they must in some way acknowledge the reality of
others who make claims of their own, and who cannot be controlled unless
forced into dependence and controllability.*

For the capitalist who seeks limitless power, no such acknowledgment is possible. To the extent he or she pursues a goal of limitless
power, the modern capitalist cannot acknowledge that as a human
being, he or she is not only independent but dependent as well. (As
we will see in the discussion of gender in the next chapter, this predicament is shared by a socialized masculinity; it may not be coincidental
that capitalism persists in being a male-dominated social system.) The
capitalist is in this respect quite analogous to the sadist, who pursues a
similarly impossible goal. That the pursuit continues despite its
absurdity means that the capitalist, by virtue of the dynamic in which
his or her enterprise is embedded, can never be content. Complete
power forever eludes his or her grasp because, as with the sadist who
continually innovates out of frustration, contingency and dependency
upon one's workers or employees can never be eliminated.

Given a capitalist who is analogous to a sadist in pursuing unlimited
power, could he or she also wish, secretly and unconsciously, for real
dependency to be discovered so that this mad and impossible pursuit
can at last be abandoned? (Remember Weber's primitive Protestant
capitalist who acted in a subordinately masochistic way in relation to
God, motivated by an obsessive desire to gain approval in heaven.) If

so, the capitalist will find himself, or occasionally herself, just as out of luck as was the sadist. The problem of recognition indicated in philosophical terms that we can only feel satisfactorily acknowledged by an other who is relatively independent of us and whom we *cannot control*: how can we believe our existence in the world genuinely recognized by someone we have forced to be dependent on us? Pursuing the analogy, how can a worker, who has been cast in a position of dominant masochism via a dynamic the capitalist himself (or herself) instigated, provide satisfying recognition? In other words, the capitalist is no more able to relax vigilance and rest than could the Weberian Protestant pursuing salvation. Perpetually insecure himself or herself (why else would the capitalist need to figuratively bind and restrict the freedom of the worker?), no level of control ever really satisfies. All that remains is the process as its own justification, even, as Marx so astutely noted, when it is highly irrational in its own terms.

But to give up the game would mean that the capitalist would have to cease to exist qua capitalist, just as the sadist was haunted by the terrifying fear of ceasing to exist qua sadist. Rather than give up the game, the capitalist can only try some new strategy, reach deeper and deeper into new forms of technology, new methods of control, all aimed at procuring a limitless power that can never be won and a recognition from others that can never be bestowed. Desperate, he or she will forever experiment with and innovate modes of investment, new ways to keep the process in motion rather than eschewing it entirely; he or she may continually create new tasks for the worker to perform. Like the sadist, the capitalist fears that death of the process will mean his or her death as well and knows no other way to live than in an endless pursuit of elusive power. What the capitalist, like the sadist, is unable to grasp is that the process in which he or she is engaged may itself point toward destruction, physical and psychological; in the capitalist's obsession with an unattainable goal, he or she is compelled to destroy not only the other and/or the environment but himself or herself as well.

Therefore, the accumulation process of Marx's description as well as the accompanying need for the capitalist to keep innovating and reinvesting are comparable to the sadist's situation. The capitalist's obsessive drive, like that of the sadist, may have to do with choosing the first strategy for resolving the problem of recognition (namely, taking away the freedom of an other) in addition to Marx's explanation of competition from other capitalists. If the capitalist is in these respects analogous to the sadist, however, yet another motive for the capitalist's continuing quest may be his or her dissatisfaction with any goal that has been attained. As with the sadist, once a certain level of power has been reached, then what? Will the capitalist, like the sadist, secretly desire the resistance of the working person/other so that control can be reasserted: how else can the (accumulation) process be kept in motion? Will the capitalist, like the sadist, paradoxically seek disapproval in the mode of approval?

If the capitalist is to remain a capitalist, he or she would desire only that amount of disapproval that is forthcoming within the rules of the game—a small degree of confrontation can be brooked, but not a challenge that threatens to topple the system as a whole. Does the capitalist boss in fact give evidence of rewarding nonthreatening challenges to his or her power? In looking at books written about personnel requirements for hiring and promotion, I noticed that managers often held "independence" to be an important element in their evaluations. For example, the author of a 1985 textbook in industrial psychology reported from a nationwide survey of a hundred personnel directors and managers (half of whom worked for Fortune 500 companies) that they preferred job candidates who were a bit distanced, favoring those who did not seem to need a job badly over those who displayed obvious eagerness; nonetheless, though overconfidence was seen as preferable to shyness, the successful applicant should be enthusiastic and responsive about the particular job prospect.[11]

Michael Lewis recorded a similar phenomenon among managing directors, who routinely selected a handful of trainees to mentor and take under their protective wing at Salomon Brothers. Clearly, writes Lewis, the worst thing one could do as a trainee who wished to be noticed was to appear desperate to be noticed; the revelation of neediness, the visibility of a sycophantic dependency, should be avoided at all costs. He cites an example of a young female trainee who made the mistake of asking one of the managers the "secret of his success" in front of a large group: to have so plainly, and therefore coarsely, acknowledged the superior's success and power earned her nothing but looks of contempt from him and from other trainees. Instead, a far more efficacious strategy is to make every effort to create an aura of scarcity about oneself, to make oneself into a hot commodity. A managing director would become interested, attracted, titillated in a sense not necessarily sexual when, as Lewis observes,

> he believed you were widely desired. Then there was a lot in you for
> him. A managing director won points when he spirited away a popular

trainee from other managing directors. The approach of many a trainee, therefore, was to *create the illusion of desirability* [my emphasis]. Then bosses wanted him not for any sound reason but simply because other bosses wanted him. The end result was a sort of Ponzi scheme of personal popularity that had its parallels in the markets.[12]

Note, too, that this prototypically male managing director is simultaneously concerned about winning "points" in the eyes of other managing directors. Though occupying the relatively more sadistic position vis-à-vis trainees, he may be subordinately masochistic toward the most powerful of his managing director colleagues, in his own turn wishing to please, to be noticed, and to construct an aura of desirability about himself as director/directed.

Other examples spring easily to mind. In the world of academia, the graduate student most sought after by the established distinguished professor will probably not be the one who simply reiterates his or her well-worn conclusions and perspectives. This student might be seen as boring in comparison to the sharp young person who challenges, firmly but respectfully, the professor's authority. And it is well known that leading candidates for an assistant- or associate-level position at a given college or university are often those in demand at other institutions as well. While this is not to deny that candidates are also considered on their merits, there is at the same time no doubt that the perception of the applicant's desirability to external others builds an aura and exerts a powerful influence all its own. For this reason, candidates learn and are encouraged to advise search committee chairs when they have received offers from other schools. A self-fulfilling prophecy can be set into motion, and even manipulated, so as to affect a given outcome: an astute candidate, like the trainee, may more or less consciously try to have his or her name become known so as to produce a bandwagon effect. School "A" now also makes an offer, spurred into action by competition with schools "B" and "C," and the commodified value and worth of the candidate increases even if nothing about his or her qualifications or intelligence has in any way been altered.

Or take the publishing business, another case in point. Editors are only too aware of the often subjective criteria at work in sifting through thousands of manuscripts of which only a small proportion will eventually be published. But if a given property—and, therefore, a particular author—begins to become hot, a manuscript previously little noticed may suddenly become the object of a high-priced auction among houses. A similar case could be made for actors, for models, for a huge number of instances in which simply informing a prospective employer about other offers produces a noticeable effect.

All of this accords with commonsensical understanding drawn from day-to-day experiences of the person who is good seeming to possess a certain independent self-assurance, even if that person is an applicant (a position that structurally implies acknowledged dependence). Assuming two applicants with similar credentials, why does the more confident job candidate appear preferable? Returning to the analogy between the capitalist and the sadist, one would expect a person who seemed unambiguously dependent to be preferable. Yet, for the capitalist/sadist who projects his or her own feelings and sentiments, the acknowledgment of dependency accords with inferiority and is to be feared and avoided. (Such sentiments are compounded by the brand of individualism so particularly rampant in the United States. The society feels contempt for neediness, for those who openly display or admit their vulnerabilities—this may be one way of understanding the cultural animosity exhibited in the United States toward obesity, a state of being that suggests a strong need for external gratification. Or, for that matter, toward poor people, who are blamed and disdained for their own glaring impoverishment.) The capitalist, like the sadist, thus desires *disapproval in the mode of approval* and is drawn toward the challenge of bringing the candidate who is characterized by a certain degree of independence under his or her control.

Just as much to the point is that the person who seems needy is a little too capable of being controlled and therefore incapable of providing authentic recognition. On the other hand, managing to hire someone who is slightly distant and therefore seems a more valuable commodity to the capitalist contributes to his or her sense of personal value as well. This dynamic also recalls the interaction between an infatuated person and the beloved, the example with which I began this book. Their, and my, relational dynamic was also commodified in this sadomasochistic direction. The more valued lover, whose approval needed to be captured, also tended to be the one who was relatively more distant, unavailable, and disapproving, though not so disapproving that interaction was impossible.

On the other hand, it is critical to keep in mind that while the capitalist/sadist is drawn toward a trainee, a candidate, or any worker/ masochist who shows some degree of independence, this challenge must be played out within the rules of the game. It is disapproval *within the mode of approval* that is sought, and so the titillating challenge to authority will be brooked only so far. The trainee or the graduate student who has managed to create an aura of desirability around herself or himself has to remain a player or the capitalist/sadist won't play, either. The ideal would be someone both independent and clearly cognizant that ultimate authority rests with the more powerful superior, who is both bold and knows when boldness is about to exceed the limits of tolerability, who is clever at remaining within the boundaries of these seemingly contradictory, yet coexisting, parameters.

This point can be further elucidated by delving into the industrial psychology literature, where promotions are seen as influenced by a desire for some independence within the generally dependent character of the capitalistic employee/employer situation. In a how-to book on employment entitled *Survival in the Office,* Andrew Durbin urges the company up-and-coming subordinate to help the boss succeed, to remember that the boss has problems also, to discover the boss's objectives, and to display loyalty rather than disloyalty.[13] These tidbits of advice seem consistent with traits one would expect the capitalist/sadist to require of the worker/masochist—like Hochschild's flight attendants, the workers are encouraged to be concerned almost entirely about bosses or client others, and to accord priority to their needs and judgments more than to the workers' own.

But just a few pages later, Durbin goes on to say that if the employee wishes to get a promotion, to "stay on the move," more than loyalty is required. One must take "initiatives," as someone he names Gloria did not. "Hardworking, dedicated Gloria made the mistake so many loyal employees make. She waited passively for promotions to come to her without taking the initiative to alter her career path. . . . Gloria should have displayed much fancier footwork earlier in her career." In chapter 2, entitled "A Guide to Power Grabbing," the first rule mentioned is to "Be Distinctive and Formidable," the second to "Maintain Alliances with Powerful People."[14] No contradiction between the two rules is mentioned but then, certainly, demonstrating contradictions is not the object of *Survival in the Office.* Employees are urged to show independence and take initiatives, yet *too much initiative is just as problematic as no initiative at all.*

In *Top Executive Performance: 11 Keys to Success and Power,* authors Cohen and Cohen (who also run management training seminars) present the hypothetical case of two vice-presidents. Only one of these executives eventually rises to be the company's president. The first vice-president worked just as hard as the second and may even have been more productive than his competitor. However, the second vice-president, unlike the first, consulted with and constantly reported back to the boss. According to the Cohens, the second was better at "marketing himself," and they conclude: "Therefore, take note: Successful marketing to your boss will determine how well you do. . . . Try to find out about what kind of communication (written or verbal) your boss likes, and then use it. . . . Positioning has to do with where you position yourself relative to other managers as perceived by your boss . . . you want to position yourself for your strengths so that you will be perceived as strong" (this last exhortation, of course, whether or not you actually are strong).[15]

As Robert and Dorothy Bolton put it in a 1984 American Management Association publication, one must learn to adjust one's own "social style" to that of others if *performance* is to be improved and one is to fit in well with the workplace and one's boss. Even the word *performance* brings us back full circle to the situation of the prototypical masochist, from whom resistance is desired only within the system of regulation promulgated by the sadist. These regulations demand, on the one hand, that the masochist (and, by analogy, the worker) place the interests of the other ahead of her or his own, and, on the other, that she or he nevertheless display strength, initiative, and relative independence. The sadistically oriented capitalist or boss may wish some degree of disapproval to be forthcoming but ends by reasserting power, only to wish for yet another challenge, on and on into the indefinite future. This syndrome may also explain the capitalist's constant innovation and search for new tasks, new research, new markets for investment. Like a child who is forever testing, the capitalist, like the sadist, weaves back and forth between the desire for challenges to his or her power and the frightened need to squelch them.

How does the *worker* cast masochistically respond to the capitalist's restless pursuits and innovations? Does she or he rebel, demonstrating that the capitalist (like the sadist) has intentionally or unintentionally nurtured resistance by causing so much discomfort or pain that the worker tries to reject the dynamic altogether? Obviously, rebelling is not an easy option for most workers for whom, as we have seen, the job is linked to survival. If many people must therefore remain in their jobs, will they, like the masochist, paradoxically seek "approval within the mode of disapproval"? A debate exists around the nature of worker reaction to the workplace situation within Marxist-influenced writing on this subject. According to Michael Burawoy's account of this controversy in *Manufacturing Consent*, workers form a separate and distinct culture in opposition to capitalist imperatives; other writers depict workers as having to participate in the capitalist "game." Aligned with Burawoy are both Marxists and industrial psychologists who believe workers (particularly factory workers) purposely restrict output as a form of sabotage and protest. Based upon his experience working as a machine shop operative at a small plant in Illinois, however, Burawoy suggests instead that workers may come to participate in a "game" that contributes to the system's maintenance and perpetuation. Burawoy calls this game "making out." "Making out" is the process of workers coming to participate actively to do their best on a particular job, regardless of monetary gain and of their greater output accruing predominantly to the capitalist's benefit. Since the machinists Burawoy studied worked on a piecemeal basis, they earned more money with greater output.

But the deeper motivations in making out, Burawoy contended, were workers' desires to make repetitive labor more challenging. Consequently, workers were hooked into a systemic game from which they gained satisfaction, even if the effect of making out was to maintain the capitalist system that they perceived to be controlling them. Even rebellion, then, takes place within the rules of the game. Not surprisingly, making out was reinforced and approved of by capitalists, managers, and chiefs within a given plant, all of whom perceived the usefulness of the "making out game" in maintaining the structure of work as a whole. Indeed, if the dynamic were not reinforced by the capitalist, making out would not have the capacity to engage the worker's energy for no rewards and no "approval" would be forthcoming.[16] For the game to continue, it has to have a certain degree of uncertainty—the worker has to work for rewards. Yet, it cannot be totally unrewarding lest the demoralized worker comes to abandon the game altogether. Here, the game is reminiscent of sadomasochistic processes of the sort I described between the lover and beloved in chapter 1. The worker can be cast in a masochistic position only if she or he receives approval of an inconsistent nature. Similarly, for a masochistic lover to take part in a sadomasochistic dynamic requires that the sadistic beloved be at least sporadically approving: without some positive feedback, there would be no basis for interaction to be initiated or continued. If, on the other hand, the beloved were loving on a more consistent basis, the dynamic would not by definition be sadomasochistic. For the masochist to be involved in a sadomasochistic social psychological system may mean that she or he must work for an approval that comes only with the meeting of certain conditions, but that is never entirely certain. In this way, the masochist, and possibly the worker as well, stays hooked, rarely questioning the rules of the game itself.

In terms of the sadomasochistic dynamic, perhaps making out and the approval it generates for the worker from the capitalist is in fact analogous to the masochist's paradoxical seeking of approval within the mode of disapproval. Thus, Burawoy's study can be interpreted as demonstrating the paradox deduced from an example of the sexually sadomasochistic dynamic to be at the heart of masochism. By conventional definition, a masochist is self-destructive, taking pleasure in painful experiences. I am arguing that, on the contrary, the worker comes to be in a masochistic position only defensively, because of her or his need to work for psychic and psychological survival. The absurdity of viewing masochism as innate and static is demonstrable in the worker/masochist seeking the goal opposite that conventionally associated with masochism. The worker/masochist seeks approval within the mode of disapproval precisely because she or he is trying, possibly unconsciously, to separate from the dynamic, to garner an independence from inside a relationship that fosters excessive dependency by fiat.

The structure of the capitalist workplace, however, does not permit separation anymore than does a certain type of family permit the emergence of simultaneous dependence and independence (see chapter 3 on object relations theory). The capitalist interacting in a sadistic mode has no more intention of allowing separation to occur than does a parent who, intentionally or not, clings tenaciously to a child. The worker qua masochist who longs for approval within the mode of disapproval is thereby also on a quixotic quest, looking for recognition and independence the capitalist/sadist can grant only sporadically and conditionally if he or she is to remain a capitalist/sadist. Yet, the strivings themselves are real and crucial insofar as they evidence a recurring desire on the part of the worker cast masochistically to break from a sadomasochistic dynamic in the realm of work. At the same time, this recurring desire also demonstrates the system's potential for demise: if the masochist were to break from the dynamic, the sadist would be forced to alter his or her form of interaction as well. The demise, like Godot, can never come unless the worker/masochist is able to break entirely with the capitalist/sadist and look for approval elsewhere—toward self or toward supportive others (perhaps family, or a union, or a social movement) as intervening third parties. In the meantime, either coercively or by injecting new and seductive doses of approval into the situation, the capitalist/sadist will regularly resist attempts on the worker's part to break from the dynamic. This statement is borne out by a brief look at the history of the capitalist/sadist's strategic attempts to control the work force. The history of industrial psychology is, in this sense, also the history of the capitalist's efforts to maintain the capitalist/sadomasochistic system and to discourage the worker/masochist from breaking away.

American labor history gives ample proof that gaining approval in the mode of disapproval through defensive methods like Burawoy's "making out" has not been the only response of the worker to the capitalist acting sadistically. Workers have also rebelled directly from experiences of pain (psychic and/or physical) produced by capitalism. Edwards's *Contested Terrain* details a zigzag pattern of interaction in the twentieth century: periods of direct coercive control on the part of the capitalist, followed by labor struggle, followed by new paternalistic methods on the part of the capitalist, met by still more labor struggle that leads to renewed coercion. Succeeding what Edwards refers to as "brute repression" of worker rebellion against a rigid industrial capitalism at the turn of the century came a period of "welfare capitalism." It was hoped that welfare benefits

> would persuade workers of the corporations' genuine concern for their well-being and, by actually improving their existence, undermine worker militance. In a somewhat more heavy-handed vein, the participating corporations also sought to bind their workers to them by creating stronger dependence—a dependence based not only on the worker's income but also on essential services. For example, workers who joined strikes found that their leases required them to vacate company-owned housing immediately. . . . Throughout the period of the most intense strike threat, McCormick family members dangled before McCormick Works employees the prospect of substantial stock bonuses for faithful workers.[17]

Yet the underlying inequality of the structural situation remained untouched. This structural situation was fundamentally sadomasochistic insofar as the attempt to revitalize the socially symbiotic bond through excessive conditionality. Only workers who did not object to, question, or express anger at the power relations of the workplace would be rewarded with welfare benefits or stock bonuses. Workers who attempted to separate from the social symbiosis the capitalist wished to perpetuate would be punished with rejection and abandonment, both physically and psychologically. Not surprisingly, the ungrateful workers rebelled, and a series of huge strikes occurred at International Harvester and U.S. Steel in 1916 and 1919.

When welfare benefits calculated to provide a dose of approval within the mode of disapproval failed to prevent the worker/masochist from moving away from the capitalistic/sadomasochistic dynamic, a more coercive mode of control was seized upon. Scientific management, a method developed by Frederick Taylor and made (in)famous in the term *Taylorism*, was adopted in many places where welfare capitalism had failed—not coincidentally, it would appear.

Taylor, the son of a wealthy Philadelphia family, rejected a law career in favor of four years' work as a gang boss at the Midvale Steels works and based his system of scientific management on impressions garnered from his own everyday experiences of work. According to him, the grave error of capitalist efforts to dominate labor was that too much potential for independent control of the work process rested in workers' hands. The capitalist, Taylor daringly admits, in this way becomes uncomfortably dependent on workers. Scientific management would correct this problem by instituting time-and-motion studies aimed at wresting this control from the workers, allowing management to calculate and rationalize a work process and raise it to new levels of technological precision. In terms of characteristics of sadism deduced in chapter 2, scientific management represents a new set of tasks specifically designed to resuscitate the flailing, potentially dying sadomasochistic process at the workplace. The enduring results of scientific management's influence would be to generate "technical control" of the bureaucratic workplace by speed-up and other processes that would be built into the structure of work itself.

The sadomasochistic texture of scientific management was not the least bit subtle. Here is Braverman, quoting from Taylor's *Principles of Scientific Management* in regard to a worker named Schmidt who had the misfortune to encounter the would-be lawyer turned industrial scientist:

> "Schmidt, are you a high priced man?"
> "Vell, I don't know vat you mean." . . .
> "Well, if you are a high-priced man, you will do exactly as this man tells you to-morrow, from morning till night. When he tells you to pick up a pig and walk, you pick it up and you walk and when he tells you to sit down and rest, you sit down. You do that straight through the day. And what's more, no back talk. Do you understand that? When this man tells you to walk, you walk; when he tells you to sit down, you sit

down, and you don't talk back to him. Now you come on to work here to-morrow morning and I'll know before night whether you are really a high priced man or not." . . .

"This seems to be rather rough talk. And indeed it would be if applied to an educated mechanic, or even an intelligent laborer. With a man of the mentally sluggish type of Schmidt, it is appropriate and not unkind."[18]

If one substituted sexual commands taken from Reage's *Story of O* for those barked by Taylorites at people like Mr. Schmidt, the tone of voice might be similar: in both cases, a pattern of dominance and subordination is acted out from within the characteristic patterns of dynamic sadomasochism.

For all its blatant coerciveness, however, scientific management failed as a perfectible mode of labor control even as its technological rationality became widespread and as speedup still continues to be used in production processes. It failed, Edwards notes, because workers simply fought it to a standstill.[19] Labor opposition to the imposition of time and motion studies and speed-up was considerable, reflecting the clear realization on the part of the "mentally sluggish" workers that even the illusion of their independence was being appropriated. Scientific management of the Taylorist variety had nothing but money to offer the worker, an incentive Burawoy, Garson, and others have observed provides insufficient satisfaction. Again, as a strategy, not enough approval and recognition was proffered for a socially symbiotic bond to be successfully manipulated.

Still another form of management control arose in the late twenties and early thirties to deal with the contradictions Taylorism did not resolve. Prominent in the human relations school of industrial psychology were Elton Mayo and his colleagues at Harvard Business School, whose work drew inspiration from the well-known Hawthorne experiments conducted at the Western Electric Company's facility of the same name. By Mayo's account, the experiments were initially undertaken to discover the effect of variable quantities of lighting on worker performance and job satisfaction. This part of the experiment was abandoned when it was found that workers who labored under conditions of dimmer lighting produced no less than those who worked in full light.

A second experiment was then commenced over a five-year period, from April 1927 to mid-1932. A group of six operatives who assembled telephone relays, all women, were segregated from the majority of their co-workers into an isolated physical space. The experiment proceeded to vary their work conditions over a thirteen-period sequence, with most of the early phases corresponding to an improvement in the workplace atmosphere. Workers' output was then tested and seen to increase during the course of these reforms. The reforms themselves were extremely radical for their time, being relatively civilized: short breaks were provided in the morning and afternoon, with refreshments paid for by the company served during these breaks; the women were let out half an hour early each day; they were allowed to rotate jobs, and so on.

But the experiment also yielded the result that the workers' output increased even during ensuing phases in which each improvement was suddenly withdrawn. Mayo's conclusion, and that of the human relations school generally, was that output continued to increase because of a fundamental change in the quality of attention the workers were receiving. Output was affected by the workers' sense of having acquired a greater degree of self-determination: the women had been consulted about subsequent phases and could occasionally even veto them, indicating that by my definition, the dynamic in which they participated was being shaped in a *less* sadomasochistic, *less* socially symbiotic, direction. Mayo writes that "what the Company actually did for the group was to reconstruct entirely its whole industrial situation . . . the individual workers and the group had to re-adapt themselves to a new industrial milieu, a milieu in which their own self-determination and their social well-being ranked first and the work was incidental." The new milieu included the women's perception that they no longer were being bossed (though, as Mayo notes, their "opinion is of course mistaken: in a sense they are getting closer supervision than ever before") and their enjoyment of a situation in which there was no one, no bogey or boss or slavedriver (or sadist) to please.[20]

The obvious conclusion was not lost on Mayo, namely, that contrary to bosses' conscious or unconscious fears, loosening or eschewing altogether the hierarchical dominance/subordination structure of the coercive capitalistic workplace did not result in the grinding to a halt, the anticipated death, of the economic system. In fact, output sharply increased when the capitalist relaxed the tightness of his historical grip—an apparent but existentially comprehensible paradox. Mayo therefore hoped to father a sophisticated and enlightened paternalistic approach: his goal was not to overthrow capitalism but to reform and humanize it for its own good, its health and longevity. In *Human Problems of an Industrial Civilization,* he chronicles with approval a

Western Electric program in which workers were encouraged to express their feelings to interviewers (Mayo even prefers the use of the term *analyst* over interviewer or supervisor) trained to listen to and not to interrupt the workers. Mayo reports the remarkable effect of this experimental interviewing procedure on a former "problem" worker: owing to the "emotional release" of having been able to express and acknowledge to the interviewer his dislike of a supervisor who resembled a hated relative, the worker's attitude improved and she was no longer a problem case.[21] (It is interesting how often problem cases in the history of industrial psychology literature happen to be women.) Mayo thereby incorporates the Freudian method itself in his enlightened capitalism.

The Hawthorne experiments provide another case study in the worker/masochist's desire to separate from the sadomasochistic dynamic and to seek recognition and approval of self supposedly alien to the masochistic pursuit. The experiments also demonstrate the usefulness for capitalism of acceding to this desire for at least some approval within an intrinsically disapproving mode, a mode that in fact structurally undermines authentic fulfillment of these desires. By providing a series of perks, Western Electric showed how capitalism could hook the worker into a social psychological system that served its own self-interest.

The historical story took yet another twist. With the coming of the Depression, Mayo's human relations approach was discredited. For one thing, in hard times, it was expensive. For another, it could be perceived as too threatening to the basic framework of sadomasochistic social psychology. In the eyes of many capitalists less progressive than Western Electric owners and managers, the notion of worker autonomy over conditions of the workplace and the idea that many workers enjoyed working without a boss may have been too anxiety provoking—such principles might lead to the game itself being overturned rather than to its rules simply being altered. Nonetheless, it seems to me that just as Braverman doubts reports that Taylorism was completely discredited (arguing instead that it was incorporated into capitalist technology), Mayo's message was not entirely lost on capitalists. Quite the contrary. Fears aroused in the Depression era that the Communist threat would come to the United States, coupled with the necessity of reviving a failing economy, led to the revitalization of welfare capitalism in the welfare state designed by the likes of Keynes and Roosevelt. Much more recently, the proliferation of stock-option plans and other benefit packages that include some degree of worker management attests to capitalism's having adopted and perfected Hawthorne-inspired paternalism (the now-defunct People's Express Airline venture was one such project). Simultaneously, this strategy revitalizes sadomasochism. As with former methods of control, the underlying hierarchical structure with its accompanying polarization between dominant and subordinate, superior and inferior parties to the dynamic remains untouched.

In sum, my argument in this chapter is that the relationship between the capitalist and the worker is analogous to a sadomasochistic one: sadomasochism may be a social fact of life under capitalist systems like that in the United States. Like sadomasochism, U.S. capitalism is based on a conditional form of social psychology that brings severe repercussions—the potential loss of livelihood, itself symbolic of the ability to live—should it be questioned too independently. An excessive form of dependence, or social symbiosis, is thereby created. I would remind the reader of the earlier comparison between capitalism and organized crime. Just as associating sadomasochism with its more blatant sexual/violent manifestations masks its wider presence in social interactions, so organized crime may be only the tip of a work-related iceberg. It is not difficult to see the structure of organized crime as sadomasochistic, yet this seemingly deviant instance may be only a highly dramatized manifestation of the vague threats that underlie work relationships and of the fear that pervades them on a more ongoing and less visible basis.

The point is demonstrable from even the brief survey of U.S. labor history I proffered above. Efforts on the part of masochistically cast workers to challenge either workplace conditions or power relationships have met enormous resistance, both of a coercive and of a seductively paternalistic variety. The power of the capitalist, positioned sadistically, to call the shots seems in one sense to be overwhelming: by controlling one's livelihood, the capitalist also has the ability to affect the worker's sense of psychic security and peace of mind. It is the capitalist, as dominant sadist, who can create social conditions for the employed person, as dominant masochist, that are not of the latter's making, because the worker needs a job to survive. Only the worker, therefore, like the prototypical masochist, is in the structural position to clearly perceive her or his overt dependence upon the capitalist. On the other hand, the never pleased or pleasable capitalist is indeed a driven human being, unable to admit dependence because allegedly the independent party. Thus, like the masochist, the worker is more likely than the capitalist to reject the insidious system because of the various forms of pain experienced through it.

At the same time, the capitalistic process, the game that I have likened to a master/slave dialectic as it develops destructively over time, only *tends* to drive the worker/masochist toward the eventual overthrow of the whole dynamic. As with sadomasochism as a whole, no law exists by which to predict a given outcome. The process may go on indefinitely, seemingly ad infinitum; by now, it is widely acknowledged that advanced, or late, capitalism, has far more resilience than Marx ever anticipated. Perhaps another way of explaining this resiliency can be culled from the characteristics of the sadomasochistic system itself. Thus far, the sadomasochistic dynamic I have outlined stresses the characteristics of the dominant sadist/capitalist and the dominant masochist/worker, leaving out the complications that ensue when their subordinate sides are also enacted in history; I have assumed, moreover, a capitalist and a worker who perceive themselves as such. However, when the characteristic of internal transformability so fundamental to sadomasochism is taken into account, a different set of conclusions simultaneously emerges. That more and more workplaces are highly stratified and bureaucratized in an economy increasingly oriented toward the service sector means that the worker often finds himself or herself both boss and bossed. Her or his position shifts back and forth, often including a dominant persona controlled from on high and a subordinate persona controlling others below. This is true for the middle manager, the secretary, the prison guard, and perhaps for the low-level capitalist as well. In fact, reintroducing the complexities of bureaucratic capitalism into the picture tends to erase, and to level, the differences between capitalist and worker; it tends to breed incestuous forms of intercourse between them, between sadist and masochist, masochist and sadist, oppressed and oppressor, bossed and boss. Each is more enmeshed with the other than before. At a dominant level, the fact remains that the capitalist does have greater power than the worker; on the other hand, daily experience makes the distinction less and less palpable for the employed person who over time does not clearly identify either with capitalists or with workers.

The significance of this perspective is that it focuses attention on the role of an internally transformable sadomasochism in the reproduction and perpetuation of capitalist relationships. Anger felt at extreme dependence on the arbitrary decisions of one's boss does not fuel collective politicization in any automatic sense. Rather, feelings of impotence are channeled subordinately; a seductive and immediately gratifying sense of satisfaction is gained from bossing others in relation to whom one is superior. At the same time, the traditional Marxist strategy of organizing the working class is called into question via this social psychological analysis. It may be that new ways of thinking about personal and political transformation, as well as about dominance and subordination more generally, are desperately needed.

5

Engendering Sadomasochism: Dominance, Subordination, and the Contaminated World of Patriarchy

> Once upon a time I loved a man I couldn't please. I lived with him for twenty-one years, had two beautiful children with him, and tried in every way I could to make him happy. But nothing worked . . . I realized I had developed a type of phobia after so many years of putting others first and myself last. This phobia took the form of an irrational fear of looking at or expressing myself without validation or approval from him.
>
> —Karen Blaker, *Born to Please: Compliant Women/Controlling Men*

It is not especially controversial to assert that men act sadistically with greater frequency than do women in sexually unequal societies, or that women more often than men find themselves in positions conducive to masochistic behavior. Like work relationships, gender relationships have been steeped in routinized patterns of power and powerlessness that permeate many aspects of day-to-day life. Broad and clear-cut examples are easy to cite: sexual harrassment is almost always the expression of men's disproportionate ability to control the economic and social conditions of women's lives, often in a sadistic manner; domestic violence from battering to rape as well as violence outside the home continue to be aimed predominantly at women by men. Heterosexuality, in fantasy and reality, is often still experienced as inseparable from the eroticization of dominant/subordinate relations along male/female lines. Cultural images and ideas in the United States—from advertising to gothic romances to popular psychological treatises—consistently contain sadomasochistic allusions divided along gendered lines. A subset of the wide-ranging dynamic we have been scrutinizing as a whole, gendered sadomasochism itself varies in form from the overt and bodily to the subtle and platonic, occurring in one's home or in an office or on the streets. But merely to observe that sadomasochism does assume a host of gendered faces is to beg two ultimately more significant questions. The first is why gendered sadomasochism comes into being in the first place, and how it operates in mundane situations such as intimate relationships between men and women. The second is how sadomasochism transcends gender at the same time it is shaped by it.

Concerning the first question, how does the socialization of men into the masculine generate a regular and repetitive tendency toward sadism, while women's socialized femininity inclines them in a more masochistic direction? Whereas in chapter 4 I contended that the structure of capitalism encourages a sadomasochistic propensity in those who work, now I inquire if male-dominated (or patriarchal) societies tend to engender a similar social psychology. In most respects, "patriarchy" and "capitalism" refer to two distinct ways of systematically organizing the social world. Yet on a deeper level, both may be organized around several common principles closely akin to those that underlie sadomasochism in general. In this chapter, I focus on the patriarchal (rather than capitalistic) character of American society, speculating about why sadomasochistic interaction is so often present in gendered relationships between men and women.

Regarding my second concern, how sadomasochism both transcends and is shaped by gender, I must again confront the fact that women are capable of the sadistic and men of the masochistic, even though sadomasochism in male-dominated societies is skewed by gender. Women do in fact abuse their children, while female bosses can sometimes exhibit even more controlling behavior toward secretaries who work for them than do male bosses. Men do on many occasions play, and wish to play, masochistic roles in their encounters with women (sexually, as did *Venus in Furs*'s Severin, or nonsexually), or they may be submissive toward the female or male superior at their jobs. In addition, as noted earlier, the sadomasochistic dynamic may be present in some relationships between men and men or between women and women; it is certainly not confined to heterosexual associations. There is consequently nothing intrinsically sadistic about the physiological state of being male just as there is nothing intrinsically masochistic about being female.

By now, this gender transcendence should be self-evident. Nonetheless, essentialistic arguments for an intrinsic and biologically based connection between men and sadism and between women and masochism have a long history of affecting commonsense impressions about the relationship between gender and sadomasochism. Within the psychoanalytic tradition, for instance, Freud had little hesitation about positing biology as a causal factor. In *The Three Essays on Sexuality*, he envisioned sadism as a primordial vestige of male aggressivity; in both that work and "The Problem of Masochism," he took for granted the existence of a feminine masochism that he called the most "easily observable" of the three types of masochism he wished to identify.[1]

To be sure, Freud's determinism met with some degree of criticism among successors otherwise sympathetic to psychoanalysis. American psychoanalyst Karen Horney called Freud to task not only for his association of women and masochism but also for his theory of penis envy, both of which she convincingly argued stem from social conditions rather than from biological inevitability. On the other hand, from another feminist perspective, Juliet Mitchell later interpreted Freud's ideas as descriptive rather than prescriptive of the formation of women's psyches in sexually repressive patriarchal milieus. Mitchell argued, I believe aptly, that feminists ought not overlook the theoretical significance of basic Freudian insights into the workings of the unconscious and the centrality of sexuality. Unlike Horney, Mitchell did not wish to treat Freud as a biological determinist, believing instead that he diagnosed (rather than approved of) the results of cultural inculcation. "To Freud," she wrote, "society demands of the psychological bisexuality of both sexes that one sex attain a preponderance of femininity, the other of masculinity: men and women are made in culture."[2]

Even if Freud's legacy for women has been controversial among psychoanalytically oriented feminists, a conservative tendency was present within his thought and has been elaborated by other more orthodox post-Freudians who have continued to seek biological explanations for feminine masochism and male sadism. This theme was reiterated and supposedly clarified by analyst Helene Deutsch in her massive *Psychology of Women* (1944).[3] In Deutsch's treatment, masochism is not a defense against an intolerable social and psychological environment but a biological mechanism of human adaptation. Only the biological life of the human female contains the painful experiences of menstruation and childbirth. According to Deutsch, women would be unwilling to bear these strains unless they also took pleasure in their pain. And, since reproduction is clearly not a luxury the race can afford to eschew, female masochism is rendered necessary to human survival. It is not to be changed, nor is it changeable. The well-adjusted woman would be one who resigns herself to it gracefully, with humility and without developing a rebellious reaction formation against it. (It is odd that Deutsch was so concerned about women's failure to accept their destiny: why would human beings supposedly masochistic by nature bridle at all?) Not only biology but psychology, too, was apparently destined.

Consequently, neither Freud nor Deutsch—as representative of any biological or sociobiological theorist with a will to interpret sadomasochism's gendered shapes as inevitable—seriously considered the possibility that the remarked association between women and masochism stemmed largely from social factors rather than from an innate predisposition.[4] And biological claims have continued to have an impact in other intellectual quarters as well, whether the connection made is a direct one between the term *sadomasochism* and gender or simply between maleness/femaleness and other character traits (such as, for instance, in the opposition of aggressivity and passivity). Sociologist Cynthia Fuchs Epstein has recently proposed that even feminist scholars in many disciplines outside psychology have fallen into a deterministic or essentialistic pitfall. Contrary to their original intention to reveal gender as a social and changeable creation, they have in many cases unwittingly treated the products of enculturation as biological givens.[5]

But it is precisely in regard to an issue like debunking past and present forms of biologically based thinking that the sadomasochistic dynamic may be most conceptually illuminating. Viewing relationships of gender through the framework of sadomasochism has the virtue of theoretically ensuring, indeed guaranteeing, that essentialist and/or biologically based thinking cannot return through the back door unheeded. For how can sadism be "essentially" the province of males or masochism that of females when nearly every observer of sadomasochism (including, ironically, Freud himself) has noted that the two dimensions coexist and are opposite sides of the same coin? Given the characteristic of internal transformability so fundamental to sadomasochism, be it described here or elsewhere, men who are predominantly sadistic still have the ever-present potential for subordinate masochism (a potential regularly enacted). Correspondingly, women's having been situated in a predominantly masochistic position does not preclude their capacity for and realization of subordinate sadism. The possibility of a successful biologically based or essentialistic argument is thus implicitly precluded.

Patriarchy and the Sadomasochistic Dynamic: From Theory to Experience

Let us begin with the issue of how patriarchal, or male-dominated, societies, could produce features akin to those of the sadomasochistic dynamic, generating dominant sadism and masochism in men and women, respectively. Take the first characteristic of the dynamic, a hierarchal arrangement coming to exist between sadist and masochist that simultaneously accords with the promulgation of a superior as opposed to an inferior, a primary as opposed to a secondary party: the sadist takes pains to render the masochist not only unequal but also demeaned. Certainly, the structure of patriarchy itself is an unequal hierarchy. As Kate Millett defined it in *Sexual Politics* (1969), an early classic of radical feminist theory in what has often been called the second wave women's movement of the late 1960s and 1970s, patriarchy

> is a case of that phenomenon Max Weber described as *herrschaft,* a relationship of dominance and subordinance. What goes largely unexamined, often even unacknowledged [yet is institutionalized nonetheless] in our social order, is the birthright priority whereby males rule females. Through this system a most ingenious form of "interior colonization" has been achieved. However muted its present appearance may be, sexual dominion obtains nevertheless as perhaps the most pervasive ideology of our culture and provides its most fundamental concept of power.
> This is so because our society, like all other historical civilizations, is a

patriarchy. The fact is evident at once if one recalls that the military, industry, technology, universities, science, political office, and finance—in short, every avenue of power within the society, including the coercive force of the police, is entirely in male hands. As the essence of politics is power, such realization cannot fail to carry impact.[6]

By these criteria, of course, U.S. society is still decidedly patriarchal. While women have made notable strides and now have some representation in spheres from which they were totally excluded at the time of Millett's writing, major institutions of power—including the political, corporate, academic, scientific, military, and police domains to which she alludes—are still overwhelmingly under male auspices in 1991. In addition to positions of power being mainly occupied and controlled by men, patriarchally organized societies are also identifiable by their proclamation of the masculine world as superior to the inferiorized feminine domain that springs up by contrast. Here, too, is an analogue with the sadomasochistic dynamic: like sadism, patriarchy involves the devaluation of the subordinate party or parties. As has by now been amply documented by gender studies, the sexual politics of patriarchy mandate women's confinement to the domestic realm because of their biological connection to reproduction. (I am here outlining the traditional patriarchal paradigm, modified by women's entrance into the labor force en masse in the United States and in other Western societies, and never entirely true for women of all classes and races in any event. Yet, the association between women and domesticity clearly remains valid: even when women work/have worked, they continue to do double duty and are held differentially responsible for childrearing, household chores, and other tasks linked to nature.[7])

Thus, as anthropologist Sherri Ortner has contended, all patriarchal societies—in her view, all known societies—have created and reinforced an association between women and the world of "nature," leaving men the projects of "culture." Culture, declared Ortner, came itself to be viewed as the business of "transcending" and "dominating" the uncertain, contingent, and forever decaying reality of the (read: inferior and feminized) natural world.[8] From this polarization between masculinity/culture and femininity/nature spring other dichotomies that are likewise accorded differential social valuation: the world of politics and publicity in contradistinction to that of personality and privacy; the split that arises between objectivity and reason counterposed against subjectivity and emotion. These divisions par-

take of sexual politics to the extent that men have had the power—
and women, relative powerlessness—to perpetuate this hierarchical
inequality. It is hard to believe that women stayed at home with their
children as wives and mothers in the traditional nuclear familial structure described by Betty Friedan (for instance) in the fifties because,
given the choice, they had curiously all come to the same decision
simultaneously. Rather, they became gatekeepers of emotion and intimacy, protectresses of home and hearth, because they had been given
no choice.

These structural imperatives that confine women to a domestic
realm that is consistently devalued are apparent in a book intended to
show the opposite, one written in direct response to the success of
Millett's radical feminist treatise. In *The Prisoner of Sex* (1972), Norman
Mailer indignantly opined that the public/private split between masculinity and femininity reflected not the overvaluation of the former
realm (and inferiority of the latter) but the superiority of women because of their proximity to the world of biology and nature. If Mailer
believed this, however, it is unlikely he would have been so horrified
at the thought of women taking their superiority public by desiring
equal power with men in all spheres of life; in fact, he railed against
Millett's "masculine" body as though to stigmatize her for daring to
challenge her biological place in a gendered status quo.[9] Mailer's work
is therefore self-contradictory, interesting primarily insofar as it doc-
uments and reveals the contemporary ideologies of male domination.
Not really about women's much-appreciated and God-given superiority, his book instead demonstrates the repercussions that ensue
should women step out of the secondary position into which they have
been placed by fiat. An analogy to the sadomasochistic dynamic is
once more implicit, in this supposedly academicized context: both entail a relationship of dominance and subordination in which any move
on the part of the party cast masochistically to question the sadist's
power will almost invariably meet with opposition and an effort to
punish.

On the other hand, Simone de Beauvoir's classic *The Second Sex* began with and was premised upon the open recognition and acknowledgment of the secondary or "inessential" position traditionally
accorded women. With regard to sadomasochism, de Beauvoir's recounting of socialization processes shows the operation of patriarchy
in and over time, affording insight into whether the second and third
traits of the dynamic (involving differential experiences of dependency and the paradoxical longings of sadist and masochist for the

repressed sides of themselves) are also fomented in and through the dividing lines of gender.

The Second Sex can be read as a developmental account of the consequences for male and female psyches of the sociopolitical reality addressed by Millett and others, tracing the divergent experiences of little boys and little girls as they age within the traditional nuclear family. De Beauvoir stated that infants of both sexes will in the first year of life face a primordial trauma: they must be weaned from a sense of oneness with the world (and another) to the realization of an irrevocable physical separateness. De Beauvoir conceptualized this experience philosophically, couched in phenomenological terminology: "The nursling lives directly the basic drama of every existent and experiences with anguish his being turned loose, his forlornness. In flight from his freedom, his subjectivity, he would fain lose himself in the bosom of the Whole."[10] This potentially universal source of sadomasochism, human dismay at physical separation, suggests that particularly in its erotic forms sadomasochism could express a longing to return to an original state of oneness and symbiotic immersion.[11] Such yearning may characterize both sexes; there is no reason to believe that altered social situations would in any way dislodge it.

But even if all children undergo this trauma, it unfolds differently for the boy and girl within the huge world of gender influences that even de Beauvoir's own quote reflects. Very soon, de Beauvoir tells us, the little boy learns that if he is to enter the polarized universe of men linked to the objective, the rational, and the public, a particularly abrupt farewell must first be paid to his childhood longings, to that nongendered desire for unity with the world. He must deny his yearning for closeness to another, for connections and emotions that fall outside the manly role. The achievement of masculinity requires severing ties with the domestic world associated with the subjective, the emotional, and the familial. For a moment, then, the little girl appears to be privileged because she is allowed to remain longer within that "bosom." De Beauvoir astutely called attention to the oppressive ramifications of patriarchal imperatives for both men and women:

> The boys especially are little by little denied the kisses and caresses they
> have been used to. As for the little girl, she continues to be cajoled, she
> is allowed to cling to her mother's skirts, her father takes her on his
> knee and strokes her hair . . . bodily contacts and agreeable glances
> protect her against the anguish of solitude. The little boy, in contrast,

will be denied even coquetry: his efforts at enticement, his play-acting, are irritating. He is told that "a man doesn't ask to be kissed . . . a man doesn't look at himself in the mirror . . . a man doesn't cry." He is urged to be a "little man"; he will attain adult approval by becoming independent of adults. *He will please them by not appearing to seek to please them* [my emphasis].[12]

In forcibly separating the public and the private, the personal and the political realms, rationality from emotionality, these cultural dictates demand that the "little man" renounce, repress, and belittle his own desires for dependency. He is required to make this sacrifice in order to win legitimacy both from parental figures and from the outside world they at once reflect, influence, and have been influenced by. Given the typical family form in which the mother was (and still is) the primary caretaker of children, it is from her that he must separate and move away. At a social level, he is required to do so *in order to gain approval* within the patriarchal world dominated by men, so as to feel he is not deviant or feminized (a form of intimidation containing implications both sexist and heterosexist).

Nonetheless, the little boy only appears to separate in response to the gendered mandate. This point is implied but not developed in detail by de Beauvoir. He still feels tied, dependent, and in need of the caretaker: the process of achieving socialized masculinity cannot erase the reality of his quite human vulnerabilities and insecurities. (Why else would he "seek to please"?) Still needy and dependent, he must yet define himself in opposition to the mother, to a woman; simultaneously, he cannot so neatly sever his emotions and simply cut off that part of himself he is now forced to alienate and objectify. He must therefore please without *letting on that he seeks to please.* Like the second characteristic of the sadist in S/M sex, the little boy is in fact dependent and emotionally needy but has learned early on never to admit to this vulnerability. He must deny it at all costs, to himself, to others, to women who little by little will come to represent this displaced and alienated part of himself he may one day wish to reclaim, to somehow recapture. In the meantime, he will have to project confidence, to premise his association with others on a macho indifference and bravado, to appear invulnerable.

To cull this conclusion from de Beauvoir's text is significant because in *The Second Sex* she frames the conditions of gender enculturation in terms entirely social, entirely sociological, without recourse to psychological concepts drawn from either Freud or the object relations brand of psychoanalytic theorizing. For de Beauvoir, this anti-psychologistic orientation was purposeful: she shared with Sartre a disdain for what she considered deterministic elements in Freudian thinking, including the idea of the unconscious so central to Chodorow and Benjamin's more psychoanalytic discussions of gender socialization. In *The Second Sex* she instead intimates that more than a merely individual and psychological phenomenon must be at stake if a tendency toward sadism is imbibed with masculinity. At the same time, her observations can be restated in psychological language in spite of their original intention; to do so further validates and enriches their verity. A Freudian formulation is that the little boy is forced to render unconscious to himself his human yearnings for dependency and continued connection. Stated through an object relations-oriented framework like that of Mahler (reviewed in chapter 3), he must separate before he is actually ready to develop beyond a symbiotic stage. He must act as though he were independent. (As I discuss later in this chapter, this psychoanalytic observation informs Chodorow's later object relations account of little boys pushed prematurely by their mothers out of symbiosis into "separation-individuation" within gender-divided Western societies.)

Therefore, as was the case for the sadist regarding his or her second characteristic of implicit need in a hypothetical instance of S/M sex, the boy's dependency remains and is arguably even greater because it must be hidden. And so a foundation for an eventual analogy between the sadist and the person socialized into masculinity has been laid. The sadist (in the case at hand, the masculine sadist) continues to be symbiotically connected to an emotionally needed and usually feminine other. At the same time, his very existence in a cultural universe that compels him to separate in the first place has placed him in a rather powerless, even subordinately masochistic position vis-à-vis both the literal and the figurative patriarchal father. (This may provide a clue to the internal transformability of sadomasochism within the structure of the nuclear family as a whole and in relation to the outside world.)

Yet, de Beauvoir continued, the boy is soon compensated for his emotional sacrifice. Although he is angered at the separation forced upon him, patriarchal privilege awaits.

If the boy seems at first to be less favored than his sisters, it is because great things are in store for him. The demands placed upon him at once imply a high evaluation. Maurras relates in his memoirs that . . .

his father took his hand and drew him from the room, saying to him: "We are men, let us leave those women." The child is persuaded that more is demanded of boys because they are superior . . . this abstract notion takes on for him a concrete form: it is incarnated in his penis.[13]

A feeling of power is now constructed, embodied in the shape of the penis (a symbolic privilege French psychoanalyst Jacques Lacan theorized by substituting *phallus* for *penis*); this power, of course, is only possible relative to the little girl not possessing or (in Lacan's view, "lacking") this overvalued organ. The boy learns to think of himself as superior and essential compared to the girl who is seen as inferior and inessential—the "second sex." It is a privilege with which, like the sadist, he will be loath to part. Like the sadist, in later life the grown man may be unable to let go of gendered prerogatives even when or if they should become destructive to himself and intimate others. Early on, the gender system (trickling down into and also created by childhood) convinced him that these privileges were in his interest, so intrinsic to masculine identity that he fears he will cease to exist without them. He learns to believe that his emotional renunciation will eventually pay off because he will be able to regain connections to others (specifically, to women) from a position of control and superiority. He will be rewarded, if later in life.[14]

On the other hand, a very different (though corollary) scenario meets the little girl, who did not have to renounce the world of her mother. If initially privileged, she too soon surmises, de Beauvoir explains, that she will come to be treated as inferior: "Mothers and nurses feel no reverence or tenderness toward her genitals . . . she finds herself situated in the world differently from the boy, and a constellation of factors can transform this difference, in her eyes, into an inferiority." Although she has not been forced to separate as brusquely from her mother as has the little boy, she watches with envy as he commences to act upon and test his environment in a more direct manner than she has been permitted. She feels that she cannot venture out so freely and confidently into the world, that she remains attached to her mother's separate sphere even after she might have chosen to move gradually away from it. She is physically independent, yet her situation demands that she experience herself indirectly, not as a subject directed outward to the world but as a person whose goal is to be an object both to herself and to the growing little boy. "Thus a vicious cycle is formed; for the less she exercises her freedom to understand, to grasp and discover the world about her, the less resources she will find within herself, the less will she dare to affirm herself as subject."[15] She is taught to remain relatively dependent.

That the girl learns to fashion herself in a mode of dependency is evident throughout the course of her psychosocial development. Like the masochist, she finds herself in a situation that forces her to acknowledge that she needs someone else. As de Beauvoir elaborates, an array of cultural stimuli nudge the adolescent girl to turn for approval to the male other, toward pleasing him more than herself. From playing with dolls when she was younger, she may now spend hours fussing with hair, makeup, fashion, and fashion magazines. Her socialized goal is to attract the gaze of an interested other, and in this regard she then and now will worry about her sexual attractiveness, her weight, the size of her breasts, or other physical attributes. That anorexia nervosa and bulimia continue disproportionately to affect young women (rarely young men), and that the multibillion dollar cosmetic industry draws the vast majority of its customers from women, are merely two of many possible indicators that de Beauvoir's observations have not yet become outdated. Reading *The Second Sex* more than forty years after its 1949 publication, many of my college students over the last three years—of varying classes, races, and ethnicities—continue to relate to de Beauvoir's account of classic female gender socialization when she describes how, for the woman,

> everything invites her to abandon herself in daydreams to men's arms in order to be transported into a heaven of glory. She learns that to be happy she must be loved. . . . Woman is the Sleeping Beauty, Cinderella, Snow-White, she who receives and submits.
> Un jour mon prince viendra. . . . Someday he'll come along, the man I love—the words of popular songs fill her with dreams of patience and of hope.[16]

The songs are no longer the same and, in many ways, the words ring somewhat crudely in 1992, relative to the huge socioeconomic and ideological shifts that have challenged and altered the position of women. Nonetheless, MTV images, the themes of commercial hit films from *Pretty Woman* to *Working Girl*, the content of gothic romances read by teenagers that continue to idealize happy-ever-after marriages and heterosexuality, the lyrics of contemporary popular music—all persist in alluding to the joys of romantic love and of union with male saviors in a way not terribly dissimilar from the cultural prescriptions of de Beauvoir's account.

One day he may indeed come along, and the young girl will find herself transformed from child/adolescent into wife and, possibly, mother. By this time, however, a tendency toward masochism may have already taken root in her accustomed interactions between self and male other. For the young girl rapidly surmises that her social legitimacy will come not from self-assertion but from efforts to please the boy who, like his father, represents power in the world. In the traditional nuclear familial model, the girl realizes that the only avenue to the kind of power held by men is to find someone willing to allow her to experience it vicariously, indirectly. Thus, parallel to the boy, she hopes renunciation of her desires for independence will one day be rewarded; she, too, seeks to find eventual pleasure and satisfaction. Like him she has been taught to own up to just one side of herself: she is everywhere urged to admit only her dependency. In this respect, of course, her experience is much closer to that of the masochist in the hypothetical instance of S/M sex than it is to that of the little boy (or, by extension, of the sadist). She has been encouraged to *seek to please others even if in reality she longs to please herself.* For the young girl, it is her (corollary) yearning for independence that through socialized femininity is repressed and denied, and becomes invisible; she learns to believe that hiding this desire is in her self-interest, given the extreme and often symbiotic closeness to others she is supposed to want (in marriage, or motherhood, with her presumed-to-be heterosexual mate).

Again, the young girl's situation can be analyzed both sociologically (as a phenomenon of collective proportions) and psychoanalytically. In Freudian language, it is now the desire for assertion, for breaking away, that the little girl must render unconscious. In the object relations terminology both Mahler and Chodorow employ, the little girl's situation keeps her symbiotically attached to the mother longer than is the boy; whereas he experiences difficulty admitting his symbiotic longings, she feels conflicted about growing toward a relatively separate sense of personhood. Yet, just as the little boy (reminiscent of the sadist) can never really escape his very human dependence on others, her paradox—like the masochist in the hypothetical instance—is her inability to escape the existential reality that, on one level, she is separate and relatively independent. It is just that the young girl has learned to act as though dependent, to shape her life (to *put* on make-up, to *dress* up: note the paradox revealed even in language, the frequent choice of active verbs to describe processes supposedly passive in character) as though in the mode of prioritizing an other, to seek approval only in the mode of disapproval—all of this in the hope that perhaps she can find someone/something to restore that part of her being she senses has been alienated and displaced. Far from masochism's being a biologically based seeking of pleasure in pain, then, the young girl comes to fashion herself *as though* she were a masochist, as *though* she were an object, in order to attain the secure and pleasurable place in life she has been promised.

Implicit in de Beauvoir's work, then, is a diagnosis still relevant to patriarchal societies that exert a contaminating influence on men and women by repressing in each a dimension of human existence. Socialized masculinity brings in its wake both an emotional dependence on women and a strong need to deny this vulnerability (lest one be socially ostracized, seen as not living up to gendered expectations); with socialized femininity arises the acknowledgment of dependency on men and a relative inability to admit one's own separate abilities (lest one face, again, social unacceptability). Each gender comes to feel an extreme need for the other, for seizing back aspects of oneself that have been forcibly displaced onto the other. This is because patriarchy is organized to prevent the realization that both sides—the desire to depend on someone else as well as the desire to preserve a sense of independence from them—exist within oneself: both must be present for a satisfactory sense of recognition (à la Hegel and Benjamin) between others to occur.

A form of splitting of oneself in relation to such others instead takes place so that men project onto women their own dependent side, women onto men their own independent longings. Each views the other's experience vicariously, recognizing in the other that which cannot be admitted in themselves. (In Spanish director Pedro Almodovar's re-released film *Tie Me Up, Tie Me Down,* for example, a young man who has kidnapped and bound a woman looks at his captive with both anger and deep love in his eyes. Through her, he visually objectifies himself, expressing sympathy outward that he is unable to feel toward his own being.) A specifically *social symbiosis* comes into being in which the other is needed much more desperately, and ferociously, than if the parties were able to acknowledge their existential equality.

At this point, the gendered and nongendered faces of sadomasochism come together. In general, a sadomasochistic type of interaction results when simultaneous needs for autonomy and connections to others, for dependence as well as independence, are denied. These needs may be sundered by the demands of capitalism, or of patriarchy, or of any other form of social organization that does not recognize the importance of both parts of human existence, rendering one group or class predominantly dependent and the other predominantly independent. (Capitalism, as already seen, appears to glorify individual initiative and scorn social neediness; at the same time, and paradoxically, it renders people utterly dependent on the system for their very survival.) When this division occurs, as Fromm suggested, people may seek either to control others (the sadist, perhaps the boss or the patriarch) or to endure others' control of them (the masochist, perhaps the worker or the woman in a patriarchally structured relationship).

But the third characteristic of the sadomasochistic dynamic deduced from the earlier hypothetical instance reminds us that sadism and masochism are insatiable strategies, ultimately unable to resolve the dilemma they are supposed to redress. As already argued, the dynamic is likely to fail at its own goals because the sadist can never be content with a masochist he or she has had to control. Just as the sadist secretly wishes to acknowledge denied feelings of dependency, so a masochist is needed through whom such feelings can be genuinely acknowledged: paradoxically, furtively, the sadist needs the masochist to be free. At the same time, the masochist wants her or his own strivings for freedom to be recognized by a sadist who cannot qua sadist ever really acknowledge these desires, too frightened to relinquish his or her investment in the masochist's lack of freedom. From this proposition it is but a short leap to imagine how a gender-divided society must plant the seeds for a similar chronically self-defeating situation to arise between the (masculine) sadist and (feminine) masochist. *This is because the organization of patriarchy itself necessitates that a group positioned masochistically, or women, cannot be truly equal to the one positioned sadistically, or men.* That women's secondary status has been legislated in all walks of life—from the worlds of politics and economics to the worlds of culture, the family, and sexuality—means that men cannot be genuinely acknowleged by this other they have rendered, collectively, unfree. Like the sadist, their secret wish remains unfulfilled and unfulfillable in such a system; and, like the masochist, women will continue to be discouraged from admitting their own desires for freedom. It would not be surprising, then, if a sadomasochistic dynamic tended to be set into motion between them, in flux and in a state of ongoing tension as each struggles to find the impossible within the rules of the engendered game.

Such a dynamic does indeed seem to be commonly present in male-female relationships of everyday life, running the gamut from mundane interactions to those that can and do turn violent. In the former category are the types of encounters described in the how-to literature on intimate heterosexual relationships. Books in the genre bemoan the push-pull dynamics of common parlance between women who try to please men and men who are distant, critical, and never really pleased by women. All three traits of the sadomasochistic dynamic are in evidence in relationships described within this best-selling how-to form, though it is the third that is particularly visible and glaring. On the whole, the stories told are of couples who have insatiable expectations of each other; dissatisfaction between them is chronic and ongoing, dependency openly described as excessive, "codependent," or "addictive." The titles themselves are revealing, with names almost laughably clichéd and oriented toward a predominantly female audience. The best-selling *Women Who Love Too Much* cited earlier, its sequel *Letters from Women Who Love Too Much,* and *Men Who Hate Women and the Women Who Love Them* are typical of the genre, as are the later *The Pleasers: Women Who Can't Say No and the Men Who Control Them* and *Is It Love or Is It Addiction?*[17]

Usually authored by therapists who base their books on their patients, this literature presents accounts of relationships gone wrong.[18] Yet, most of the authors do not employ the word "sadomasochistic" to paint portraits of destructive dynamics masquerading as love. Legitimately concerned about reinforcing past definitions of masochism that have blamed the victim by portraying women as simply desirous of or taking pleasure in pain, Robin Norwood prefers the language of "loving too much" and the metaphor of obsessive alcoholism; Brenda Schaeffer comments on what she refers to as "love addiction"; and, in *Born to Please: Compliant Women/Controlling Men,* Karen Blaker calls the extreme dependency she has noticed in women fearful of expressing their authentic feelings and opinions "me/phobia." On the other side of the coin, Forward and Torres eschew "sadism" in favor of "misogyny" to describe the behavior of the man who hates and is abusive toward women.[19] The problem with these alternative terms, however, is that they are decidedly euphemistic, obscuring what at root seems to be the same sadomasochistic phenomenon. Moreover, any connection between individual case studies, sadomasochism, and the larger systemic features of male-dominated societies (as documented by Millett and de Beauvoir, among others) is also hidden.

Note the definitional language: "we who love obsessively are full of fear—fear of being alone, fear of being unlovable and unworthy, fear of being ignored or abandoned or destroyed" (Norwood); "the fear of being myself in my relationship . . . was deep and complex: He might leave me if I could not be what he wanted. I might be alone. I might feel empty without him. I might fail if I had to make it on my own" (Blaker); and "love addiction is a reliance on someone external to the self in an attempt to get unmet needs fulfilled, avoid fear of emotional pain. It is our unhealthy dependence on others" (Schaeffer).[20] An unequal hierarchy of superiority and inferiority valuation, in which dependency takes different forms for men and women, is blatant enough. In addition, Torres's *Men Who Hate Women* and Leman's *The Pleasers* stress that "the systematic persecution of one partner by another" need not be physical in manifestation in order for abuse and deep humiliation to have occurred.[21] As with sadomasochism, experiences are depicted as falling along a continuum united by common patterns of behavior. The tactics of the misogynist, Forward and Torres admonish, are to threaten, yell, name call, and constantly criticize. They cite the case of Paula, constantly belittled by her husband, Gerry (himself a psychologist), about her taste, how she looks, what she reads, whether she is deep or thoughtful enough. Blaker speaks of Arlene and Bill, enmeshed in a relationship in which the latter "called all the shots," not only physically but "emotionally and financially" as well, while Leman refers to hearing over and over again about "verbal attacks and put-downs that are almost beyond description."[22]

One might predict that the male partner would be content once his position of dominance had been established in these relationships. As with the sadist, precisely the opposite seems to occur. Frequently, the man will pick a fight, complain, or make an arbitrary demand just as things seem to be settling into some routine. Or he will back away when it becomes obvious that a woman is now in the more subordinate position he had allegedly and so ardently desired. Norwood records such interactions between Trudi and the married Jim: the more Trudi tried to please Jim, sexually and otherwise, the more he pulled away, until he finally returned to his wife. (His wife, of course, was the person in comparison to whom Trudi was initially a greater challenge, cast as the enigmatic and comparatively unattainable woman.) Norwood also describes Randy, an attorney Jill meets in law school whom she pursues so vigorously that he begins to avoid her altogether. Blaker, referring again to Arlene, notes that "the more she pushed, the more distant [Bill] became." A perverse progression ensues in which the more financially and emotionally dependent Arlene became on this particular Bill, the less he was interested in her.[23]

The moral of these stories, it would appear (and we are sometimes told), is that women should refrain from demonstrating excessive dependency. The books lead one to believe that if women desire longevity in these dominant-subordinate relationships, they must try to keep cool and maintain some sense of independent liveliness about them; at the same time, they should not become *too* independent. If a woman cared to try to manipulate things in her favor, it might not even be a bad idea to have another admirer herself, à la the Wanda or Odette sketched in earlier chapters. Thus, in terms of the theoretical model I have been developing, the intimacy literature implicitly advises women to transform their masochistic position into a relatively more sadistic one: they, too, can control their relationships by appearing to be more independent, even if in fact they badly need someone else. They might thereby come to resemble the (masculine) sadist; like him, they will have learned that under sadomasochistically oriented circumstances, pragmatic benefits accrue from hiding vulnerabilities one actually feels. However unconscious, this may account for part of the genre's commercial, how-to, appeal.

A similar how-to conclusion reached in the previous chapter applies to work relationships as well. The prospective job candidate is obviously in a stronger position if he or she is wanted by other employers. To be most successful at manipulating the job-hunting game, a certain amount of independence in the mode of dependence is desirable. Like the masculine sadist, the employer will not be satisfied by an overly dominated employee. Sadomasochistic social psychology may operate beneath the surface of these seemingly disparate examples.

My analogy between the sadist in general and the person socialized into a certain form of masculinity should by now be obvious. Rather than feeling contented once a situation of control has been established in the sexual politics of these relationships, the male party to them, like the sadist, frequently feels discontented and restless. He may start fights with his partner; if single, he may move from one relationship to another. (Another branch of the popular literature is explicitly addressed to men who exhibit such behavior, books like *The Casanova Complex: Compulsive Lovers and Their Women* and *Why Can't Men Open Up?*) If married, he may turn to an affair. In this last eventuality, the classic split between good woman and bad woman, madonna and whore, or wife and mistress can enter his life. His wife is legitimate to and for him, yet she seems somehow boring, drab. Life with her is routinized, sexually and in general, while the extramarital partner is exciting, bedecked in the charm and allure of newness. But what both the man and the authors of the literature that describes him fail to understand is that this good woman/bad woman division stems directly from an *inegalitarian form of social organization*. Where there is a patriarchal society, I would argue, we may logically expect to find good women and bad women. By virtue of having rendered his partner subordinate, purportedly in his own interest, the patriarchal husband, like the sadist, paradoxically legislates his own frustration. His chagrin stems from having denied existential equality to the very person who could recognize him for who he is, including the dependent part of himself. Confused but not necessarily unhappy, ready to seduce or be seduced, he may search outside the marriage for satisfactions impossible to obtain from within the structure that he has erected and that he perpetuates.

On the other hand, in turning to the woman's dilemma, it is hardly surprising to discover that male-dominated societies rarely generate an analogous split in her mind between good men and bad men or faithful husbands versus sexy lovers. This situation, however, may change with increasing movement toward gender equality. Certainly, there is no innate reason why women cannot (or do not already) feel split between sexy lovers and relatively boring husbands. Nonetheless, it is hard to imagine madonna/whore terminology being similarly applied to men in a society where they are still largely in control. The roles of power and powerlessness have been reversed. Consequently, men who engage in multiple sexual relations are often viewed positively; by virtue of sexual double standards, they may be dubbed studs rather than sluts, playboys rather than nymphomaniacs. As with the masochist, the problem of obtaining recognition from an unequal and subordinated other (such as the good woman) will generally not exist for women. At present, they rarely have the power to command a bad man, even if this circumstance should slowly change as gendered inequities diminish for individual women. Rather, for women, the corresponding dilemma is usually the opposite: how can one be recognized as a relatively independent being by a male partner who believes that his interests entail never providing any such acknowledgment?

As with the masochist, it is not a desire for independence that is initially apparent. On the contrary, the women in the pop literature seem at first glance to be quite needy, indeed to be in a subordinated position. According to the therapists' accounts, many women fear being without their lovers, their boyfriends, or their husbands, suspecting an internal void the relationship had filled. Satirizing these feelings (but calling no more attention to their social roots than does the popular literature), the Spanish film *Women on the Verge of a Nervous Breakdown*, also directed by Almodovar, features a heroine, Pepa, falling apart when her lover, Ivan, leaves her. We watch her spiking her gazpacho with sleeping pills, ignoring a female friend's desperate pleas for help, and spending nights outside her married paramour's apartment gazing emptily into space. Judging from the commercial success of the film in the United States, its images resonate with familiarity even as *Women on the Verge* pokes fun at and reflects stereotypes at once sexist and sadomasochistic. As I described in the Introduction with regard to my own relationship with the first young man, ambivalent feelings of self-worth are a catalyst for the cool man taking on greater value; the woman who loves too much runs away when a man is interested in her, while Leman sees her as having "to earn their [or her] value and their [or her] worth."[24] If Ivan were extremely interested in her, Pepa might have devalued him along with herself, feeling attracted instead to the more distant other who confirmed her low self-image and required her to work for the approval she had lost or had never been given.

On closer inspection, however, this analysis of the woman who loves too much is much too pat. It does not take seriously the complexities of the back-and-forth, dialectically push-pull interaction that unfolds over time. For one thing, might not Trudis, Jills, and Arlenes at one level be trying to push themselves out of the very relationships they seem to be pursuing, albeit in an alienated and often self-subverting manner? If so, their motivations would not be dissimilar to those of the prototypical masochist of chapter 2. The books recount stories in which not only men but women partners to relationships also make trouble, starting fights and exhibiting forms of dependency that are often covertly and understandably hostile. What appears to be an internally generated suicidal tendency within the relationship may instead be unrecognized mutiny; the rebellion may be aimed, apparently aimlessly, at escaping from a dynamic the woman senses is not in her interest. Simultaneously, pleasing behavior on the part of women may often be as ironic as it was for the masochist, revealing a contradictory desire not only for approval within the mode of disapproval but for an exertion of control and power that cannot be expressed directly. Take the figure of the Marquise in the film and play versions of *Les Liaisons Dangereuses*, enmeshed in behind-the-scenes, quietly malevolent manipulation of intimate upper-class relationships in prerevolutionary, decadent eighteenth-century France. Like Odette in Proust's depiction, it is only too clear that her abilities and powers then (and, for many women, now) could not be exercised directly given the socioeconomically based realities of her power-lessness.

Moreover, the demands of the sadistically oriented man may in and of themselves have the effect of emboldening the woman, pushing her slowly but steadily away from a dependent position in the direction of independence from the relationship. The pain she experiences may become unbearable, steadily worsening as he becomes more and more frustrated by the structural inability of the situation to provide him a sense of contented equilibrium. She may gradually back away until finally there is no choice but to take drastic action for her own sanity and survival. Again, the pain experienced by women in sadomasochistic relationships is not only psychological, as in cases drawn from the intimacy literature, but frequently physical as well. A similar sadomasochistic pattern extant in everyday intimate encounters between men and women is typically present in violent interactions. In *Terrifying Love*, for example, Lenore Walker writes about battered women who kill only after being driven and beaten to the edge of desperation. Notice that in Walker's description of the marital life of one such woman, Joyce Hawthorne, she uses virtually identical language to that which abounds in Norwood's accounts, or those of Torres and Forward, or that of Karen Blaker in the quote from *Born to Please* that opens this chapter. Shades of de Beauvoir come to mind.

> When Joyce had married Aubrey Hawthorne, she had been a seventeen-year-old bride who dreamed of being a good wife and mother. She'd believed strongly in the traditional values that assign women and men to different family roles: women stay home to take care of the house and kids, while men go out into the world to earn a living. . . . But, no matter how hard she tried to please him, to be a good wife, he would never really change. Lately, Joyce had felt that she was "living with a time bomb," "walking on eggshells." Nothing she did seemed to please her husband; he always found fault with her.[25]

Joyce went on to take control of her life by killing her husband in self-defense after a series of ongoing and worsening beatings that threatened her and her children's lives.

In other cases of domestic violence, of battering or of rape in marriage, women may defend themselves by leaving when the push-pull dialectic finally drives them out of the relationship. At this moment, still another analogy with the sadomasochistic dynamic presents itself as the extreme dependence of the (here, masculine) sadist is revealed.

Supposedly, the male is the partner in control; he is the boss at home, regardless of how powerful or powerless he may be outside it in other spheres of day-to-day life. But should the woman cast in the masochistic position be forced by pain to reject the dynamic, books about domestic violence attest to the fact that the abusing male will resort to greater and greater measures to resuscitate the symbiotic connection now severed.[26] It can be predicted in advance that something will happen that illustrates the depth of the sadist's need just when the masochist decides to depart. He may, as Walker confirms, hunt down his wife or girlfriend, enraged, banging on doors, or threatening to kill her. This reality is only too well known to feminists and social workers who try to help battered women escape to safe 'shelters.' Just the fact that 'shelter' is required attests to the sadist's dependency: now his worst fears of abandonment have been realized and his anger is inseparable from his desire to punish the one who has abandoned him.

This aspect of the dynamic is also present in relationships characterized more by psychological than by physical violence. The sadomasochistically oriented boyfriend or husband may endlessly call the girlfriend or wife he has formerly abused or ignored. In divorces, he may at first hound the spouse who has left him and then attempt to punish her not violently but through unreasonable legal measures and/or economic retribution.[27] Just at the moment when the woman in the relationship has found the strength to break from it, her supposedly independent paramour may suddenly reappear on her doorstep with words of love, apologies, and even a momentary declaration of need. For an instant, as in the hypothetical sexual paradigm, their roles may undergo a reversal to reveal both his hidden vulnerability and her hidden power. Generally, though, the overall rules of the game are far too entrenched and habitual to be so easily overthrown. Perhaps she will take him back until the pattern recurs and, one day, she is able to leave for good. Then the extremity of the sadist's dependency—which, of course, was always present—will be reexposed even more nakedly as his frustrated desires can accelerate into threatened or actual violence. We come full circle: along the continuum that potentially unites them, psychic sadomasochism may turn into physical, physical into psychic, all within the parameters of the same underlying dynamic.

A connection clearly exists between the structural tendencies of a male-dominated and patriarchal society like our own, and a particular social psychology it encourages between men and women. My argument has been that this social psychology often resembles sadomasochism in general as sketched throughout this book, showing similar characteristics to those deduced from a hypothetical instance of an S/M sexual dynamic. Though this psychology frequently pervades marriages and affairs, relationships both violent and just chronically tense, too often the traits of the woman who loves too much or of the abusing or emotionally distant man are seen as individual anomalies, abstracted from the larger sociological system of which they are a part. Thus far, I have explored only the predominantly masochistic and sadistic sides of the dynamic, so that my account has tended to link sadism with men, masochism with women even though this association is by no means essential or intrinsic. To examine sadomasochism's internal transformability and the subordinate side of the dynamic, I return to Chodorow's work on gender reproduction, reinterpreting it through the lens of sadomasochism.

Engendering Male Masochism and Female Sadism: Chodorow Revisited

In *The Reproduction of Mothering: Psychoanalysis and the Sociology of Gender,* Nancy Chodorow incorporated object relations theory to overcome the limitations she perceived in purely sociological renderings of gender development like de Beauvoir's. For Chodorow, a question like why mothers would pass on to their daughters a sense of the world that clearly devalues both of them (or, for that matter, the issue of sadomasochism's internal transformability) is unanswerable unless unconscious motivations are taken into account. A review of her theoretical perspective follows.

Chodorow began *The Reproduction of Mothering* with the assumption that parenting is a potential capacity of anyone who has been parented: both men and women have the ability to parent even if only women are called upon to do so within the skewed organization of gendered social systems. In the mothering relationship that develops between a woman and her child, memories of the woman's own childhood will in some way be reactivated; she will project onto the child her own experience of having been mothered. Consequently, since the mother was raised in a gendered social world that dealt differentially with little girls and little boys, she is likely to reproduce this divergence in parenting her own children. More specifically, Chodorow stated, the effect of gender differences on a mother's treatment of a daughter in the pre-oedipal period of development (infancy to the discovery of genitalia in the first oedipal stage) is that the daughter is perceived as an extension of the mother. The mother will have difficulty recognizing her daughter as a separate person. Chodorow cited numerous studies conducted on mother-child relationships, all of which showed a large number of highly symbiotic relationships. The mother initially appears to be empathetic with her female child, to support her desires and perhaps to wish to live vicariously through her. This approval goes only so far, however, and is limited by the mother's desire for the child not to grow away from and abandon her. Thus, the already gendered mother may keep the daughter in a symbiotic or "hypersymbiotic" state well past the pre-oedipal period when separation and individuation ought already to have occurred.[28]

Quite another picture, however, emerges with regard to the mother's relationship to her son in the pre-oedipal period. Chodorow argues that as a result of the structure of the nuclear family as described at the beginning of this chapter, the mother may turn to her son as a substitute for the relatively absent husband/father who is immersed in the business of the public sphere. She will tend to sexualize and differentiate him at an early age, experiencing him as "a definite other—an opposite-gendered and -sexed other." Seeing him as this 'other,' as exactly the opposite of the daughter she perceives as an extension of herself, the mother pushes the son into the sexualized oedipal phase long before she does his sister. By virtue of this process, Chodorow tried to resolve the dilemma of gender reproduction: again, critical as she is of socialization theories that describe mothering rather mechanically, she shows the gendered mother's possibly unconscious motivations for reproducing the same roles she herself had inherited.

The oedipal phase, when the child begins to perceive parents in sexual terms, is a crucial one because with it comes the explicit introduction of a triangular rather than dual relationship. For the young girl, the daughter, the oedipal phase poses a particular problem: if symbiotically or semisymbiotically attached to her mother, how will she come to transfer her sexual interests onto the father? Chodorow's answer is that the daughter makes this transfer only ambivalently, retaining strong affectional ties to her mother that are later the basis of the greater emotional intimacy felt by and between women. However, the daughter's rationale for turning to her father is not merely learned gender expectation or innate heterosexuality. Rather, the gendered hierarchy of the traditional nuclear family structure within a larger social system causes the daughter to turn toward the father to help her separate. He, after all, is a symbolic representative of the outside world of potentiality and freedom. Moreover, because of her own desires to keep the daughter close to her, the mother provides insufficient encouragement in this child's process of individuation. The young girl cherishes hope that in the superior world of men she can meet this frustrated psychological need for a sense of her own separate identity. A large degree of continuity may exist between the pre-oedipal and oedipal phases as this struggle for the daughter's recognition is sexualized in relation to the father. Usually, the father will encourage these symbolic gestures toward him on the part of the daughter, reinforcing the young girl's turn toward heterosexuality even as the mother continues to exert a strong influence in the background.

For the boy, on the other hand, Chodorow contended, the oedipal stage is not nearly as complex and loaded. He has already developed a sexualized relationship to his mother in the pre-oedipal phase. Consequently, unlike his sister, he does not have to transfer his sexual loyalties from one sex to another. Yet, it is interesting that Chodorow devoted far less attention to the oedipal experiences of the young man, seemingly persuaded that his situation was far less conflictual than that his sister faced. In general, the situation of the boy and his relationship with his father remain relatively untheorized. But perhaps this omission is too hasty. Certainly, Chodorow was correct to indicate that the little boy's and little girl's positions are asymmetric: because both children were raised by a female parent, only the girl will have to transfer her sexual feelings onto the opposite gender. Yet, the little boy nonetheless may feel a particular desire to please the father he is to emulate. The father may remain to him a problematical background figure, just as the person of the mother continues to haunt the daughter even after she has transferred her affections to a male.

The implications of Chodorow's work for understanding the emergence of gendered sadomasochism can now be explored. Both daughter and son were parented only by a mother who, because of the way she was raised within a gendered social system that devalued women, tends to treat her children differently on the basis of sex. She is not necessarily conscious of this unequal treatment, the effect of which may nevertheless be to thrust the boy into a false and premature separation/individuation. In this way, the little boy can develop a tendency toward dominant sadism, unable to acknowledge continuing dependency on a woman. The daughter, on the other hand, often remains in a prolonged symbiotic relationship with her mother from which separation comes late, only superficially, or not at all.

However useful in helping explain how sadism and masochism develop along gendered axes, Chodorow's analysis is not as fruitful for gleaning insight into why sadomasochism also appears to be genderless. Again, patriarchal structures and the corresponding socialization they engender produce a tendency toward dominant sadism in men and dominant masochism in women. What happens to the subordinate tendencies of both?

One possibility is that the subordinate tendencies of the S/M dynamic could emerge in relation to children, compared with whom parents are clearly empowered. As both de Beauvoir and Chodorow indicate, it is usually the mother who rears the children rather than the father. She may find that in regard to her children, she thus has a subordinate potential for sadism (a seductive possibility given her inability to exert power and control elsewhere), even as she is conditioned toward dominant masochism in relation to her socially and economically more powerful husband. (I am only suggesting a potentiality within the structure of the traditional nuclear family. Many mothers may and do not enact this tendency at all.) The implications of this potentially subordinate sadism for Chodorow's model would lead one to conclude that both children should emerge masochistically if the mother enacted her subordinate sadism toward them. And yet we know that not only gendered roles are reproduced within the family but gendered sadomasochism as well. We know that eventually it is the boy who will grow up with a tendency toward dominant sadism in his masculine persona vis-à-vis women, and the girl who will grow up with a tendency toward dominant masochism.

Pursuing Chodorow's argument, I would agree that the mother may perceive the son as an extension of his father, and therefore as heir to similar privileges. The son is another representative of the first sex and therefore powerful; she may be drawn into acting toward him as she would to the (absent) husband and father. Her socialized persona of dominant masochism thereby turns toward the son who, as de Beauvoir described existentially and now Chodorow psychoanalytically, may then be thrust abruptly from the symbiotic vise.[29] If the mother has indeed been socialized to share the characteristics of the masochist, she does not want the son to be powerless but powerful. How else could the son become an other to her, a vicarious and supposedly independent legitimator of her own frustrated aspirations toward this very sense of autonomy? When the gendered mother turns her dominantly masochistic persona toward the son, he may learn a tendency toward sadism. Such a tendency, given the sadist's need for a masochist and the masochist's for a sadist, would be impossible except in relation to an other who plays the opposite (here, masochistic) part. Within the patriarchally structured family, then, the son emerges with a sense of his ability to have power and control over the mother: he takes on the socialized persona of dominant sadism in response to her socialized persona of dominant masochism. On the other hand, his own subordinate masochism may be enacted only in relation to the father, compared to whom he knows he is relatively powerless within the family structure. At the denouement of this process at once social and psychological, the little boy has emerged with a dominant tendency toward sadism and a subordinate tendency toward masochism. This, of course, mimics the orientation of his father as well as of the patriarchal order in which the family partakes. (The reader may recall the preceding chapter's analysis of the usually male capitalist who, like Weber's Protestant, is predominantly sadistic toward workers below while subordinately masochistic toward a God he has endowed with transcendent authoritarian powers.) Simultaneously, the son's sadistic side has taken shape in relation to a woman, his masochistic side in relation to a man. (Here the reader may recall the characters of René and Stephen in Reage's *Story of O:* they are sexually sadistic in relation to women while, on a subordinate level, playing the masochistic part in relation to each other or any more powerful man.)

Like the masochist in S/M sex, the mother's efforts to win approval from the sadistically situated son are no more likely to succeed than her analogous attempts in relation to her husband. She may find herself more and more demoralized and despairing; she may sometimes be resentful and angry. The result of this demoralization may be to create in the mother a great need and desire for someone—a third party, perhaps—upon whose approval and affections she can count. Now the daughter enters the frame of the familial system. Though powerless relative to the mother, she is of the same gender; unlike the boy, therefore, she is not associated with the same longing to recoup a socially withdrawn sense of approval and legitimacy. Rather, it is the little girl who looks to the mother for love, legitimacy, and the blessing of her developmental progress from symbiosis through individuation. The mother nevertheless may not wish the daughter to separate because of her own engendered loneliness; according to Chodorow, the mother is motivated to keep the daughter close because she is like her.

This realization eventually dawns upon the daughter, who senses that nothing she does can altogether convince the mother to let her go, to approve of her desires for autonomy as well as for connectedness.

On the other hand, as Chodorow indicated, the father waves the flag of individual power and redemption. Perhaps he compliments the daughter, sexualizing her pre-oedipal desires. Or perhaps it is simply that the young girl perceives the father's greater control over family and within society compared to the mother's relative powerlessness. Given this experience, she turns her dominant masochism toward the father, although a latent potential toward subordinate sadism persists in her now more disinterested attitude toward the mother. At the end of her developmental process, the daughter has imbibed dominant masochism in relation to men (her father, later her husband, her son) and subordinate sadism in relation to women (her mother, later her daughter). (In *The Story of O*, recall that O's masochism is enacted vis-à-vis men, her sadism only taking shape in relation to women lovers with whom she is more in control; at SAMOIS, O both is beaten by and beats women.) As with the son in relation to the father, the daughter is left with the same dominant and subordinate orientations as those with which the mother began the parenting process. Based on this analysis, it is not difficult to imagine how specifically gendered sadomasochism can be reproduced in ensuing generations.

It seems to me that the advantage of this reinterpretation of Chodorow's work in terms of the sadomasochism paradigm is that it allows for S/M to take form within, but not to discriminate by, sex. At the conclusion of *The Reproduction of Mothering*, Chodorow called for a change in the asymmetric relationships of parenting so that both mother and father, man and woman, husband and wife, are present to restore to the whole of the family its bifurcated, gendered halves. Though certainly important in focusing attention upon the crucial need for both sexes to participate in and take responsibility for child rearing, this solution is nonetheless only a partial one. For the mother did not push the son out of the symbiotic bond prematurely because he was male and physically different from her, but rather as a result of his legacy of having been cast in a privileged position. Were the daughter to have been similarly privileged by society, chances are the mother would have done the same with her. In other words, the mother may not be responding so much to the physical *sex* of the son or daughter, as to the perceptions of socially constructed *gender* and what it means to be masculine or feminine in our society. Similarly, the son is positioned sadistically in opposition to the mother not so much because she is a member of a different sex as because she belongs to a devalued gender group: under patriarchy, sex and subordinate status are coincident. Thus, in sum, Chodorow may have inadvertently confused these two dimensions by (unconsciously) resting her argument on the mother's response to physical likeness or difference; in so doing, she illustrates Cynthia Epstein's previously cited point about the subtle seductions of essentialism in contemporary feminist scholarship.

Given this analysis, there are both advantages and disadvantages to Chodorow's call for dual parenting. The implication that people of two different sexes should raise a child can reinforce a deep and biologically based prejudice feminists have tried to avoid. Such a belief presumes that there is something intrinsic about male versus female identity. At the same time, Chodorow ignores the reality that many households (such as single-parent families) no longer conform or wish to conform to the traditional model. I would therefore prefer to call for parenting that is not sadomasochistic, in which both women and men can attain simultaneous independence and dependence, dependence and independence, in which they can find love and approval of their strivings toward both dimensions of existence. This requires caretakers who are not themselves embedded in sadomasochistic dynamics and can therefore allow children to satisfactorily experience needs for both connectedness to others and autonomy from them. By implication, such caretakers and parents do not necessarily have to be part of a couple or single, married or unmarried, heterosexual, lesbian, or gay, though they may be any of the above. Hopefully, caretakers and parents will increasingly include men as often as women, a transformation possible only if accompanied by corollary alterations in social attitudes and the provision of social services valuing childcarelike leave and daycare for both sexes. The assumptions of patriarchal society itself would themselves have to slowly alter, since dual parenting cannot affect or resist the sexist connotations of dominance and subordination we imbibe from the culture at large.

There is little doubt that the position in which both women and men find themselves under patriarchy is problematic and skewed, sadomasochistically engendered. My own position is that transforming sadomasochistic interaction leads outside the dynamic itself to the heart of our social organization before turning back again to haunt the psyche and habits of individuals. Making matters more complicated, what happens to the father who—even if dominant within the structure of his family—is a powerless worker in the mode of subordinate masochism? Does this somehow perpetuate and expand the infinitely regressing chains of the system as a whole? Perhaps he looks elsewhere, above or below, to justify his impotence; here, race or homophobia as well as simply gender may work in similar ways within the sadomasochistic system.

In the next chapter, I relax the assumption of sadomasochistic interaction resulting from direct interaction between people. Certain types of everyday experiences become sadomasochistic even if they are not created directly by institutions or the interaction of two persons within institutions. What about other forms of social inequality such as racism or homophobia: how do these affect us, and is there any relationship to sadomasochism? Chodorow's solution of dual parenting is inadequate insofar as it does not take into account the many possible origins of gender bias (and its reproduction) across our culture, as numerous as the roots of sadomasochism itself.

6

Creating Enemies in Everyday Life: Following the Example of Others

Sadomasochistic dynamics may also exist beyond the everyday life contexts of work and gender already described. Outside one's family or job—on the streets or in a bar, for instance—small indignities can suddenly escalate to become sadomasochistically charged. Envision the ire of an assaultive homophobe or of a racist or of any person who denounces other groups or persons, indignantly shaking a head at a television set or among friends. These instances often create an inimical other or others, or the experience of being created as such. Unlike the previous cases, interactions like these need not occur within institutions already stratified, structured in space and time by rules and regulations set in advance. Unlike work or gender, they cannot be ascribed neatly to the tendencies of abstract systems, to a capitalistic or patriarchal form of social organization. Perhaps they do not even conform readily to all the specifications of the dynamic earlier defined.

Still, I intend to explore the possibility that the examples that punctuate this chapter bear some resemblance to the characteristics I have ascribed in this book to sadomasochistic dynamics as a whole. Since these phenomena are also both social and psychological, analyzing them via sadomasochism may be relevant and even illuminating. At the same time, I wish to stress at the outset that this is only one among many possible interpretations of why and how otherness comes to take the form of specific prejudices. Certainly, the complexities of these prejudices are best not oversimplified or reduced to functions of any single conceptual framework, as they vary historically from culture to culture and relate to complex economic, political, and social psychological processes.

I start, then, with very quotidian individual situations and progress to those linked to the expression of open prejudice on a group or collective level. Lastly, I consider examples from the contemporary U.S. context, focusing upon forms of bias (some of which are encouraged through imagery and the technological mediation of television or print). Uniting all of these examples, I will argue, is the constructed nature of the sadomasochistic element in each: it must be literally structured out of situations that are initially not structured, or less so, compared to our prior examples. An opportunity for the expression of sadism (and, by extension, for the establishment of persons situated masochistically, usually not of their choosing) arises or is generated, differing from situation to situation, and rationalized before or after the fact. Some justification or rationalizing idea would likely be called up, since no institutional justification (such as, at the workplace, a chain of command) exists to legitimize the sadomasochistic tendency a priori.

The circumstances with which I begin are microcosmic, indeed everyday, in the types of interactive opportunities they introduce. (In sociological terms, they may be the types of examples that interest symbolic interactionists, being somewhat Goffmanian.) Suddenly, a particular power differential can or does spring up between two parties, one now disproportionately dependent on the other even if for only a brief duration. A sense of superiority is simultaneously seized upon by one of these parties, the other belittled and intimidated by contrast. Other traits of the 'dynamic' may not be pertinent, particularly those relating to tendencies that would only emerge in situations ongoing in time. And yet, only if partially applicable, something about these occurrences smacks of the sadomasochistic. A person who picks a fight in a subway, who flares up and leaves surrounding others in an extraordinarily impotent position, trapped, may take sadistic satisfaction in this existential moment. So may a man who harrasses a woman on a more deserted subway platform, experiencing pleasure in the power of observing her evident fright and discomfiture. Perhaps the dynamic occurs even in interactions in which one person regularly and consistently keeps another waiting, thereby in a sense demeaning that other and exerting control by rendering that individual momentarily dependent. (In psychological jargon, this might be called passive aggressive behavior, a term I prefer to eschew so as to treat such circumstances more sociologically.)

Other incidents may in fact entail work-related situations wherein the interacting parties often relate in the mode of server/serviced: their ties are temporary, and their relation not necessarily one between people in the same bureaucratic organization. Examples include a physician who abuses the knowledge and power exercised over an anxious patient; the department chair or office manager who seems especially in his or her element when dealing with relatively less powerful outside others, perhaps while interviewing or in other business capacities; the taxi driver dimly or not so dimly aware of a (maybe out-of-town) passenger's confusion and temporary helplessness, who enjoys a heightened feeling of being in control while cruising too slowly or taking a circuitous route. Even waiter/waited upon situations come to mind, suggesting myriad combinations and permutations of this particular dynamic. Perhaps a frustrated customer in a restaurant demeans the waiter and loudly demands service, for a moment constructing him/herself as a member of an oppressed group and the waiter oppressive by consequence. (I have a relative who used to embarrass me greatly when he did this in restaurants, making me wish I could disappear under the table each time the waiter came into sight. Scenes in Peter Greenaway's controversial film *The Cook, The Thief, The Wife and His Lover* portray a graphically extreme version of this demand to be served, one by conventional definition more apparently sadistic.) Alternatively, a given waiter may not entirely mind the vexation of a customer evidently eager to be waited upon, purposely taking his or her time to get to the table.

As a preliminary observation, it interests me—and will be worth elaborating later—that small-scale turnarounds seem to occur in many such cases, and in ways reminiscent of other sadomasochistic reversals. A person who on one level is in control (say, the one being served) momentarily becomes out of control, rendered for this instant quite dependent: simultaneously, someone at one level more controlled (the server) may be tempted to exert compensatory power from within a position/job of relative powerlesssness. It is not entirely farfetched (even though, I admit, relevant to only very specific instances) to compare the interaction between such parties to that of our erstwhile sadist and masochist, respectively. The particular conditions of that powerlessness may provide the grounds or the opportunity for facilitating a temporary transition from a structural position of (coerced) masochism toward a more sadistic exercising of power (think of that cab driver or waiter). In some cases, the line between the rationalization that is built into one's job and that which stems from the existential situation blurs: a clearly abusive prison guard or brutalizing police officer may act as though sadism were justified by the job, even as other motivations are simultaneously being satisfied.

In one respect, the most mundane of these examples seem so common that it is hard to believe similar incidents do not occur on a regular basis in any society. On the other hand, it is also hard to believe that some forms of social organization more than others do not exacerbate people's ordinary sense of powerlessness and frustration, thus contributing to such dynamics en masse. As observed in chapter 4, for instance, the especially insecure and conditional psychology that goes along with capitalism certainly could affect the frequency of this phenomenon overall. The more persons in the United States (as the focus of this particular work) are overwhelmed by feelings of insignificance, the likelier that they would look for moments of powerfulness—consciously or unconsciously, for however brief a duration.

The observation that many people do not act out such everyday chances rightly alludes to the complexity of social life. As with sadomasochism in general, many factors can and do offset what I am once more suggesting is a large-scale *tendency*. Viewed as such a broad tendency, however, sadistic opportunities would become more alluring the more we feel out of control and powerless in different parts of our lives, perhaps economically, perhaps sexually, perhaps both and more than both. This feeling would not only alter from one society to another but is likely aggravated during a particularly insecure era within any country. At such times, we may more eagerly fall into picking on different kinds of others who are at best annoying, at worst our enemies.

Let me raise the stakes by moving more deeply into the question of motivation and of the appeal of constructing a demeaned other more generally. Otherness has alternate meanings and occurs in situations dissimilar from those noted above. It can be much more insidious and venal, recurrent and patterned, and its creation takes place not only on individual and microcosmic but on group and macrocosmic levels as well. Evidently, it is often ongoing, commonly associated with social groups (perhaps classes, races, genders, or persons associated by age or sexual preference) who exert control by negatively labeling others.

Within both sociology and philosophy, numerous well-known writers have posited versions of the following thesis: an important reason for the creation of others may be to provide boundaries and definition for groups otherwise amorphous, insecure, in their sense of self-certainty. In the course of defining outsiders, a given collectivity transforms this uncertainty into a perception of superiority, with others rendered inferior human beings in comparison. Indeed, as seen in the last chapter, it was exactly this type of analysis that informed de Beauvoir's theory of women as the second sex, a categorization that enables men to become first by contrast.

Within the sociological context of structural functionalism, Durkheim used the example of crime to make an analogous argument. For Durkheim, a society without crime is virtually inconceivable. As he asserted in *The Rules of Sociological Method,* crime is not only a matter of right or wrong intrinsic to acts in and of themselves (not only because to see crime in completely relative terms also poses problems of its own). Members of a society may consciously believe crime to be merely a function of the content of criminal behavior, oblivious to the repetitive form implied by that society's own continuous participation in its definition. Unconsciously, society needs a construct like crime: it requires something to be seen as bad for purposes of self-clarification. In the course of expressing the outrage of the collective conscience, social identity is forged in contrast to an other. Thus, society nurtures deviants and would manufacture them were the old to obsolesce off the face of a particular historical landscape. If certain types of crime were to vanish, others would arise. Criminologist Edward Sagarin paraphrased this idea:

> Furthermore, as one can see in the attitude toward traitors, renegades, and apostates and in the witch-hunting that has taken place on many occasions throughout human history, a drive against those who would break the rules by which a society abides is something that can bring about social solidarity of those who remain "the good people." They are brought together with one another, in common conscience, to express their disapproval of or indignation at those outside the law. In this view, societies are sometimes driven to *create deviants where none exist*: witness the Inquisition, the Salem witchcraft trials, the Communist purges, the deliberately created German anti-Semitism, the lynchings in America, the red-baiting of the McCarthy era, and other all too numerous examples.[1]

But I would like to become more specific than this categorical emphasis on "society" suggests. One would hope that the creation of deviantized others does not have to occur universally but becomes seductive on certain "occasions" more than others, and then for particular historical reasons and "functions." In a well-known application of Durkheim's theory to U.S. history, Kai Erikson suggested that three "crime waves" promulgated over the course of the seventeenth century in the Massachusetts Bay Colony—the Antinomian controversy of 1636, Quaker persecutions of the 1650s, and the witchcraft hysteria of the 1690s—served a common purpose.[2] Each functioned to provide an insecure society that had not yet established itself with a greater sense of identity and self-confidence. It is fascinating that the colony's rate of "deviance" tended to remain the same throughout the century; as soon as the prisons had been emptied of one group that had been labeled an enemy, another one was pointed out to take its place. Erikson's study showed with great lucidity that it was precisely this creation of an other that allowed the fledgling community to better define its own boundaries. The construction of a "Devil" who changed from crime wave to crime wave successfully deflected attention from the colony's internal divisions toward an external enemy around whom people could conveniently unify:

> It is quite natural, then, that they would seek new frames of reference to help them remember who they were; and it is just as natural that they would begin to look with increasing apprehension at the activities of the Devil. One of the surest ways to confirm an identity, for communities as well as for individuals, is to find some way of measuring what one is *not*. And as the settlers began to take stock of themselves in this new and uncertain land, they learned to study the shapes in which the Devil appeared to them with special care—for he had always loomed in Puritan imagery as a dark adversary against which people could test the edge of their own sainthood.[3]

Take, too, the example of anti-Semitism that Sagarin cited, which was elaborated at length by Jean-Paul Sartre in "Anti-Semite and Jew." Now it is the Jew who is forcibly molded into the shape of the Devil. Sartre propounded a comparable thesis at once philosophical and political, also calling attention to the group tendency to establish hated enemies when groups feel especially powerless themselves. In this essay, Sartre broached issues of displacement and transformability that are even more relevant for helping us segue back toward sadomasochism.

I would like to take "Anti-Semite and Jew" as a starting point for again raising the question of how, and if, the social construction of disliked/despised others relates to characteristics of sadomasochism already outlined. It is interesting that Sartre himself made explicit reference to "sadism" in this classic essay on prejudice—the anti-Semitism example drawn, of course, from the history of German nazism. That anti-Semitism involves a hierarchy between one party defining itself as superior in relation to an inferiorized and hated other is almost obscenely obvious. Different as is anti-Semitism from other prejudices in its specific contours and features (from, say, sexism or racism), in this respect a commonly sadomasochistic element is present.

The characteristic of excessive dependency seems to apply as well. Just as it is clear that there can be no sadist without a masochist, so does Sartre describe the extreme dependence of the anti-Semite on the Jew: "To this end he [the anti-Semite] finds the existence of the Jew absolutely necessary. Otherwise, to whom would he be superior?"[4] Like the sadist (and other creators of deviants as well), the anti-Semite can't really perceive the profundity of this dependence. He or she doesn't realize that, as with the sadist, to destroy the other is also to destroy himself or herself. The need is so deep that were there no Jew to function as other, a replacement would have to be found, just as the Puritans replaced the Antinomian with the Quaker, the Quaker with the Witch. Piecing together several of Sartre's remarks:

> A destroyer in function, a sadist with a pure heart, the anti-Semite is, in the very depths of his soul, a criminal. What he wishes, what he prepares, is the *death* of the Jew. . . . Thus, the anti-Semite is in the unhappy position of having a vital need for the very enemy he wishes to destroy. . . . The anti-Semite chooses finally a Good (extirpating Jews, for instance) that is fixed once and for all, beyond question, out of reach; *he dares not examine it for fear of being led to challenge it and having to seek it in another form* [my emphasis]. The Jew only serves him as a pretext; elsewhere his counterpart will make use of the Negro [the black] or the man of yellow skin.[5]

From Sartre, too, can be extracted one explanation of why the sadistic anti-Semite so desires and needs the hated other. Partly, yes, for reasons of Durkheimian self-definition. But to explain how this need changes from moment to moment, and why it comes into being with such ferocity at certain times, I think the concepts of dominant and subordinate sadism and masochism, which emphasize the transformability of sadomasochism itself, are useful, fitting Sartre's own explanation into a larger theoretical schema. When viewed in specific social and historical context, the tendency of the predominantly sadistic anti-Semite is to be also subordinately masochistic. This would seem to be the case in two distinct ways.

First, as Sartre posited (along with other scholars of the period, concurrently and later), a significant portion of German nazism's mass base was lower middle class. The position of this group was declining, both by the criterion of class and in terms of a compensatory nationalistic pride it was no longer able to feel in the post–World War I era. Anti-Semitism gave this group a feeling of power, elite status, and national pride relative to Jews that otherwise it had lost. Whether or not Sartre was as precise as are historians today about the class composition of German nazism, it can hardly be disputed that the latter was more than just a ruling class phenomenon. That large numbers of people voted for Hitler, indicates that a sadistic streak was being exercised by many who were objectively and relatively less powerful, situated in this sense masochistically within a German society, demeaned not by their own choosing:

> Many anti-Semites—the majority, perhaps—belong to the lower middle class of the town; they are functionaries, office workers, small businessmen, who possess nothing. It is in opposing themselves to the Jew that they suddenly become conscious of being proprietors: *in representing the Jew as a robber, they put themselves in the enviable position of people who could be robbed* [my emphasis]. Thus they have chosen anti-Semitism as a means of establishing their status as possessors.[6]

The anti-Semite thus depends on the Jew. Without someone to cast into a coercively masochistic position, the anti-Semite's real situation of powerlessness would be much more apparent: "he would find himself nothing but a concierge or a shopkeeper in a strongly hierarchical society in which the quality of "true Frenchman" would be at a low valuation," Sartre wrote, "and that profound equality which brings him close to the nobleman and the man of wealth [i.e., to others positioned relatively more sadistically] would disappear all of a sudden."[7] Thus, the anti-Semite uses an other as the excuse to turn from masochist in one respect to sadist in another: here is the first application of the characteristic of transformability. Power is seized from within a position of relative powerlessness.

It will be much easier, much more pleasurable, for the masochistically sadistic anti-Semite to direct anger at a relatively powerless other (below) than toward more powerful others (above). And, as Sartre quite astutely pointed out, it was in the interests of German elites that the anti-Semite do so. One would not expect many members of this class to be against a social movement that directed social psychological energies away from itself. More likely many would approve of, sometimes support financially, and perhaps vote in favor of such a movement. It would be in the interests of *any* elite that less powerful fractions of society be encouraged to focus their attentions away from *them*. "Anti-Semitism channels revolutionary drives toward the destruction of certain men, not of institutions," Sartre pronounced. "It represents, therefore, a safety valve for the owning classes, who encourage it and substitute for a dangerous hate against their regime a beneficent hate against particular people."[8] It does not take all that much imagination to realize that such dangerously displaceable sentiments are not limited to the Vichy France or late Weimar/Nazi Germany of Sartre's 1930s and 1940s description. A version of it is fomented today (and, extending the example, in France at that) as a politician like LePen resuscitates nationalistic sentiment by directing the gaze of many working- and lower-middle-class persons, whose class position may be declining, toward less powerful foreign others. With disturbing effectiveness, LePen has thereby managed to deflect vague dissatisfactions away from more powerful classes in French society (above) onto targets constructed xenophobically (below). Perhaps these dissatisfactions—this *ressentiment,* to borrow the Nietzschean term—stems from relative powerlessness perceived in relation to a persistently wealthy capitalist class that gives new form to hazy vestiges of older aristocratic privilege in French society.

The second way in which sadomasochism's transformability illuminates Sartre's soliloquy on otherness is equally important. Clearly, the anti-Semite does not perceive himself or herself either as predominantly sadistic or subordinately masochistic. As would be true for most sadists of the sadomasochistic dynamic I have been describing, he or she is no more able to admit to being sadistic than to see his or her extreme dependence on the masochist. (By definition, sadists who realize that they are contingent and sadistic would thereby be less so, undermining their own sadism from within.) A major reason for this book being predominantly theoretical and not founded on interviews or other empirically oriented methods of social research is precisely this: the type of sadomasochism that interests me at the moment is usually unconscious to individuals or groups, unbeknownst to the actors who engage with/in it.

Nevertheless, Sartre's anti-Semite did and does act sadistically yet keeps this sadism from coming to conscious awareness possibly through another twist on the theme of sadomasochistic transformability. For, as Sartre reported above, the predominantly sadistic anti-Semite may turn things around in his mind so as to believe that he is the predominantly masochistic one. *But he does not see himself cast masochistically by oppressors above, who actually do have power in a given social order, but in relation to a powerless other below, an oppressed group who he convinces himself is really the oppressor.* "In representing the Jew as a robber, they [the anti-Semite] put themselves in the enviable position of people who could be robbed," said Sartre. Even though anti-Semitism allows the anti-Semite to be as though possessed, the "proprietor" Sartre described, the resulting sadism is justified through seeing him or herself as dispossessed. (In the end, the anti-Semite feels some of the same emotions after the reversal that he or she felt before it: anger, dispossession. He or she has somehow managed to reproduce the real emotional state that was bothering him or her in the first place.) The anti-Semite is the victim, the Jew the victimizer. The latter is seen as usurping the rightful place of others by becoming too economically and socially powerful, the supposed source of all Evil. The Devil. The anti-Semite believes he or she is acting for Good, as a righteous rebel with a cause. (When I turn shortly to examples taken from U.S. society, sociologist Jack Katz's perspective in *The Seductions of Crime* becomes quite apposite. Katz contends that in most forms of crime, the criminal's existential state is to believe he or she, too, is acting for Good. Role reversals frequently result, and victims are cast as victimizers, so that a "righteous slaughterer," for example, believes his adulterous wife brought him to the climactic moment of her own killing.)

The specifics of a given historical situation thus become raw material for building elaborate ideological systems of rationalization and justification, the stuff out of which opportunities for mass sadomasochistic turnabouts can be constructed. What reverses is *at whom* one feels angry, and *by whom* one believes one has been dispossessed. By projecting this anger onto an other who actually had nothing to do with the problem (and casting this other by force into a masochistic position), a sadomasochistic system is reproduced, both in miniature and writ large, both in the structure of the psyche and in the polis. At the same time, the sadistic class, in this case the German ruling elite, is let off the hook. This, too, Sartre perceived, as he bemoaned the ways in which a highly stratified and inequitable capitalist society aggravates this dynamic:

> This means that anti-Semitism is a mythical, bourgeois representation of the class struggle, *and that it could not exist in a classless society.* Anti-Semitism manifests the separation of men and their isolation in the midst of the community, the conflicts of interests and the crosscurrents of passions: *it is a phenomenon of social pluralism* [my emphases]. In a society whose members felt mutual bonds of solidarity, because they are all engaged in the same enterprise, there would be no place for it.[9]

Unfortunately, from the intellectual and political vantage point of 1991, Sartre's call for a classless society—though admirable, a hope I share—is nonetheless simplistic, a happy ending tacked onto the more intractable set of problems posed by "Anti-Semite and Jew." The phenomenon Sartre analyzed is certainly one of social pluralism insofar as complex layers of inequality exacerbate the possibilities and opportunities for prejudice, for the blaming of various others. It is also apparent by now that anti-Semitism didn't wither away with communism, nor have other forms of oppression, from diverse racisms and sexisms to homophobia. I hope that our present theoretical sophistication is such that we recognize how, generally speaking, one form of oppression is not reducible to nor simply vanishes with another. Even more germane to this work, however, is another crucial point that Sartre may have missed by not giving full weight to the transformability of power relations. He may not have sufficiently noted that a sadomasochistic character structure tends to make its way into all of us, capitalist and communist/socialist alike, just from living in a sadomasochistically enmeshing culture, one that fosters complex reversals from masochist to sadist and back again. Such a culture incubates a great deal of anger, while not overtly generating much loving recognition and pleasure on the erotic side (from fulfillments sensuous and sensual to sexual).

Therefore, it would be surprising indeed if we were not prone to take some of that anger out on each other on a day-to-day basis, to lash out, to pass it down from generation to generation or across social subgroups, and perhaps to do so even within the very social movements we spawn to fight given forms of oppression. It would also be surprising if any of this were easy or pleasant to recognize, if it is not disconcerting just to have it brought to conscious awareness that sadomasochism may have been reproduced inside ourselves. Maybe a given reader will become angered merely reading this. Not only does the experience of being oppressed oneself fail to guarantee that as an oppressed group, we will not in turn oppress others; but if it is true that sadomasochism is transformable, the opposite is more likely: one would have to be wary of, and on guard against, a propensity to do onto others as someone did onto us. Thus, to call for a classless society in the economic sense alone, while critically important, does not ensure a society shorn of the coercively sadomasochistic dynamics this book has been depicting. Not necessarily, not at all. Israelis later came to discriminate against a Palestinian other. A bureaucrat, now propertyless, may now exert sadistic power toward other party officials in relation to whom he or she has applied new forms of distinctions. The person racially or religiously discriminated against may be quite prejudiced in his treatment of some other group, railing against an ethnic minority or against homosexuals, or behaving shabbily toward spouse and/or children. We may rationalize a different oppression than the particular form we have personally suffered.

(I strongly believe that it does not in any way detract from the validity of his—or her—writings to point out that if Deirdre Bair's autobiography of Simone de Beauvoir is accurate, Sartre himself was less than entirely ethical in the way he treated women in his own life.[5] In fact, he was extremely sexist, thoughtlessly setting up a dichotomy between a good intellectualized woman—de Beauvoir—and a host of relatively more sexualized others. From this might be gleaned a possible source of his blindness with regard to the specific observation I am making.) And I could go on, and will, to provide more examples of transformability when returning below to contemporary American society.

In other words, just because a given person or group of persons is committed to greater degrees of freedom ideologically and in public does not mean that they will automatically act this way in practice and in private (and vice versa). Rather, both levels—the personal and the political, the public and the private—would have to change for Sartre's vision to be realizable. They would both have to conform, to correspond with one another. Indeed, herein may lie one explanation as to why eliminating one form of oppression is not followed by the eradication, or even necessarily by the diminution of others. This common and underlying character structure—our psychic/sexual patterns, the ways and directions in which we learn to channel our feelings—can remain untouched by external changes that are at once key and all too superficial. Better, perhaps, to look toward a society not only classless but less sadomasochistic in this book's particular usage of that term, a society not characterized by unfreely mandated *sadomasochistic dynamics*. The latter may be a deeper-going conceptualization of the same intention. Better yet to do something truly innovative historically: to bring these dynamics to the surface as a focus of study in and of themselves, and to thereby bring about alterations that would come simply from sadomasochistic patterns being paid serious and conscious attention.

But this rumination, important though I believe it to be, has taken us somewhat adrift: the question remains as to whether other traits of sadomasochism apply as readily to the creation of otherness, including anti-Semitism. As in sadomasochism, a hierarchical dichotomy between superiority and inferiority along with excessive dependency has thus far seemed to likewise characterize the dynamics of prejudice. What about the paradoxical leaning of the sadist toward turning into and being attracted by his or her opposite? Or the supposed tendency of the dynamic to fail and be irrational in its own terms?

In one respect, the sadist of the hypothetical sexual example with which I began this book cannot easily fool the observer about his or her need for the masochist. The former may try to act independent and in control, but the very fact of being in the same room with this bound other physically attests to the reality of dependence and desire. Less obvious may be the underlying feelings of a particular anti-Semite or racist. These prejudiced persons may allege to the world how much they hate and are unattached to the other, remaining distanced and at some remove—apparently, then, self-consistent. Nevertheless, this anti-Semite's or racist's having to dub him- or herself so superior in relation to a demeaned inferior reveals that he or she is not very secure at all. If secure, why be so intent and sometimes obsessed with belittling others? Rather, the bigot's attachment to the other is much more enormous, excessive, and symbiotic than he or she admits or may appear. The bigoted person needs the other badly, for many interrelated reasons. He or she depends on the other to try to gain a feeling of mutual social recognition and legitimacy which may have been denied by society (as in Sartre's case of the lower-middle-class anti-Semite). By in turn denying recognition to the inferiorized other, forcing this other into a less powerful position, the prejudiced one becomes more powerful and supposedly recognized by contrast. At the same time, insecure and inferior beliefs about oneself (within) can be projected onto the other (without). In so doing, the bigot doesn't entirely lose those feelings (after all, they are part of and originate within the self). Simultaneously, the disconcerting realizations that would come from having to own up to and take responsibility for these feelings can be avoided.

There are, however, many instances in which the biased person does not keep his or her distance. In many cases, certainly, a version of the sexual analogy did and does very much apply to this chapter's examples. It is interesting that not only Sartre but other writers on the subject of prejudice as well, from Frantz Fanon to Joel Kovel to Wilhelm Reich, have observed the paradoxical attraction of sadists to others by whom they are supposedly repulsed. Sartre spoke very plainly in "Anti-Semite and Jew" about one element of the former's hatred being a profound and "sadistic" sexual attraction toward Jews; this is so strong that the anti-Semite will sometimes surround himself with "exceptional" Jews whom he rationalizes to fellow bigots are different from the rest.[11] In *Black Skin, White Masks,* Frantz Fanon expounded the now familiar argument about the sexual repression of the white male racist who projects his own sexual conflicts onto black men. Fanon referred explicitly to sexually sadomasochistic transformability, depicting the white man as sadistic at some times and masochistic at others:

> Since his ideal is an infinite virility, is there not a phenomenon of diminution in relation to the Negro, who is viewed as a penis symbol? Is the lynching of the Negro not a sexual revenge? We know how much of sexuality there is in all cruelties, tortures, beatings. One has only to reread a few pages of the Marquis de Sade to be easily convinced of the fact.

Fanon also believed masochism to be latent as the sadistic racist's other side, manifest at certain moments when whites try to ingratiate themselves into black culture with a suspiciously persistent zeal. Therefore, some pages later:

> There are, for instance, men who go to "houses" in order to be beaten by Negroes. . . . There is first of all a sadistic aggression toward the black man, followed by a guilt complex because of the sanction against such behavior by the democratic culture of the country in question. This aggression [the black man's] is then tolerated. . . . In any event, it (this schema) is the only way in which to explain the masochistic behavior of the white man.[12]

In addition, of course, as many black feminist writers including Bell Hooks and Angela Davis have detailed, the sexual desires of white men have also been projected onto black women. An alleged promiscuity was mythologized, conveniently fantasized, in a way that rationalized the many rapes of black women that have taken place in U.S. history before and after slavery.[13] Another form of patriarchal good woman/bad woman (or madonna/whore) split was therein affirmed. Racism and sexism were allied in a specific conjuncture and locked into the same class-ridden economic system, operative not only among white women but between white and black women as well. The white woman was set up as the good wife, as predominantly masochistic but nonetheless accorded a potential (whether or not realized) for subordinate sadism through her relative power over black women others. From the point of view of the predominantly sadistic white male, the good white woman was rendered sexually boring, having been cast coercively as pure, controlled, predictable. (I think of the wife/mistress split described in the last chapter, then as though only an *intra*racial phenomenon.) Consequently, the split that originated within this white male's own mind required a construct like bad woman for the sadist's subordinate masochism to be enacted, even from within a sadistic mode. Black women were therefore invested with the fascination of otherness, forced to represent sexual and ontological desires that sprang (in part) from the paradoxes of a sadomasochistically oriented social and psychosexual system.

The attraction on the part of the prejudiced person toward the object of prejudice can be even further elucidated by the psychoanalytic concept of splitting. As the sadist with the masochist, so the prejudiced person has split off parts of himself or herself, projecting that which must be alienated or disavowed onto others. Joel Kovel defined the term to some extent in *White Racism: A Psychohistory,* using language that hearkens back to Benjamin and the Hegelian problem of recognition reviewed earlier in this work:

> As humans we demand self-expression and recognition. We insist on the integrity of the "I," which recognizes itself in the other person and is recognized in turn. Racism, however, is the domain of the Other. When the self becomes Other, it is denied recognition and, by extension, self-expression. . . . The Other is assigned some part of the dominant self which is unbearable yet desired; therefore, the Other is not recognized for him/her self, but as the repository of some split-off element of the dominant self.[14]

For the sadist, as we saw, it was the desire to be vulnerable and contingent that is split off and projected onto the masochist: it is the other who seems to be dependent, certainly not the sadist. (Likewise, the masochist assigns independence to someone else, last of all to her or himself.) For a racist who is also sexually repressed, it is the black person (or person of color in other cases), male and female, whose sexuality may be mythologized to suit this white fantasizer's forbidden desires. And of course it is the other, not the self, who will be punished for inspiring these feelings. Victim becomes victimizer yet again. For the homophobe, clearly, it is one's own fears of homosexuality/homoeroticism that are often foisted onto the other as though he or she were to blame. I am often amazed at the vehemence of the disdain that can be expressed by those (including those who consider themselves otherwise progressive) who nurture discriminatory feelings toward others who are gay. A particular man, for instance, may construct a machismo and virile identity only possible in comparison to a demeaned gay male other, seemingly oblivious to the insecurity about self he has thereby revealed. Why would one react so strongly and hatefully were not something being aroused that one feared existed and that had to be defended against, perhaps within oneself?

No matter how one looks at it, then, it seems inarguable that just as society plays a role in defining the criminal (usually failing to recognize its own participation in the process), so the projected fantasies of the splitting process originate from within the consciousness of the sadist himself or herself. Still another reason for the paradoxical (and often sexualized) attraction between bigot and object is that the former tries to seize back, to merge again with, parts of the self that have been denied and repressed. The bigot tries to overcome self-alienation, albeit in a warped and subverted way, recognizing feelings outside that cannot be seen or admitted within. This was also true for the sadist and the masochist (see chapter 2). But the only way his or her desires can be admitted by the sadist qua sadist is if they take a form that somehow punishes the alleged provocateur. If, that is, intercourse takes place in a form decidedly sadomasochistic, decidedly sadistic.

Though they are appealing and undoubtedly true in many ways, one ought be a little cautious about reducing prejudice to a function of only these sexual and individual dimensions I have been exploring over the last several pages. I do not wish to fall back into an overly psychologized explanation, as did Fanon from time to time. My intention is exactly the opposite. I hope to describe the psychosexual and the sociological as inseparably as possible. Therefore, it might be preferable to declare that the prejudiced person (the anti-Semite, the racist, the sexist, the homophobe) projects onto created others a whole set of ideas, frustrations, forbidden desires, and angers that have been aroused *within a particular society at a given historical moment.* Splitting then becomes a notion both social and psychic, the specifics of what is projected being greatly affected by the context of people's varying, situated experiences.

Given how common it is for societies to be sexually repressive, we would anticipate being vulnerable to blaming others for the unfulfilled and seemingly unfulfillable desires we think they have inspired in us, but such hatreds are neither universal nor inevitable. They tend to flare up with special strength at times when traditional morality is being demanded or reasserted. In *The Mass Psychology of Fascism,* for instance, Reich analyzed the sexual symbolism and representational imagery to which the Sartrean anti-Semite also seems to have been attracted, emphasizing the repressive sexual/heterosexual fascism of the Nazi order. One wonders also how it could be entirely coincidental that hate incidents (including the phenomenon of gay bashing) are on the rise in a late 1980s/early 1990s United States wherein sexual conservatism is being reimposed. This is a time when other violent crimes involving sex, too, are widespread. Moreover, split-off projections need not only be sexual in their variable content but may involve other sorts of political, economic, and social fantasies, as well. Supposedly Jews were involved in a conspiracy to take over the world (at the same time national socialism was trying to do just that). Several years ago, the Sandinista government in Nicaragua was still being labeled part of the Communist other by the Reagan administration, alleged to have covert designs on the whole Central American region (at the same time we were waging a covert war, with our own designs on the Sandinista government). Again, what I am suggesting is that history provides specific opportunities for rationalizing and justifying sadistic acts that arise out of generally sadomasochistic insecurities and contradictions.

It is obvious that the prejudiced sadist must really believe these insecurities will be assuaged by virtue of having created a demeaned, devalued, and mistreated other. I wonder if here, too, there isn't another analogy with the earlier paradigm of sadomasochistic dynamics. Does sadomasochism genuinely work for the bigot or does he or she, too, remain as dissatisfied as our Weberian Protestant/capitalist appeared to be. Does the sadist stay insecure, perhaps becoming even more so, in the process of the dynamic's unfolding? One would think it indicative of something going awry that the hierarchical inequality set up between sadists and masochists regularly produces a division within the class of masochists, a structural tendency toward the promulgation of good and bad masochists. For example, evidence of discontent lies in the fact that the sadistic imagination in its incarnation in the gendered category of male repetitively spawns a good woman/bad woman split within the group of all women who have been cast masochistically by patriarchal societies. *It would seem indicative of a tendency toward triangulation,* testimony toward an internal split the sadist has exteriorized without. (This triangle consists of the sadist, the good masochist tolerated because controlled, and a bad masochist who may consciously be hated but is yet the object of obsession and/or sexual titillation because relatively *uncontrolled.* The bad masochist represents the part of oneself that has been involuntarily denied.)

That the good masochist alone does not appear either to satisfy or in the long run to sufficiently interest the sadist is because, as I have argued elsewhere, the sense of recognition and superiority the good masochist accords the sadist has been coercively bestowed and not freely given; he or she has constructed the ensuing sense of superiority, manipulated it, into existence. All of this, somewhere deep down inside, the sadist knows and thus remains frustrated, his or her original insecurities not assuaged. In fact, the sadist may sullenly resent and scorn this good masochist for exactly this reason, mistreating her or him even more. At the same time, the sadist will often wish to keep the good masochist in tow as an anchor of both loved and/or hated security, going out into the world to compulsively hate and/or love a freer, rebelliously bad other.

This dynamic is an extremely complicated one, and I will leave the possibility of querying it more precisely to other writers on the subject. For now, however, I add only that there is something about this structural split between good and bad masochists that seems to recur. I suspect it is rather generalizable, not at all limited to the example of the good and the bad woman bequeathed from the structural imperatives of patriarchy. The reader may recall, for instance, Sartre's observation that the sadistic mind of the anti-Semite also triangulates. He or she erects a category like the exceptional Jew, one who can be kept closer at hand because opposed to those who are not exceptional and bad. It is not uncommon for a racist to think something similar, promulgating a belief in good minorities as opposed to bad. In a study of racism entitled *Canarsie,* Jonathan Rieder mentions a distinction often made between "niggers" and "blacks" by biased persons in the Brooklyn neighborhood he studied; beneath this dichotomy was "the foundation of a ranking of the profligate lifestyles of lower-income blacks and the respectable lifestyles of middle-income blacks."[15] The same racist distinction was represented cinematically by Spike Lee in a scene from *Do the Right Thing.* A white Italian named Pino tells Mookie, the young black (played in the film by the director) who works in a pizzeria owned by Pino's father Sal, that there are plenty of good blacks he does like and respect, such as, if I recall his listing correctly, "Magic" Johnson and Muhammad Ali. Of course, the others are bad, feels the enraged Pino: "niggers."

A propensity for sadomasochistic bigotry to dissatisfy or, at least, to destabilize itself from within, can likewise be intuited from speculating now on a grander historical scale. Just as with the sadist in general, groups of the sadistically prejudiced may tend to subject their coerced masochists to greater and greater depths of oppression. Frustrated by a recognition that can never come because systemically impossible, driven themselves, they may drive the other sadistically through more and more repressive measures. (I suppose this could happen instead of, or in addition to, the splitting process just outlined.) Each time the group cast masochistically resists from psychic and/or physical pain, the sadistic may punish this oppressed group still more, on and on in a vicious dialectical progression that causes masochists to resist yet again. Out of such dialectics, of course, revolutions sometimes result. The former group of masochists, now in power, may have to not only defend against counterrebelling sadists but decide how or if to satisfy the rage and desire for punishment these sadists have undoubtedly generated. Other times, the sadistic class (or fractions of it) may realize that in destroying the other, it is also destroying itself; it may stop the process, suddenly fearful and self-protective, cutting its losses by embracing reform rather than revolution and by becoming seemingly more reasonable for the time being.

I think of an example like the South African apartheid regime, under which racist repression seemed for a while to worsen alongside rebellion against it. After a while, though, the sadists' tactics may alter somewhat, as they did in this case, which was also affected by another kind of dialectical interchange with the outside world. A more paternalistic and liberal response may then be forthcoming, as though generously conceded, so that some of the others' more palatable demands are met. This may amount to the concretization of yet another form of splitting, now between good and bad protesters (good reformers versus bad radicals-and-revolutionaries), promulgated from within the sadistic mass psyche onto the coercively situated masochistic group. As I suggested in chapter 4 this process seems to have occurred in U.S. labor history as well, characterizing the response of capital to periodic rebellions, a zigzagging pattern between overt repression and placating concessions, between the brutalizingly scientific measures of a Frederick Turner and the supposedly enlightened paternalism of someone like Elton Mayo and his school of industrial relations. Indeed, someone could contend that the contradictions of a system like South African apartheid (or, for that matter, like German nazism) are inclined to worsen over time precisely because they are capitalistically organized. Their tendency to self-aggravate would then relate to more than just racism and the traits of an allegedly psychologized dynamic—to, additionally, the structural demands of intracapitalist competition. At one level, this seems true enough, and yet such economic tendencies can themselves (as in the analysis of the accumulation dynamic in chapter 4) partake of and correspond with those that are sadomasochistically oriented. Whichever interpretation one adopts, though, the argument can be made that systems of prejudice revolving around the forced creation of an other appear to generate their own set of internal and paradoxical instabilities. In this respect, their dynamic tendencies bear comparison with those of sadomasochistic systems more generally.

By now, I hope to have indicated that there is indeed a resemblance between the workings of prejudice and the dynamics of sadomasochism. Each of the characteristics deduced earlier seems relevant to the creation of outsiders. But I wonder how this analysis could be merely an abstract one, germane only to the past, a Germany of the 1930s (à la Sartre and Reich) or the seventeenth-century settlement of a not-yet United States (à la Durkheim and Erikson). To the contrary, I would like to speculate for the remainder of this chapter on the thesis that creating "enemy others" continues to serve special functions and to have highly loaded meaning in the historical context of the contemporary United States.

For one thing, as I suggested in chapter 1, late 1980s and 1990s U.S. society faces insecurities that make its situation not entirely dissimilar from that of the amorphously defined Massachusetts Bay Colony. Even more disturbing, certain analogies with the late Weimar Republic come to mind insofar as the United States is no longer the preeminent world financial power it once was relative to Japan or to reunited Germany, having amassed mind-boggling international budget deficits. And before military confidence was resuscitated by the recent Gulf War (itself dependent on the construction of a Middle Eastern Arab other to replace the obsolescent Red Menace), we had lost Vietnam and been left with a nagging sense of embarrassed defeat and self-doubt.

Domestically, the picture is no rosier. We wait as though for Godot for recessions to recede, euphemistically avoiding use of the 1929 word *depression*. Of late, the human cost in massive employment layoffs and shutdowns and the insecurities both engender have become more and more worrisome—across class, as attorneys and Wall Street bankers as well as factory and municipal workers are finding their jobs abruptly terminated. Meanwhile, the federal government has been sadistically abandoning inner cities to deteriorate more and more precipitously, crime ridden in ways that frighten all of the residents within and outside them. Such cities are being both destroyed and allowed to self-destruct, their budgets decimated as basic health and human services are withdrawn. (This situation, of course, disastrously affects the poor, themselves composed in disproportionate numbers of minorities who have already often suffered the effects of past and present discrimination and of prejudice.) At the same time, as just noted, traditional moralities are being reasserted, and gay persons may face new forms of discrimination consequent upon the advent of AIDS. A number of individual rights are progressively/regressively being abridged and delimited, judicially and legislatively, and sexual conservatism is being advised, something that has to sow confusion when combined with the desires for erotic freedom and liberation associated with the 1960s. Perhaps it isn't coincidental that Weimar-style garb—black leather, studs—became visible in recent years, attesting at once to perceptions of and mocking rebellion from a sadomasochistically charged environment.

In the midst of such a historical predicament, how could the creation of demeaned others not serve as a handy pretext to distract from this host of internal and external problems? Groups in positions of power would have to be grateful for, and to unconsciously or consciously encourage, any construct that helped to deflect critical attention from above to below. If a common enemy is perceived without, one need not look too hard at political divisions and inequities within. Consequently, it is also not surprising to find a zigzag pattern emerging in recent U.S. history with regard to the construction of late 1980s and early 1990s devils.

In addition, demeaned others seem to shift easily from foreign to domestic incarnations (while both can exist simultaneously, one may be especially emphasized at a given point in time).[16] The important point, though, is that something is continuously being pegged to fill a conveniently deviantized hole. As the recurrent forging of enemies did for the Puritans over the course of an earlier century, the process today provides a sense of sadistic identity, however fragile and specious it may be. In the United States, if not the Sandinistas, it was the Granadians, or the Panamanians, or the Iraqis personified in Saddam Hussein who seemed to occupy this constructed slot of foreign other. Regardless of how we evaluate the rights or wrongs of a particular cause, a function of distraction is also being served in such cases, sociologically speaking, whether or not recognized. Reiterating Durkheim's point, societies get so caught up with the content of deviantized behaviors that the repetitious forms of their own not entirely innocent involvement are overlooked. Yet, one has only to study before-and-after newspaper headlines and top TV news stories to remark how coverage of domestic economic hardship and budget deficits was displaced as focal points of media, and therefore public, attention with the coming of the 1991 Gulf War.

Domestic enemies have been named and pointed to as well. Politicians' and media references both to the "war on drugs" declared during the Reagan administration and to crime are usually linked with people who are poor and members of minorities. Since the social issue of most concern in the United States after the economy *is* crime, this connection means that members of a so-called underclass—a term overlaid with historical deviance attribution itself—are portrayed as at the root of our most serious problems. Image after image, conservative speech after speech, the impression is semiotically reinforced that a group overwhelmingly constituted of black and Hispanic males (who comprise over 80 percent of the jail population in New York City, for instance) are the major criminals of U.S. society. Attention is focused on them: the individual behavior of these others is examined as they are placed as under a social magnifying glass.

But focusing on the other also means we barely look at how crime is defined, or at whether the history of past and present racism should be seen as criminal itself. Simultaneously and not coincidentally, the public stops reflecting with even a modicum of intellectuality about what causes this phenomenon that has such generally destructive effects. If we had to think about it, wouldn't it strike us as highly peculiar that violent street crime (committed disproportionately both against and by minorities) should be so concentrated among particular groups? Were this question persistently posed, we would have to admit either to underlying racist presumptions about "their" essentialized behavior or that something social must be going on that relates to inequality and the ramifications of just such racist attitudes.[17] In a sense, there are really just these two possibilities. Were we to seriously consider the second proposition, though, it might not be so easy to ignore power structures (above) or to hold these structures blameless for placing minorities in a position (below) wherein decent jobs, housing, and education are often not to be found. Empowered elites would then have to bear some of the responsibility for the ghettoization that is having an almost genocidal effect on inner-city communities.

Instead, the spotlight is turned away from the powerful onto the powerless, and the possibility that we as well as "they" (both above and below) might be at fault rarely crosses our minds. Rather than becoming angry at these elites (and divided against them), we achieve unity at the price of targeting the ghettoized other. The victimized become the victimizers, only to be victimized again. This is not to say, of course, that in the case of violent street crime, those who have been victimized are not in many cases victimizing others. Just the opposite. As already contended, the sadomasochistic paradigm's usefulness is to illuminate how those hurt can tend to take their anger out on others, lashing out and reproducing more horror by channeling their own rage below rather than above, at the system that generated the problems in the first place. Again, the trickiness of sadomasochistic dynamics is that both socially and psychologically they facilitate such displacements as they pervade the psyches of oppressed and oppressor alike. Tendencies for subordinate sadism are thus enacted by those cast in predominantly masochistic positions, and the same cycle threatens to start anew.

In analyzing contemporary problems of crime or poverty, I do not mean to disregard the critical role of human agency and individual responsibility. I do mean to observe, however, that it tends to be only the victimizing acts of the powerless that we are urged, politically and by the media, to notice. Only relatively powerless others are blamed, in reality as well as in our psyches; only this "they" who become ghettoized and reghettoized through a tautological maze of systemic self-justification. As sociologist Loic Wacquant recently proposed (coining a term highly appropriate in this context), it is only the other whom we tend to "devilize" and represent as demonic.[18]

Perhaps the most horrifyingly brilliant aspect of such a sadomasochistic setup is that it not only manages to let the powerful off the hook but also aids in "saint-izing" them relative to the foreign and domestic devils it has created. If one were to argue that the past and present racism I outline above has itself been sadistic, then sado-masochistic transformability must again be coming into play. It appears that the sadistically racist—those who are prejudiced and exclusionary in their social practices—are themselves the ones who have been cast masochistically. In the Gulf War, for example, we became convinced that the Iraqis alone (the Arab other not seen as fully human, as the Vietnamese were similarly dehumanized in the prior war) were the bad guys endangering Western interests. Much of the gratuitously sadistic violence exercised by the U.S. side, along with the eventual death of l00,000 Iraqis, was thereby obscured. Or, returning to the domestic side, the profoundly individualistic tenor of U.S. culture facilitates the belief that poverty and crime among inner-city residents must somehow be their fault: again, it is the other who is doing something to us, and not vice versa.

Thus, drawing a second time on Katz's conceptualization, those with far greater power somehow become the ones acting in and for the Good: something like a war on drugs is waged with the self-righteousness of a crusade. I think here of another disquieting analogy with the late Weimar–early Nazi period when fascism managed to represent itself as a liberating force, a national socialism, borrowing the language of socialists who, of course, did not share the fascists' convictions about racial superiority or about concomitant inequalities. In our present era, now often dubbed postmodern, something similar has happened. Leftist terminology is once more being adopted and co-opted, splashed across television screens and mainstream magazine articles so effectively as to be virtually surreal. The contras, a few years ago, were "freedom fighters." Across the electoral spectrum, from right to center to left, the idiom of "political correctness" is being bandied about, stripped of its contextual origins in 1960s cultural radicalism. On the front page of the 30 June 1991 *New York Times,* Housing Secretary Jack Kemp, whose past views have been extremely conservative, talks about fighting poverty through measures of "empowerment." This confusing muddle is also a major vehicle by which sadomasochistic transformability is achieved: through language, it becomes that much more difficult to tell the devils from the saints, the victims from the victimizers, the dominant from the subordinated.

Such examples bring up the interesting theoretical problem of just where the media fit into this particular piece of the sadomasochistic maze. Much of the targeting of others I have been depicting is effected through television and print imagery. How, if at all, does this relate to sadomasochism? In *White Racism,* Kovel distinguishes between three forms of racist bias: (a) dominative racism, which involves direct physical assault and possible "sexual obsession," going back to slavery; (b) aversive racism, which characterizes "bourgeois life" and is a phenomenon of avoidance in "stable urban zones of segregation and suburbs"; and (c) metaracism. This last category, the one most relevant here, Kovel defines as no longer dependent on direct human agency, but a

> racism of technocracy, i.e., one without psychological mediation as such, in which racist oppression is carried out directly through economic and technocratic means. . . . Metaracism characterizes an internally pacified late-capitalist society, in which it inherits the racist mantle from the inexpedient and odious forms of aversion and direct domination.[19]

Metaracism, therefore, requires no person-to-person contact but becomes hidden much more subtly within the technocratic and economic organization of society itself. I would add to Kovel's characterization that the technocratic and everyday operations of media may also be metaracist in their impact, so that interpersonal mediation is no longer required: it is wrought anyway, albeit in a different manner. A phenomenon one could perhaps name "postmodern sadomasochism" has arisen, working something as follows. The attention of a given television viewer sitting at home is directed toward minorities who are linked by symbolic representations with social problems like drugs and crime. This viewer may become angered at members of the groups being portrayed, even sadistically so, and be therefore that much more eager to see harshly punitive criminal justice measures imposed, including capital punishment. Crime and sadomasochism thereby become interrelated and intertwined in complicated and multidimensional ways.

I would also submit that such sadistic feelings are aroused in the subordinate mode by persons who are often situated much more predominantly masochistically. The passivity intrinsic in sitting in front of a TV would seem to affirm this observation to some extent. Should the viewer feel overwhelmed by local and world events in the news, there is no place to channel such emotions but onto the deviantized minority on the screen or in the papers. (Even the aversive racist, who has ghettoized the others and supposedly tries to avoid them, is likely to encounter such metaracist exposure anyway.) There is no other place for general feelings of powerlessness about one's social situation to go, no media commentary to validate suspicions one might quietly harbor about whether powerful others exist above and behind the surface imagery. After all, one can't get mad at a TV screen or at *The New York Post*. Hostilities engendered therefore don't go anyplace but down, toward the powerless. Simultaneously, to the extent elite groups are situated in a predominantly sadistic structural location, they are able to take advantage of this position, both postmodern and metaracist in its utter invisibility. This isn't even sadomasochism with a human face, but sadomasochism with no face at all.

Lest a reader think I have lost my mind in positing some vaguely postmodern sadomasochism, at the same time overlooking the truism that viewers become anesthetized to (rather than maddened by) all the images that bombard them, let me provide a few speculative analyses by way of example. During the Bush-Dukakis presidential campaign, the winner's advertisements were especially successful at directing anger toward targeted others—Bush's famous Willie Horton commercial, for instance, an offensive thrust from which Dukakis never recovered. Throughout the eighties, politicians in general tried to outdo one another over the issue of crime and the degree of toughness each promised to, and believed political efficacy required he or she had to demonstrate.

What I conclude from all of this is that the importance of crime as a social problem in contemporary American life includes but goes well beyond the reality of crime itself. In addition, crime may take on a special meaning *because it is the perfect issue to facilitate the expression of the mass, and subordinately sadistic,* racism I refer to just above. Fears about crime are more than well grounded, but it is hard to believe there is not a sadistic element also being satisfied, one quite emotional indeed and reinforced by the media imagery that plays a not insignificant role in its arousal. Think of how media coverage differentially applies wolf-pack language to describe crimes committed by groups of minority youth.[20] Or how whites can talk of criminals as "animals," their faces often contorted with rage. Since a disproportionate amount of violent crime involves minority defendants, and animalistic allusions are inseparable from the history of social Darwinism, both usages carry clear racist connotations.

Given the depth of this sadistically racist hostility, then, it is hard to believe that anger at minority criminals is not an overdetermined reaction. It may express not only frustration about crime but also a sense of powerlessness that goes beyond the particularities of the problem itself. Again, if only crime were truly at stake, why wouldn't we demand massive redistribution of economic and social resources to the ghetto neighborhoods where crime is concentrated? Why not continue the War on Poverty only half-heartedly begun in the sixties to at least neutralize the possibility that crime indeed has root causes that can be socially altered? It seems to me that we would do this, and be encouraged to do this by both politicians and media analysts, if crime alone were really the issue on the table.

That we do not or cannot make such demands, however, seems to indicate that crime is serving unconscious functions also (in true Durkheimian/Eriksonian fashion), uniting around the identification of racialized others at a moment of decided historical confusion. This outward focus may be operating as a crucial sadomasochistic safety valve whereby angry energies that could be criticizing centers of power in our society are channeled instead toward attacks on the powerless. (So said Sartre, too, about the energies of the relatively dispossessed anti-Semite, however else the cases are in other respects extremely different.) Postmodernism or no postmodernism, television or no television, crime remains an exceedingly emotional and charged signifier. It is simultaneously vital to the sort of "devilization" Wacquant describes and to processes of systemic reproduction. Last, crime serves as another catalyst for actuating sadomasochistic transformations. What better way to transpose victims and victimizers than to turn a social mirror so that its reflection goes only one way, so that it makes only the other into a criminal? Little wonder that right-wing ideology is so consistently persistent in its sadistically punitive approach to crime, characterizing it solely as the product of faulty individuals.

I wish to look at a slightly different twist on the relationships between this possibly postmodern sadomasochism, the media, and crime. Even though Kovel indicates that the direction of racism in society has gone from the "dominative" toward the "metaracist," the former is by no means bygone, and, in certain cases, the two types come to be insidiously combined. For example, a rise in hate incidents, attacks on persons targeted simply because of their race/ethnicity, sex, religion, or sexual preference, has been reported in numerous places over the last several years.[21] One such incident constitutes an instance of dominative racism only too plainly: the murder of Yusef Hawkins in Bensonhurst, Brooklyn, by a group of white teens who "mistook" the black youth for an unidentified minority member allegedly dating a young Italian woman in the neighborhood.

Clearly, a highly sadistic racist act was committed. Whether or not this act was committed in a predominantly or subordinately sadistic mode, I leave to others to assess. Indeed, it may have been that a subordinate mode was being enacted at least in part, class and other forms of masochistic powerlessness the youth experienced being madly displaced. But a mediated metaracism was also involved. There is no doubt that whatever else was transpiring social psychologically, hostilities were being aroused (and fed back to further reinforce racism) by the huge degree of media coverage accorded the Bensonhurst case. As I sensed in regard to another highly publicized crime (the gang rape of a young woman in New Bedford, Massachusetts),[22] media saturation of such instances often amplifies the sensitivities of communities already insecure about their place in the larger society; the process can foment a strongly defensive response and an anger toward the media, which signifies the powerful judgments of society itself. Again, how can one express anger at a TV set that exerts power invisibly and that hides so totally the power structures behind it? When people are situated masochistically relative to media, their subordinate sadism, customarily expressed through racism, is channeled and displaced into a metaracist reblaming of the victim, into another version of what feminists in rape cases have called a second assault.

Here, then, was a case study of media's role in the postmodern sadomasochistic transformation of victims into victimizers, victimizers into victims, and the symbiotic enmeshment of both. For at the end of the process, it was the victims who were at fault. When a group of sixty to seventy protesters marched through the streets of Bensonhurst less than a week after Hawkins's killing to "reclaim the streets of New York," it is horrifying but unfortunately not surprising that they were met with an enraged response. It was the protesters who became reconstructed as the intruders, the troublemakers, the victimizers, while members of the Italian-American community (including the defendants themselves) came to see themselves as victimized. They were the ones who were truly under siege. As occurred analogously in the New Bedford case, the defendants (and the community in their defense) were transformed from a sadistic identity into the ones cast masochistically, not of their own choosing. And they had been cast this way not by the sadistic effects of a media standing in for social powers that be, but by the victims themselves (now transformed, and themselves cast sadistically).

And, so in a counterdemonstration so redolent with overtly domi-native racism that some journalists compared it with 1960s Mississippi, this social psychological displacement grew to mass proportions. Local white residents shouted "Niggers, go home," "You savages," and "Long Live Africa," holding up hate-mongering signs and water-melons. At the same time, and confirming in one final allusion Katz's thesis of how "self-righteous slaughter" comes to be rationalized, the arrested young men were seen as "good boys . . . they were defending the neighborhood"; at the same counterdemonstration, the white crowd shouted, "Let the boys from Bensonhurst go!" and "Central Park, Central Park!"[23] They were referring to the Central Park rape case (in which a young white woman was brutally assaulted and raped by a group of black teens), familiar to the Bensonhurst residents largely by virtue of their exposure to it as yet another "media"ted representation—a very metaracist one at that, given the prominent use of charged wolf-pack language in media coverage of the crime. Central Park was thereby placed in competition with the murder of Yusef Hawkins, used as yet another vehicle for transforming a sense of collective defensiveness and insecurity (that may arise from pre-dominantly masochistic experiences) into a predominantly sadistic an-ger and blaming of the black demonstrators qua other.

Moreover, as I have attempted to show throughout this book, the other is frequently cast in the shape of a woman in patriarchal soci-eties. In the New Bedford case, analogous ire was aroused by media saturation of a group rape of a young "Portuguese" woman assaulted by six young "Portuguese" men on a pool table in a crowded bar. Since the Portuguese community of New Bedford saw itself as having suffered both ethnic and class discrimination in the past (that is, hav-ing been cast masochistically by the white Anglo Saxon dominant cul-ture), it felt victimized by this young woman's victimization. But the young woman was held responsible—not the media, or class or ethnic or gender discrimination, or any system of power that contributes to any or all of the above. Having received death threats, she was com-pelled to move out of town in the aftermath of the rapists' trial. Sim-ilarly, in the Bensonhurst case, Gina Feliciano—the young woman whose right to date whomever she pleased was also being assaulted—was seen as partly to blame for an alleged assault on Bensonhurst. In both cases, prejudicial gender ideology is trotted out as rationalization and justification for sadomasochistic turnarounds. And, since sexist belief systems often exist across class and race and ethnicity, they may indeed provide a ready excuse for creating she-devils, too, in the course of mischanneling anger yet again.

But it is not just that sadists in power (above) are often exonerated. To think only in these terms is to continue the tradition of bad guys and good guys that I suspect still keeps one going round and round in the same dynamically sadomasochistic circles. More important, perhaps, is to try to somehow not recreate "enemy others." At one level, of course, there are bad guys, and it is extremely important not to lose a sense of individual agency and responsibility within social theory and social movements. But there are also bad ideas and coercive social processes. It is interesting that Marx, for example, was much less interested in thinking about the traits of individual capitalists (that is, in blaming them) than in altering the systemic imperatives by which he believed those capitalists were victimized as well. Similarly, it may be important to focus attention on the structure of coercively sado-masochistic systems within which both sadist and masochist are enmeshed, often not of their own choosing. At the same time, one would hope to do both, to effect changes both within and without: to try to affect our own self-awareness (even if we are limited in ability to affect others') at the same time one tries to influence the course of social ideologies and institutions. One would hope to "fight the power," in the words of the rap group Public Enemy (a rebelliously self-satirizing name also appropriate in this context), while still trying to maintain one's humanity, minimizing the reproduction of sadistic dynamics this power tends to arouse—somehow keeping all of this in mind.

Sadomasochistic dynamics are reproduced so very insidiously, as we come to attack ourselves and each other over and over again. One ethnic group hates another group or another race, a given class or race oppresses others within it by gender, homophobia may be extant among them all, and so on. And all of this becomes entwined and enmeshed with the more microcosmic dynamics of our families and intimate others, as we may take it out on them in a host of small ways of the sort with which I began this section.

A related point was portrayed more poignantly than it ever could be in an academically oriented book in a film directed by nineteen-year-old Matty Rich entitled *Straight Out of Brooklyn*. The film centered around the situation of a black family in the Red Hook projects of this New York City borough: the father has been beating his wife to the point of destruction, himself clearly victimized by racism and haunted by his own father's past. The entire family is beset by financial worries and impoverishment. The son struggles to help the people he loves to escape, tending to reproduce the cycle in the very process of struggling not to reproduce it. At the end of the movie, the words flash onto the screen: "What is first learned is hard to forget. It passes from generation to generation. We have to change." Perhaps we have to stop blaming enemy others and begin instead to change both ourselves and the sadomasochistic social/psychic system in which we are embroiled.

7

A Theoretical Finale

This book has evolved to the point where the prospect of reaching static conclusions is as elusive as the dynamic I have tried to depict. The guises sadomasochism can assume, the motivations by which it is fueled, its suspectibility to historical variation, and the numerous intellectual traditions through which it can be interpreted attest, above all, to an exceedingly complex and multifaceted phenomenon. Even now, the subject changes kaleidoscopically as I reflect on the issues it raises, continuing to both fascinate and compel. Because it appears rather differently to me now than two or three years ago, it is hard to believe it will not develop in my mind still further. Nonetheless, I wish to record those political and social implications that strike me as most noteworthy thus far, taking responsibility for the book's past if only speculating about its future. In the process, I return to the allegedly just personal level from which I began.

I have argued for broadening the vision of sadomasochism beyond the individual and sexual manifestations with which S/M is so commonly and primarily associated. Of course, in some respects, sadomasochism is exactly this, sexual *and* individual, and so it is simultaneously critical that these dimensions not be lost in the process of a widened formulation. If I have focused too much attention away from the specifically sexual in the preceding chapters, this will have been a shortcoming I would hope others (or other versions of this manuscript) may eventually correct. For some—say, someone approaching sadomasochism from a Reichian angle—sexuality cannot be separated from other spheres of life: it is present even when sadomasochism is enacted nonsexually. Consequently, the prison guard or the Nazi of Reich's own description,[1] and much less dramatically the sadistic boss, may take decidedly sexual pleasure in physical and/or psychic exertions of control that link repressed desires to socially legitimized opportunities, pleasure denied elsewhere, stifled within most (individual) families and/or (individual) cultures. A similar analysis applies to the masochist whose denied sexuality reasserts itself, in or outside the bedroom, in situations of relative powerlessness wherein sensations of power and pleasure are sought.

While agreeing with this view, theoretical precision also requires acknowledging that sadomasochistic dynamics can no more be completely reduced to their sexual incarnations than the opposite, or Reichian, possibility can be eliminated. In many cases, the sadomasochism of the verbally abusing lover or of the racist may indeed refer to ontological desires for control that are more global, cosmic in a different way. These desires may often take shape within, and meld themselves to, the sexual, yet they are not necessarily identical with it. It is hard to believe that other forms of social impotence would vanish automatically, or simply, if the day-to-day world of that lover or racist were to become less sexually repressed. He or she might yet act masochistically or sadistically in other spheres and for other reasons.

Whether one adheres to one or both of these interpretations, it seems safe to conclude that sadomasochism exists both in and outside the sexual locale inherited from its linguistic, literary, and psychoanalytic origins. Not only is it present in both loci, but it can take shape as a *dynamic* I have characterized as an "ideal type" with typical features.[2] I contend that this sadomasochistic dynamic operates as a social psychological tendency sufficiently common in contemporary life as to be virtually *normal* (by Emile Durkheim's usage of that term), built into the structure and fabric of many forms of social life and organization. As I have noted several times, this dynamic ought to be distinguished from consensual forms of S/M sex, which are often far enough from the more compulsive (and at times nonconsensual) pattern of interaction I have been describing to be almost *non*sadomasochistic by this particular definition.

Before turning to those aspects of contemporary social life to which sadomasochism corresponds (and that it in turn can reinforce), let me restate these "ideal typical" features. Without one more overview from a position of hindsight, it will be hard to discern with any clarity those social facts that may encourage and nurture this particular dynamic on both the individual and collective planes. In part 1, sadomasochism was defined through three frameworks: phenomenological, psychoanalytical, and sociological. Each features its respective concepts to frame a similar slice of reality. Or so, this far from the Introduction, I hope by now to have convinced the reader.

From a phenomenological perspective, dipping into the theoretical terrain of Sartre, Hegel, and Benjamin, my hypothetical instance in chapter 2 revealed a sadist and a masochist who exist within an unequal and hierarchical ordering, superiority imputed to the former and inferiority to the latter; the freedom of the masochist has been deflated, that of the sadist inflated, by virtue of their relation. Once this hierarchy is established, certain tendencies logically arise. It is apparent that both sadist and masochist depend upon the other symbiotically (only the latter has no choice but to admit this extreme and built-in dependency), looking to the opposite for recognition through the experience of controlling or being controlled. They search for satisfactions that may be sexual, ontological, or perhaps both. But structured into the sadist's act of having controlled the other is the impossibility of ever being freely acknowledged by her or him; similarly, the masochist's existence cannot be legitimated by a sadist who has a vested interest in controlling. Paradoxes ensue. To keep the dynamic moving over time and to maintain interest, the sadist tries on one level to generate a liveliness from the masochist; ironically, on another, he or she has removed the possibility and foundation of that liveliness. The masochist wishes for what I called "approval in the mode of disapproval" and is analogously pulled in contradictory directions. Based on a given set of premises (see chapter 2), each seems to desire the opposite of what appears to be desired: each is unable to see his or her dilemma qua sadist, qua masochist. And so the sadomasochistic dynamic unfolds, unpredictably but with some predictable proclivities; it does not proceed within a predetermined mold. In its own terms, it can be said to be irrational, unable to produce its alleged aim—namely, a feeling of contented control for the sadist or of sated subordination on the part of the masochist.

So much I intuited from appearances, existentially speaking. Simultaneously, one could speak of this same phenomenon in terms more psychoanalytically oriented, with reference to Freudian concepts as well as to several ideas from post-Freudian object relations theory. The sadist of the example cannot admit he or she depends on the masochist and in this sense is quite powerless; the masochist does not have a clue as to her or his independent powers. Each is unaware, or one might say unconscious, of a side of themselves that makes its repressed presence felt nonetheless. If indeed (as we seem to) human beings exist in a state of mutual dependence upon and independence from one another, then this sadomasochism represents an effort *to capture both dimensions in the mode of not seeming to capture them both*. It is a skewed form: within it, the sadist can acknowledge his or her independence but not his or her neediness; the masochist is able to, and in fact must, acknowledge her or his dependency, yet is loath to own up to her or his inalienable powers.

Denied from view, the dynamic may be driven forward by unconscious desires for intercourse with the opposite side in a compromised manner, by fiat if necessary, through an implicit or explicit sadomasochism. At least in the masochist, the sadist can see, can feel and exteriorize, the dependence he or she cannot see internally: in the sadist, the masochist vicariously experiences and is able to visualize an allegedly stronger other invisible within. In both cases, their encounter may be highly pleasurable for this reason, even (or especially) if tinged with danger and a desire to merge with that part of oneself that one wants so badly, a desire forbidden and thus punishable. Vis-à-vis this reference to unconscious motivations, it is also possible to explain the sadist's and masochist's transformability and potential to become each other's opposite.

From object relations theory, though, can be addended another psychoanalytic point about the effect of childhood in influencing whether sadism or masochism arises in individual cases. Mahler and others have noted a developmental process in the pre-oedipal period, between birth and a child's initial encounter with genital sexuality. At this point, a symbiotic closeness to a primary caretaker is initially experienced. This stage later gives way to that of so-called "separation-individuation." In *The Bonds of Love*, Benjamin revises Mahler's model to suggest that the ideal outcome would be the maintenance of connection to others at the same time one learns to feel a sense of relative autonomy. However, if a child is pushed away from a trustful symbiotic dependency before he or she is sufficiently confident, "separation" occurs at the cost of connection with others, which must be repressed or denied. On the other hand, if the experience of establishing a relatively separate existence is discouraged, a child can remain overly dependent. Guilt ridden, she or he may feel compelled to act needy even when experience has required (and attested to the existence of) physical and psychic separateness. The former child's situation creates feelings approximating those of the grown sadist; the latter's is closer to the existential reality of the eventual masochist.

In retrospect, the object relations account attributes nearly exclusive responsibility to individual parents as lying at the root of a burgeoning sadomasochism. The extent to which the theory fails to develop its more generalizable implications is one of its pitfalls. Nevertheless, I reiterate my insistence that rigid dichotomies between the individual-psychic and the collective-social dimensions of reality are ultimately false, worthy of being at least questioned and possibly reinterpreted. In this case, one could surmise that children who experience the object relations' difficulty in attaining both a sense of autonomy and connections with others have themselves been parented by persons already socialized sadomasochistically. The parent who either demands or discourages a child's emerging autonomy may be looking to this small other to meet needs or provide recognition unavailable elsewhere. (This thesis was not only provocatively advanced by Benjamin but also figures in the work of psychoanalyst Alice Miller; it is also implicit in my critique of Chodorow in chapter 5.)[3]

Why would many parents have these unmet needs and, if sadomasochism exists in large numbers of people, how is it engendered in them and in children en masse? As soon as these questions are broached, so is a potential for connecting individual with social sadomasochism. Obviously, the experience of the parent(s) has been shaped in and outside the family, in school or at work, in relation to others and to a given neighborhood, and so on. These social experiences may themselves discourage the expression of both human dependence and independence, especially in the context of the individualistic U.S. ethos I allude to in more detail below. Or another example: as we saw, the patriarchal insistence on women's responsibility for parenting (as described by Chodorow in her *Reproduction of Mothering*) is part of a social ideology that splits dependence and independence along gendered lines. As a result, it is not unusual for little girls' relation to self and others to be felt quite differently than little boys', clearly at more than just an individual level.

On the other hand, perhaps a predominantly psychological explanation is sometimes at work, and parents are treating their children as they were treated, passing down a cyclical pattern of behavior. Even then, perhaps that cycle is constantly related to the social. In still other instances, outside social exposures may have been sadomasochistically charged, and childhood background is not germane at all. Numerous combinations are possible. My point is simply that object relations theory need not be treated in a purely 'individualistic' manner, whatever its own shortcomings. For purposes of this argument, the theory has the advantage of strengthening the existential definition of sadist and masochist as yearning for something alienated outside themselves. The childhood division between dependence and independence, and the inability to feel both separated from and connected to others, provides a second way of elucidating the sadist's and masochist's attraction for one another.

But object relations theory has one further disadvantage that ought be mentioned before turning to the third, explicitly sociological, perspective on sadomasochism. Within some psychoanalytic circles (among followers of Lacan, for instance), the theory has been accused of domesticating the radical implications of Freud's "drive" theory, employing a language that barely mentions emotions like anger and rage. At the same time, the object relations preoccupation with the pre-oedipal period focuses attention away from overt consideration of sexuality and pleasure. According to critics, the theory does not give adequate weight to the child's first oedipal encounters with forbidden sexual objects and desires. From this critique can be taken several additional observations relevant to the sadomasochistic dynamic that are worth retaining from the psychoanalytic Weltanschauung.

For one thing, the sadist and masochist do not drily, or dispassionately, yearn for aspects of themselves that have been repressed. They are anything but the cool, detached actors of a rational choice theorist's supposings. The sadist is enraged at needing the masochist, however unconscious he or she may be about the depth of this dependence: thus, the need to put down and belittle the other noted in chapter 2. The masochist, on the other hand, is equally angered at the oppressive sadist who obstructs her or his exertions of independence. But unlike the sadist, the masochist has no one readily available to beat up, literally or figuratively. What, then, happens to the anger? It can be directed inward, certainly; alternatively or concurrently, it may be subverted back toward the sadist through exercise of indirect controls. (The character of the Marquise in *Les Liaisons Dangereuses* comes to mind once more as an example. Masochist and sadist simultaneously, as a woman, her orchestration of human relations took place from within a position of relative and apparent powerlessness.)

A third possibility arises when we begin to move toward a more social set of conclusions. Consider a sadist and a masochist who are no longer artificially isolated, no longer restricted to the confines of their sexually delimited pair. If sadomasochism is really transformable so that both sides coexist in the same person (a point on which Freud and virtually all his psychoanalytic successors concur for all their other internecine disputes), then the masochist could be sadistic elsewhere, the sadist masochistic. It becomes axiomatic that when placed in a larger context, a sadist is implied by the presence of a masochist and vice versa, on and on in an apparently infinite social regress. With this, my memory is jarred back to those college relationships: my wanting the other who didn't want me, another wanting me when I didn't want him, while someone else did, and so forth.

Consequently, the masochist may displace her or his anger onto someone below, this party occupying a relatively more powerless position. At the same time, she or he is not conscious of being originally enraged by the sadist above. Concomitantly, the sadist who does have a masochist on hand below onto whom anger can be vented may not at all consciously intuit rage felt at someone else above. In relation to this third party, the sadist adopts a meek and relatively submissive, finally a masochistic, demeanor. I have tried to provide numerous examples of these transformable and displaceable phenomena throughout this text, from personal experience to that of the parent, from the batterer to the organized crime figure, the academic to the businessperson. And I will return to it once more, in proceeding a little further.

A Freudian-type emphasis on anger and displacement applies even to a social sadomasochism, providing additional terms of explanation for the dynamic's transformability. Last, object relations' omission of sex can be mixed into the theoretical brew that is emerging. A pre-oedipal experience that creates a tendency toward sadism and masochism can later merge with sexual desire, giving specific shape to the earlier set of needs and allying those needs with feelings of pleasurable bodily release. What is often felt as very passionate sex, and the iconography and images that come to be associated with it, may reflect both physical desire and a primordial reliving of earlier dramas of denied versus admitted dependency. Or, as Freud hypothesized in "A Child is Being Beaten" and as Reich also asserted (see chapter 3), the sadomasochistic dynamic could *originate* from sexual repression encountered in families and in the culture at large. The masochist may feel sexually guilt ridden, allowing herself or himself pleasure only when some form of restriction has been reproduced: the sadist may be orgasmic only when able to imagine himself or herself in control, the masochist in need of him or her rather than the reverse ("Do you like it?" the sadist inquires and demands). Therefore, reconsidering this sadomasochism cannot be separated from familial structures and attitudes that presently engender sexual repressiveness.

Conditions that generate a social (or collective) sadomasochism thus can be inferred even from within the individually oriented psychoanalytic tradition. Last, sadomasochism can also be defined in a more plainly sociological manner. For instance, though I have left this tradition largely undeveloped in the present text, a sociologist of symbolic interactionist leanings might apprehend the dynamic's transformability without recourse to psychoanalysis at all. Perhaps one could draw on Mead's concept of "taking the role of the other" to illuminate how the sadist learns to place himself or herself constantly in the masochist's position, the masochist in that of the sadist. As in dreams, the dynamic would not be possible unless the players all knew the rules of the game and could, at least in their sociological imaginations, envisage themselves in all its parts. Moreover, one learns to take these roles within the context of a particular society, in this case, an arguably sadomasochistic one. Thereby, a link between the psychic and collective is immediately implied, and yet another explanatory framework for the dynamic's transformability introduced.

But the criteria broached in the Introduction for defining sadomasochism were even more broadly social, a circumstance that leads me to a first major point I wish to underline in concluding: sadomasochism can be used as a metaphorical common denominator for translating between these psychic and collective dimensions, between the individual and the social, the so-called personal and the political. Whether stated phenomenologically or psychoanalytically, the characteristics of the individual sadist and masochist are inseparable from those of the sadist or masochist in dynamic social settings. Their psychology is also a social psychology, or psychologically social. As argued earlier, the Weberian Protestant incarnated today in the capitalistically oriented workaholic—the banker or lawyer, perhaps, or the obsessively ambitious academic—may be dissatisfied, driven toward some unspecified goal by the same sort of dynamic operating in the discontented sadist. He or she may have come to value independence and scorn dependence in others, constantly looking for new challenges when control has been established in one enterprise and boredom sets in. The Casanova-style lover of the how-to popular literature may likewise feel driven, as might a compulsive abuser who seems impelled by forces out of his or her conscious control.

And, like the sadist of the paradigm with which we started, the person with a touch of social sadomasochism evidences (paradoxically) deep layers of insecurity, often unconsciously. Seemingly confident, he or she is nevertheless haunted by doubts and fears of failure, frets about losing status and control of one sort or another, worries lest a grip on and over others may slip away. Supposedly self-assured, this person may also be surprisingly vulnerable to the opinions of others, especially alert to discovering how they have evaluated a given event, person, or product. In sadomasochism, as we have seen, independence and dependence are split from one another in such a way that relations between self and other cannot take place in the spirit of a mutual, dialectically alternating equality. Similarly, the weight given to the perceptions of self and other would tend to be analogously unequal in a sadomasochistic culture. The editor who responds eagerly when others have begun to construct a book as a best seller, contributing to a snowball effect . . . the agent who sees potential star material in an actor previously snubbed and ignored, once the actor has shown some independence and been rewarded a little . . . the corporate, governmental or academic institution that starts to go after someone newly labeled "hot" . . . all of them, and us, seem to be enmeshed in the dynamic, sometimes sadistically, other times masochistically, and always, on one level, both.

Therefore, I used the concepts of dominant and subordinate sadism to coin a now specifically *social* concept of sadomasochism's transformability. For although sadistically oriented in some spheres, the person I have been depicting will often be masochistically so in others. It is again not difficult to envision examples. Take one of Michael Lewis's sadistically bossing bankers at prestigious Salomon Brothers, who may turn subordinately masochistic should the chair of the board walk in the door. Or, as in Judith Rollins's study cited in the context of racism between women: the white female boss situated in a position of predominant masochism in relation to her husband acts out subordinate sadism relative to a black domestic worker whom she can dominate.

Related to this first major inference is a corollary one. Just as sadomasochism can be used as a common denominator to translate between the vagaries of the private and public psyche, so does it alloy and level individual with group dynamics. Thus, the transformability of sadomasochism (and of its dominant and subordinate modes) would also apply, say, to a past or present Stalinist-style bureaucracy: operating rather sadistically toward lesser officials below, it may nonetheless respond with masochistic alacrity to demands from the central committee on high. Closer to home are some of the instances of mass displacement I described in the preceding chapter. One can explain the recent rise in hate incidents as exemplifying sadomasochistic turnabouts writ large. Justifiably perceiving their class and status prospects to be dim, working-class youth may wrongly enact their subordinate sadism on relatively powerless others via incidents of racist, homophobic, or anti-Semitic assault. As also conjectured, the mass media seem to function more and more skillfully to facilitate and effect such transformations. They may quite literally mediate, focusing sadistic feelings on relatively powerless groups below who thereby become internal or external "enemies": minority youth reghettoized by being semiotically associated with crime, or Arab followers of Saddam in the 1991 Gulf War and massacre. Simultaneously, attention is distracted (and emotions deflected) from powers that be, also on high, who actually control our economic and political predicaments.

One more point of social translation. Regardless of the specific level at which the sadomasochistic dynamic is operating at a given moment, it is discernible by the consequences that ensue when or if an individual or group situated masochistically should rebel. This is the key criterion by which I adjudge its presence or absence. It is also the primary clue to assessing, retrospectively, whether extreme and excessive dependency was or is present between the interacting parties. Even if a predominantly sadistic partner seems to be stimulated by a good challenge or reverses roles under certain circumstances, he or she has no conscious intention of letting the masochist get away—at least not, in general, until he or she is ready and in control, the architect of the departure. For instance, perhaps the sadist will have rejected the masochist in favor of a more interesting substitute with whom the process can be started anew. On the other hand, if out of control, the usually male batterer will predictably become yet more crazed when a wife or girlfriend demonstrates serious intentions of leaving. Similarly, nonbattering husbands who nonetheless have a chunk of the sadistic in them will commonly try to make their wives pay, literally and/or figuratively, from feelings of vengeance aroused by a divorce the latter has initiated. Or an especially sadistic executive might become enraged at a long-suffering secretary's sudden challenge to his or her authority; because there is nothing to be done by law or custom to block the secretary's exit, the executive might switch tactics and become for awhile unusually solicitous. Similarly, the more subtly controlling lover or boyfriend/girlfriend may become temporarily repentant, unusually romantic, when faced with an unexpected threat of rejection.

I tried to provide numerous examples in the Introduction to document the analogous dynamic grafted onto a collective axis. Other case studies are as follows. Social sadomasochism is in evidence if, instead of treating the formation of a particular union as legitimate, its plans become the occasion for calling in a union-busting law firm to overtly or covertly break up the movement. A host of recent conservative movements (including, of late, the more public resurfacing of groups like the Ku Klux Klan) could be construed as sadistically reactive. Such movements may aim to punish discriminated against parties in U.S. society—women, minorities, gay and lesbian persons—who have dared to assert power and challenge their historic disenfranchisement. Outside the United States, a reactionary South African regime's response to a heightened antiapartheid movement was heightened repression: read, increased social sadism. A similar answer to Palestinian uprisings was meted out by the Israeli state on numerous occasions. Nor can sadistic responses to masochists' rebellion(s) be dismissed as an easy question of political ideology, of left versus right, radical versus conservative, of Christian Democrat versus Communist. As I have also attempted to indicate throughout this work, a previously disenfranchised masochistic group newly come to power will likely face a critical moment of decision—social psychologically, apart from its temporal affiliations. When and if the newly dismantled sadistic group should counterrebel, will that group clamp down on the former sadists more severely than self-defense necessitates, in the process of pleasurably fulfilling and enacting its rage? Will the formerly masochistic party repress the formerly sadistic one, the latter now transformed into the mirror image it had denied? Should any or all of this occur, it seems to me that at one fundamental level, the jig is up. In a sense, if perhaps only this one, the revolt would be over and dreams of authentic change concomitantly vanquished. Something remains fundamentally unaltered when the same old ball game— what I have dubbed the dynamics of social sadomasochism—is reproduced over and over again.

All this takes us only part of the way toward a denouement. Although the sadomasochistic dynamic has been portrayed in several ways, the social conditions that nourish and correspond to it have yet to be specified. Here, previous conjectures can be restated and expanded. At the individual level, sadomasochism was indicative of two parties' inability to acknowledge both their dependence upon, and relative autonomy from, one another. Their/our intensely symbiotic attachment is related to habitually looking outward rather than inside for approval; the other's eyes, body, words are scanned for some glimmer of recognition of those parts of themselves/ourselves that have been denied and frustrated.

Transposing back into a social key, dominant ideology in U.S. society likewise does not allow for the admission of both dependence and independence. Quite the opposite. (Let us leave aside, for the moment, the issue of whether to call this ideology capitalistic, capitalist patriarchal, late-industrial postmodern, or whatever. In one sense, it is all of the above; in another, for our purposes it is a mostly academic quibble.) I doubt that the extent to which myths of individual responsibility remain engraved within our culture can be overestimated or exaggerated. We are not supposed to be needy, to cry in public, to be clinging, dependent, or depressed. Any such emotions may be taken as a sign—indeed, an admission—of weakness, and possible cause for disapproval. Vulnerability may be met with subtle or not so subtle disdain; it may be taken as indicative of being a less than cool, attractive, and desirable person.

And it is not a long leap from these observations to believing that the blame for poverty, homelessness, or ghettoes really must lie with the faulty individual or family who is not able to stand strong and alone. In America, to be in need is either to be stigmatized or to face possible stigmatization. In a world of winners and losers, it is to be decisively dealt the losing hand. Even persons who publicly espouse liberal or radical ideas may in private find themselves wondering what a friend or acquaintance did wrong upon hearing that this person can't find or just lost a job, published a bad book or article, or in some other way was found to be socially wanting. Like the masochist who turns anger inward rather than toward the sadist, so we attribute blame and causality to ourselves, to each other, or to less powerful groups than ourselves, not to the system of which we are a part. As with the masochist, it is a way of trying to seize a sense of control and power from within a position of actual subordination and relative powerlessness. Simultaneously, a sadistically oriented and macho-esque notion of one-sided individualism comes to predominate and to be internalized. Via this profoundly immersed mental habit, the individual is indicted for failing to live up to social expectations. Much more accurately, it is society that is inhumanely failing individuals by not embracing and accepting the full range of their/our humanity.

For indeed, recognized or not, this humanity does include both the sensation and reality of dependency. That people frequently require various types of public and social assistance is not something that can blithely be repressed, denied, and forgotten without some consequences later ensuing. The need may be, simply, for a job: one day, a person discovers rather suddenly, arbitrarily, that a cyclical shift in the economy has taken place and a small oasis of supposed security has dissolved in the sand. Or the person never had a job in the first place and could benefit from governmental assistance to overcome disadvantages inherited from a racially and sexually discriminatory past. Similarly, it is equally basic (and simplistic, restated here only because not a taken-for-granted social presumption) that medical care is necessary for survival. Yet, how much desperation is felt by another hypothetical individual who learns of a frightening disease, only to be overwhelmed not only by the illness but by worries about money and resources? What of the aged who wait to discover whether necessary home health care services will be provided by a confusingly bureaucratic and not very generous state?

Even if denied in a given social and political order such as the contemporary United States, needs and dependencies do not just go underground for good. Rather, I suspect that real social security and social sadomasochism are antithetical realities. There may be an inverse relation between them: the less one exists, the more there is likely to be of the other, and vice versa. Hence, the fact that the provision of neither income nor jobs, nor housing, nor medical care is a secured social right generates feelings of perpetual insecurity. At any moment disaster may strike, producing neediness that an individualistic society loathes and throws right back onto the individual's overly responsible and self-blaming shoulders.

Of course this does not leave one—if the reader will pardon a bit of sardonic understatement—terribly free, for all the stress on much-vaunted individual freedoms. Again, this is quite paradoxical. Indeed, what better way to forge bonds of excessive dependency and needs for social approval, or to foment what I have defined via the concept of the socially symbiotic? Under these circumstances, it would not be surprising if one were terrified at the prospect of being fired from one's livelihood (as elaborated in chapter 4), and of the myriad repercussions for other aspects of one's life this loss could augur. Suspecting that punishment may in some way result (just as the masochist astutely intuits of the sadist), one may be that much more afraid to challenge one's boss or the rules and regulations of one's workplace. One may be scared to question other aspects of this society of which one is a part. (I feel for the moment slightly, spookily, worried even as I write these words, as though internally verifying my own argument.) And one may try to be that much more pleasant, perhaps according differential weight to the judgments of more powerful others than to one's own. Note that no chains were required to produce this creepy effect, highlighting the importance of not linking sadomasochism only with its more overt and too smugly deviantized, its whips and chains, connotations. For to associate sadomasochism merely with what we label "kinky," with the sexual and/or the violent (that is, those of its manifestations thought to be extreme) is to miss its subtler incarnations—a convenient distraction, I should one last time add, from phenomena that are more routine, mundane, and more generally distributed across the board in everyday life.

Another thought in the context of this peculiar U.S. individualism concerns a self-contradictory ideology that fosters excessive dependency in the very process of denying it, hypocritically glorifying independency alone. (This contradiction, by the way, is why I prefer the more complex concept of sadomasochism to Christopher Lasch's older dubbing of our culture as monolithically "narcissistic.") If we are insecure and unrecognized at work, chances are this will affect us elsewhere as well. Corresponding to such social insecurities may arise feelings of increased dependence on the love and affections of lovers, of significant others, of spouses, and even, as insinuated above, of children. Now, the potential specter of losing them is that much more upsetting; we are left feeling that much more unfree, bound to these others more than we might ideally wish or otherwise choose to be. Thus, social symbiosis in the world of the public (of work, of schools) can be transposed back towards the private sphere as well. The result is an atmosphere in which Benjaminesque "bonds of love" are analogously forged, at this level glued together with personal rather than with economic ties.

This brings me back, in another circular progression, to the recent interest in the popular literature on codependency and women who love too much. The reality is that this type of sadomasochistically charged personal relationship, along with comparable domestic disputes and violence, is extraordinarily common, not an astonishing circumstance in a universe where dependency is denied and the individual is isolated, often feeling alone or afraid of loneliness. Here Durkheim and Fromm again come to mind. Each was concerned about the fate of a modern individual when left too much to his or her, her or his, own devices, shorn of a larger sense of social and communal belonging. As sociologist Donna Gaines recently writes of young people, they may find themselves banding together in a "teenage wasteland," maybe suicidal and certainly sensing themselves to be abandoned and forgotten by the larger society surrounding them.[4] For all of us, whether or not a secure sense of community is experienced may be a matter of subcultural opportunity, often of chance. Certainly, providing community is not an accepted part of social responsibility, of acknowledging human neediness at once material and emotional. Rather, its lack is analogously implied from within an individualistically skewed set of premises, a lack that furthers the attractiveness of a sadomasochistic dynamic as defensive and compensatory strategy for day-to-day survival, as Fromm contended.

One last observation should be recycled regarding how U.S. society nourishes social sadomasochism through one-sided individualism. Also attendant upon devalued dependency is another social psychological ramification: in a sadomasochistic social system, one's existence is no more its own justification than was mine to my predominantly sadistic lover, cited on the opening pages of this text. On the contrary, conditional psychology prevails, here as well as there. In this regard, our experiences in the private/public and personal/impersonal worlds just alluded to are of a piece. Since approval is not presumed but must be earned (or proved), people are cast in a relatively subordinate and masochistic position; equal weight cannot be given to the evaluations of self versus other. There are tasks that must be done to please the other, whether or not they please us, whether rational or irrational for a given purpose. And, structurally, we are predisposed to prefer liking over disliking them. The deck is pretty much stacked.

Concurrent with all of this, and just as expectably, an unequal power situation is reinforced or would have to be born between the socially situated sadist(s) and masochist(s). For if conditional psychology predominates in a sadomasochistic structure, personal or seemingly impersonal, a hierarchical system will be an understandable outgrowth. I do not mean that just any hierarchical orderings emerge. As already posited, whether speaking of a relation between a teacher and a student, an employer and an employee, a parent and a child, or two lovers playing unequal roles in S/M sex, hierarchical arrangements certainly don't in and of themselves spell the presence of a sadomasochistic dynamic. Rather, it is the form hierarchy takes in accordance with conditional psychology that is telltale. As in the hypothetical sexual paradigm with which we began, this form will tend to impute rigid judgments of superiority versus inferiority, worthiness versus unworthiness, to the human beings layered within it. From this classificatory pattern comes the dynamic's distinctively sadomasochistic texture, its status as a class structure in and of itself.

So far, I have spoken of an especially U.S. cultural ethos, correlating socially sadomasochistic dynamics with a capitalistic oriented ideology that treats dependency as illegitimate. (Of course, this ideology is simultaneously patriarchal: as argued in chapter 5, male-dominated systems analogously tend to split dependence and independence along gendered axes.) It is beyond this book's intentions to do much more than this, since the United States is the country with which I am most intimately familiar. I would hope, however, that this analysis might stimulate others to raise issues and questions of a more seriously comparative and theoretic bent. For now, however, suffice it to suggest that a sadomasochistic social psychology could also come to predominate in a society that was built around the opposite ideology to the one just analyzed. I have discussed the ramifications of socially recognizing independency but not dependency. But what happens should the reverse occur and only the dependent part of our beings come to be acknowledged within a given order? What if, this time, it is desires for autonomy and separateness that are denied and repressed? (The reader may recall from chapter 3 that according to the Hegelian "problem of recognition," both sides are required for mutual recognition to occur between persons "A" and "B"—or perhaps between groups "A" and "B" as well.)

In fact, from a social psychological viewpoint, numerous Communist states did adopt the opposite ideological extreme. (Note the capital "C": I refer to historical entities that exist or existed, not the concept of communism per se.) Horrified by capitalistic indifference and social irresponsibility, it was often bourgeois individualism that came to be scorned, and loyalty to a collectivity glorified, in much of Stalinist and Maoist-style discourse. In this sort of system, one could anticipate a tendency for activities that were of a separate and independent rather than a dependent character to be devalued and overladen with guilt (in some respects, at least). Individual initiatives, ideas like individual creativity, or simply doing something that involved striking out on one's own, separating from the socially accepted way of doing or seeing things, might be frowned upon. Thus, another form of one-sidedness could and did come into being. Very happily, human neediness was acknowledged under most existing communisms (so that rights to food, shelter, clothing, and basic survival were seen as legitimate expectations); unhappily, human needs for relative autonomy and separateness were not (and were delegitimized).

Viewed from afar, with only the small amount of historical distance now possible, these two systems seem to have pitted themselves against each other as though stuck in a zero-sum game. Their ideological effect was/is to make a trade-off between liberty and equality (or what I here call independence and dependence) appear natural and inevitable, penalizing the fulfillment of one pole with the frustration of the other. This raises to an even higher plane of complexity the types of sadomasochistic turnabouts that can potentially occur en masse. Perhaps from one skewed extreme to another, a type of transformability may also occur within the dynamic that is of socially systemic and not only individual proportions. (Potentially, this could be applied to the study of social movements as well.) In regard to assessing the presence or absence of social sadomasochism, the result is another spin of the wheel, a reversal inside the rules of the same ball game of my prior metaphoric allusion. As with sadism and masochism themselves, capitalism and communism become opposite sides of a coin. Under capitalism, as with sadism, independence from the social is ideologically valorized and predominant; under much of communism, as with masochism, dependence on the social is or was the explicitly valued and prevalent side. In both antinomies, one part of interactive reality has been suppressed.

Continuing the argument, social symbiosis in the second, Communist-oriented system(s) would predictably persist even as it came to take an apparently altered shape. Now it may be the thought of being thrown out of the party more than one's job that nags at the mind. This, of course, will in turn discourage questioning, challenging, or rebelling against rules and regulations of the workplace and of the social order itself. Some might argue that being expelled from the party and from one's job amount to the same thing. Others would see this second system as flawed but historically progressive as against the first: at least under communism, as with the masochist, there is/was no choice but to acknowledge basic human dependencies because of the structural content of its own ideology. A third camp visualizes the second order as having regressed in relation to the first, any notion of progress negated by the meanings of communism and socialism having been historically contaminated.[5]

But for our purposes, it is the social psychological similarities I wish to emphasize, while at the same time not in any way denying the existence of other types of specific historical differences. Similarly, persons once again find themselves worried about losing social acceptance or approval. If one dares to question a predominantly sadistic political or economic superior, will one be rejected (sent to Siberia, say, under the old Stalinist model, or to a mental hospital), forcibly stripped of what precious little sense of community and belonging one possesses? If one is a young student at Beijing University, will one be in jail or on the run for the next ten years just because one protested then, still wishes to protest now? Again, the opinions and evaluations of others begin/began to far outweigh one's own: one nervously tries to find out what the politically efficacious take on a certain issue or decision may be; or one anxiously looks around to see what one's neighbor is thinking, feeling, or doing. Again, one would feel enchained in this second system, differently but also sadomasochistically. *And, at perhaps the deepest level, the most sadomasochistic aspect of controls exerted in both systems is that they play on our fears of death.* This being the bottom line, the ultimate stick held up behind the carrot, we intuitively fear, often silently or unconsciously, that too much rebellion may be met and punishable by physical and/or psychic extinction. This is the most fundamental basis of vindictive power, possibly at the core of socially (and sometimes individually) sadomasochistic dynamics.

Yet change occurs anyway, in spite and maybe in a sense because of all of this. Think back to the paradoxes that unfolded between chapter 2's hypothetical sadist and masochist as they worked their way through that paradigmatic example. The dynamic's tendency—though, of course, not automatically enacted—was to produce unintended effects and transformations, pushing the masochist toward the edge and outside the system altogether. And, as is typical of sadomasochistic dynamic systems in general, contradictory tendencies arise here as well. Whereas capitalism's paradox is to produce dependency in the process of devaluing it, so many Communist systems paradoxically generate independence in the course of trying to nurture just the opposite propensity. (It is interesting to recall here that the sadist was paradoxically much more dependent than was at first glance apparent, the masochist much more independent.) That which is repressed seems to return with regularity in addition to unpredictability, recurring in some other form, time, and place. Guilt can and does reverse to anger.

In this respect at least, it need not be bewildering that Western democracy and individual freedoms—indeed, capitalism—begin/began to seem relatively appealing again, resilient, full of vibrancy, suppressed life, even eros. And these signifiers come/came to also signify the seductions of difference and diversity, of sensuality and exultant pleasures, of a range of artistic and sexual individual choices that can be made from rock and rap to an iconoclastically liberating S/M itself.

Thus, the monumental post-Gorbachev changes, both in the Soviet Union and throughout Eastern Europe, are analyzable not only in political and economic terms but also in a language I have here called "social psychological." They can be seen as a case study in this return of the sadomasochistically repressed, en masse, more secure in the rebellious safety of numbers. If nothing else, the capitalistic other was perceived as allowing the independent side of personal and social identity to be freed up. By valorizing specifically individual rights— an extraordinarily critical value at that—at least, capitalism seems to do a better job of recognizing the other side of our human needs, that is, relative autonomy and separateness.

Someone might inquire if I am not wasting words on belabored description of Communist systems that have for the most part been spectacularly overturned, and this in a remarkably short period of time. Is this analysis relevant, this person could wonder, to a post-Communist, a post- rather than pre-Gorbachev era of new world order? I suspect it is extremely applicable, precisely because whether these changes betoken yet another spin of the socially systemic wheel remains to be seen. Should the pendulum swing back again, embracing a capitalism that begets poverty and homelessness by its redenial of human dependency (a denial that, of course, characterized tsarism before that), then the past will be repeating itself in ways the sadomasochistic dynamic might portend. It will be zigzagging in a circular motion, losing a sense of long-term memory and equilibrium, failing to stop somewhere in the middle.

For what I am really arguing is that, based on this form of psychosocial analysis, a new paradigm is required if compulsively sadomasochistic tendencies are not to be reiterated. This paradigm would have to emerge synthetically from the remnants and clashes of older models destabilized or crumbling amidst their own internal paradoxes. It would have to recognize both independence and dependence simultaneously, envisioning mutuality to be possible in both the political and the personal, the individual and the collective realms of our lives. Developing such an idea with any thoroughness or in any serious detail falls outside the parameters and possibilities of this book. Moreover, a similar goal informs myriad theoretical projects undertaken of late by many others in different ways: debates within feminism and other social movements, for instance, or the concerns of recent cultural theories that look toward postmodernism or representational analysis to provide fresh concepts for rethinking outmoded frameworks. Too, much of the independence-and-dependence perspective of this treatment is implicit within political theories and empirical studies of socialist democracy. Consequently, the interpretation proffered here is just that, one interpretation. And the following notes are just one version of a possible outline, some broadly drafted contours that might assist in building or evaluating a useful alternative conceptualization.

Given this perspective, a reconstructed paradigm would optimally contain several key elements. On the one hand, acknowledging dependency implies movements' assertion of the need for social security in the broadest sense: namely, that income (including but not limited to jobs), decent housing, medical care, and the meeting of other basic requirements be seen as a matter of right rather than as conditionally bestowed rewards. In the United States of the 1980s and 1990s, this is still a gargantuan proposition. Such a program, however, may strike a Scandinavian or Western European as much more self-evident, each acclimated to advanced industrial societies that come closer to accepting such measures as merely civilized. For another person, say someone from Japan, the same acceptance may be a concomitant to paternalism, or at the very least to an aesthetic sense that would disdain poverty. As I have discussed, experimenting with new shapes and modes for fostering community would also be implied by the project of fulfilling emotional as well as material needs.

On the other hand, the paradigm would also have to include independence: it makes sense to give explicit legitimation to the individual and the self, in addition to the collective side of give-and-take human interaction. Thus, to be individualistic only equates with a negative selfishness when abstracted from an insistence upon being socialistically oriented at the same time. For that matter, as half of a dialectically balanced equation, the former's theoretical place ought be a much less embarrassed, guilty, and self-conscious one. More concretely, I suppose such independence would involve historical movement in the direction of consciously excising the pejorative "bourgeois" that can sometimes still precede references to simple democratic freedoms. Certainly, it means applauding the pleasures, even the virtues, of individual diversity and choice that give U.S. society and social movements an amazing cultural richness in the midst of even more amazing impoverishment. None of this is especially novel or unprecedented. What strikes me as the greater challenge, flowing much more directly from premises related to this book, is to bring about an altered rebalancing on *both* the personal/individual and political/social levels. So far, such balancing appears to be quite an elusive historical trick indeed. Interestingly enough (and as a matter of generalization), many cultural theorists/postmodernists as well as democratic socialists, each in their own way trying to point beyond old and one-sided models, seem to have difficulty formulating a simultaneously personal and political vision. On the one hand, cultural theorists/postmodernists amply treat the world of culture, of individual difference, diversity, and personal life; yet, postmodernists often shy away from serious consideration of forms of political power that reside, quite materially, in external entities like a state. On the other hand, socialist democrats, or democratic socialists, still seem to have difficulty truly conceiving how personal issues such as sex, culture, and the familial structures in which individuals reside can be as crucially political as external ones like that state, or a fiscal crisis, or corporate wealth.

An alternative paradigm would have to bridge the gap between these two polarized dimensions, translating back and forth as we have done in the process of reconsidering sadomasochism itself. Just as sadomasochistic dynamics seem to exist on both levels, so altering those *unfreely* chosen structures from which these dynamics partially stem also implies a need for changes to occur on dual planes. This is the second, and intimately related, point I most wish to elaborate in the process of concluding.

A particular social movement motivated by an alternative vision of this sort would consider people's experiences in their families in addition to those at the workplace, the site traditionally privileged by leftists, to be a perfectly valid and important focus of discussion and for the sharing of experiences. Certainly, gendered principles imbibed in patriarchally structured settings analogously contribute to the sundering of dependence and independence (see chapter 5). In addition, traditionally oriented families still commonly reproduce sexual repressiveness and what Adrienne Rich in her famous essay called "compulsory heterosexuality."[6] They may discourage an ability to envision any other form of intimate association except that which is self-reproducing, thereby perpetuating the elite status of heterosexual and monogamous marriage as the preeminent, socially legitimated unit. It is often within families that sexual experimentation and free exploration is first denied, pointing toward another right to which alternative social movements and/or paradigms would have to insist. Finally, it may be *only* in intimate family environments (whatever form this entails, single parent or communal, gay or straight) that the explicit airing of *emotions* is permitted. Here alone is where one may be able to talk about feelings that concern pleasure and sex, sadness or fear, sometimes anger, rage, jealousy, love; where one can talk about personal relationships within and between sexes. Or on the contrary, it may be within one's family that one is *unable* to speak about any or all of this, where feelings are suppressed rather than only contained.

It seems to me that to seriously consider human beings holistically, as persons at once rational and emotional, is to open up a brave new world of alternative social theory, alternative conceptualizations. In and of itself, reconnecting private realms of feeling (including those that are sexual) to public ones of alleged instrumentality might transform the very notion of family itself. As a result of explicitly incorporating both rationality and emotionality, alternative social movements might *create* a greater sense of familial community than now exists through their own ideas, actions, modes of organization. In so doing, they would partially redress presently existing imbalances in the relationship between family, community, and society, diminishing tendencies this imbalance produces toward the socially symbiotic. To develop a language that permits sentiments both triggered by and repressed within sadomasochistic societies to be enunciated ought be as legitimately political an enterprise (albeit different) as analyzing the internal contradictions of an economic market mechanism. Similarly political would be the task of finding forums in which this range of experience could be expressed—from anxieties about one's status or lack thereof to those structurally bequeathed feelings of superiority or inferiority or worthiness/unworthiness cited earlier.

More specifically, what I am saying draws on any number of old and new ideas. Bits and pieces of relevant models are already to be found in examples set by other theoretical traditions (such as the much undervalued Frankfurt School, of which Fromm and Marcuse were part) and by several movements that have attempted parallel syntheses in the past and continue to do so at present. A clear instance of the latter is feminism's having proffered the "personal as political" as just such a synthetic theoretical proposition, however much its earliest vision has been co-opted and derailed. Looking backward, second wave radical feminism derived much of its burgeoning power and sisterhood from reliance on consciousness raising groups—a seemingly forgotten, much less common form by 1991—that were at once rational and emotional in their intentions and effects. Or, going back to Germany of the 1930s, Reich ran broadly defined sex clinics especially for young people, seeing them as altogether inseparable from socialism and a more conventionally political intervention into everyday life. That many today would see this effort as mad (along with Reich) is a measure of our culturally schizophrenic, love-hate relation toward sex; it was and is still extraordinarily transgressive to acknowledge and talk in comparative public settings about matters of bodily desire and pleasure. (I recall describing aspects of Reich's thought to students in my social theory classes on several occasions. Immediately, they perked up and laughed nervously—we joked together—very interested in and dubious about what was being said at the same time.)

In addition, whether or not reconsidered by other movements, a combined rationality and emotionality perspective might even reinterpret the value of currently individualistic psychotherapy in a more positive light. This, too, could be detached from its bourgeois associations, contents, and background (that is, its historic class and race biases) if made much more publicly available and politically demanded. Perhaps various psychotherapies might be seen as yet another special avenue for the expression of feelings elsewhere denied within one-sided social systems. Like consciousness raising, or like social movements themselves, this form also has distinctive characteristics, advantages, and disadvantages; ideally, it would be used by people in ways and toward purposes defined by and for themselves.

Perhaps psychoanalytic transformations thereby effected on an *individual* basis can't be artificially divorced from those that are *political* and *social* in character. Nor should it be presumed that the upshot of such changes at the level of an individual is to be necessarily apolitical, or even neutral. In fact, just the opposite case can be made if we accord any validity to a translatability thesis, as suggested here, between the psychic and the collective. That is, at one level an analogous relation exists between the processes and structures of individual consciousness as it operates at home and outside; between the meaning of confronting issues like psychic life and death within and responding to life-and-death physical realities we face without; between how we feel inside ourselves and in the social universe in which we are embedded. For the freer and more in control of my life I feel in its myriad aspects, the more my perspective on the larger world around me may be correspondingly affected. Similarly, translating in the opposite direction, struggles waged and lessons learned in situations more conventionally considered political may redound to affect my intimate attitudes and relationships as well. Change can go either way, from the inside out or the outside in. The beauty of according explicit recognition to this observation within an alternative paradigm might be to render prospects for large-scale transformation less overwhelming, seemingly futile, or altogether abstract. Small happinesses in one's own life, how one feels toward and treats oneself and others, are also important, potentially empowering and liberating, acts of personal and political love.

Equally important to note is that this hypothesized correspondence is by no means automatic or predictable, even as it creates definite tendencies. It is not a relation that can or should produce a predetermined result because of the indeterminate character of our symbolic interpretations themselves. For instance, it is certainly theoretically possible that a person could go to psychotherapy of a particular variety for, say, twenty-nine years—Reichian, gestalt, orthodox psychoanalytic, whatever—and yet remain virulently homophobic, racist, against provision of any and all social securities. (Somewhat dogmatically, I am inclined to doubt it: such a person would probably not go voluntarily, and certainly not stay for twenty-nine years if he or she did, but theoretically speaking, why not? I certainly can't prove the grounds of my own skepticism.) Indeed, related to the earlier argument about not oversimplifying a specifically Reichian perspective, this person might now be even more comfortable with a given set of beliefs. Likewise, as feminists know all too well, a particular man may spout compassionate political prose in public only to be highly oppressive in his personal relationships when he returns home.

Perhaps the best an alternative social movement (or a paradigm of thought associated with it) can do is favor conditions that maximize the *possibility* that changes could occur on either and/or both levels. Although an individual's or family's personal transformation does not necessarily accord with concurrent and related economic and political changes (including within that person's own attitudes), or vice versa, at least a new paradigm could itself keep in mind the existence of an other side, directing and in control of its *own* ideas toward these spuriously divided dimensions. If indeed it is to be motivated by visions of change more authentic (because more thoroughgoing) than many in the past, then there would be little choice but to recognize the importance of social movements embracing both the reasonable and the emotional/sexual (the so-called irrational) sides of our beings. Consequently, it would look not only toward socializing psychotherapy but toward psychoanalyzing the social as well. Last though not least, its efforts wouldn't be focused on particular persons but rather on *social structures* coercive on these dual planes of our lives, ones that delimit our choices and freedoms in both spheres compulsorily, not by our own choosing. Here is the alternative significance in politicizing the personal realms of family, sex, and intimacy, while simultaneously attempting to humanize the world of political economy.

The reader may be wondering what happened to sadomasochism in all of this. I would propose that these speculative remarks on the need for an alternative paradigm grow out of and were suggested by the process of analyzing the sadomasochistic dynamic itself. Presumed in an interpretation widened to include a range of manifestations—from work, school, sex, and family on through angrily discriminatory phenomena like racism and its ilk—is that the dynamic at hand relates at least partly to *socially based* experiences of an initially compulsory quality. From this would be supposed that much of sadomasochistic or nonsadomasochistic interaction is socially constructed. Likewise, I have been implying that if societies were to change along the somewhat general, somewhat concretized lines outlined here, the dynamic also would be affected. Mysteriously and indeterminably so, no doubt, but affected nevertheless. It might diminish, disappear, take relatively newer forms, or move to new locations, but it is hard to believe it would simply stand still.

On the other hand, returning full circle now to those thorny philosophical and intellectual debates that initially sparked my interest in this subject at the 1982 Barnard sexuality conference (see chapter 1), one could assert just the opposite claim. Maybe the sources of an unconscious or compulsive sadomasochism are not entirely social, or social at all. Instead, let us entertain the possibility that its roots are *transhistorical* and *universal,* hence not so susceptible to efforts at conscious change or manipulation. Continuing to play devil's advocate, perhaps feminism and other social movements were naive when they assumed in the 1960s and 1970s that when external structures were altered, internal ones would quietly or quickly follow suit. Perhaps such a presupposition underestimates the real complexity of our psyches, our sexuality, our consciousnesses. No amount of tinkering with political economy or with familial structures or with personal/political transformation can remove certain anthropological givens. Such tinkering can't change our virtually powerless dependency for a number of years after birth, for instance, a helpless state that varies but is never absent from culture to culture. Nor the fact of mortality. Nor a host of other sexual and emotional desires and longings that remain frustrated as long as we respect other persons' separate freedom and will. Moreover, no degree of social intervention can cause deep and violent reactions to any or all of this to simply vanish, Houdini-like, just because we would like it to.

To these objections I offer a two-fold response, coming to the final points I would most like to stress. Granting a universalistic argument's objections, how could we ever know what would or wouldn't change until everything social had been tried, and all else had thereby been ruled out? How can we assess what could be until those social structures and ideas that *are* responsive to our conscious intentionality have been altered, so that at least *they* no longer correspond with a compulsory sadomasochism? For what I have been contending is that prevalent social psychology in contemporary cultures does bear a suspicious resemblance to what one would anticipate finding given the imperatives of patriarchy, capitalism, sexual repressiveness, and a communism that didn't succeed at going beyond a still one-sided alternative. In other words, a sadomasochistic mind-set does empirically exist and flow rather logically, analogously, from the ways we have organized our social systems and ideologies.

In addition, I continue to find it interesting—and equally suspicious—that ardent proponents of an eternal and unchanging human nature are usually the last to favor social interventions or to call for the provision of widely general social securities, however ideologically variant among themselves in other respects. To be consistent, they ought be the first, eager to jump on a bandwagon of consistent personal and political transformation if only to prove the verity of their contentions once and for all. For wouldn't the most convincing proof of anthropological immutability consist in being able to point a finger at human nature acting up as always, biting the hand that feeds it even in a finally less barbaric and nonsadomasochistic social setting? If the same patterns of ritualized dominance and subordination recur even when social sadomasochism no longer corresponds with social insecurity—a complete disjuncture having arisen between what is and what we would expect to be—then the conservative case for an intrinsic human nature should be complete. That no such scientistic (indeed, positivistic) zeal is manifested, however, and no fully socialistic measures demanded, suggests that such proponents may not be so secure in their essentialistic views after all. Or, rather, that the belief in an unchangeable human nature may itself obfuscate fear of what it would mean (including for them) if indeed things were changeable. It thus serves to exert a very powerful inhibitory effect on the possibilities of change from within an ideological position that asserts human beings' apparent powerlessness from without.

Still, as the second fold of my response, I think one would have to concede the point of our psyches being complicated indeed, and therefore that it would also be ludicrous to expect huge meta-

morphoses in human interactions to ensue immediately, or even rapidly, in the aftermath of altering those many social structures and
ideas that badly need to be changed. Lasting changes occur much
more slowly than this, evolutionarily, like peeling layers off an onion
or moving up in small circles along an axis. This thought does bring
me back to the personal level from which I began, causing me to note
how my own sadomasochistically tinged desires have ebbed and
flowed since those college relationships of over ten years ago. Even as
I have consistently become more and more conscious of them on one
level, on another, old patterns flare up from time to time—amidst
crisis or mourning, for instance. I even observed their partial resuscitation over the course of completing this book, as though they were
putting in a cameo appearance to mock, magnify, and/or reminisce
upon the very dynamics I have tried to describe.

I am speculating, therefore, that it would be most remarkable if
some sort of sadomasochism was not deeply embedded in all of us
simply by virtue of living in a culture so sadomasochistically attuned.
It is not, consequent upon this interpretation at any rate, deviant, but
arguably quite generally distributed. Yet, admitting the difficulties of
changing those of its manifestations that are compulsive/compulsory,
that we *would* wish to alter, doesn't have to mean a gloomy prognosis.
It does not lead to a set of inexorable conclusions akin to those
reached by Freud in the morbid *Civilization and Its Discontents*. Just the
reverse, as I have contended throughout. The more we are able to
bring these dynamics to conscious awareness; the more we can explicitly include the reality of feelings like anger and rage and fear and
desire in our social theories, movements, and institutions; the more
we can recognize and acknowledge both the dependent and the independent, the rational and the emotive sides of ourselves; the more we
can deal with these phenomena honestly, whether in writing about
them or perhaps even leaving a space for exploring them in sexual
freedom. . . the less sadomasochism will control us rather than our
controlling it, and the more exertions of power could then be linked
to positive and pleasurable affirmations of self and other rather than
to the impossibility of according mutual recognition to either. Anthropological givens or not, for society to accept human beings wholly
and humanely, using its own massive powers to channel energies differently than it has until now, might certainly make a little—maybe
even all—the difference in the world.

In the United States in the 1990s, as the capitalistic economy
tightens its belt and reasserts an apparent superiority, as traditional

mores are analogously reclaimed amidst conservative backlash, and as social self-doubts reach at once new and very old heights, some greater understanding is certainly called for. If nothing else, reference to a sadomasochistic dynamic that is transformable on the individual and group plane in its dominant and subordinate modes provides some insight into one mechanism by which systemic reproduction operates at both levels. Like the sadist and the masochist, we have a tendency to blame ourselves, each other, or subordinate groups around us, for the recognition we have been denied in more systemic ways. The sadists at the top of the hierarchy are thereby accorded a distinct advantage for, as with the Weberian Protestant, they are the only parties in the system whose subordinate masochism has nothing/no one to check its reality except heaven . . . or hell. Maybe the time has come to reverse the trend, to render insecure our social assumptions rather than ourselves by creating a world where human beings can be both individual as well as sociable, dependent as well as free.

EPILOGUE

In looking back I am acutely aware both of how much and how little I have written about sadomasochism. A contradictory feeling persists, at once enlivening and overwhelming, of having just scratched the surface of a subject rich and stubborn in its theoretical multidimensionality. Consequently, this epilogue is devoted to what has been left unsaid or only implied, to assessments of commissions and omissions, and to thoughts of where another book might resume at the point this one leaves off.

As noted in the conclusion, this work was intended as a philosophical and sociological rumination on the tendency for a specific type of social psychology—in this case, a sadomasochistic one—to correlate with certain social structures and mandates. If social life is organized around a forced trade-off between human beings' simultaneous needs for dependence and independence, and between the need for both individual freedoms and communal commitments (such that only one of the two poles is acknowledged or fulfillable), then sadomasochistic dynamics of the sort I defined in part 1 will be predictably commonplace. Within sadomasochistic dynamics, parties in webs of dominant/subordinate relationships come to represent one or the other side of the bifurcated equation, and to project repressed aspects of themselves onto other(s). Put slightly differently, my argument is that these dynamics ensue as a logical outgrowth of, and concomitant to, the position in which large numbers of people are placed by the skewed structures of particular societies.

More specifically, in part 2, I have also tried to provide numerous examples of the workings of such dynamics in the contemporary United States, my particular focus of study. Our society is one that scorns vulnerability and neediness; it speciously separates these qualities from those of control and independency, bestowing cultural legitimacy only upon the latter category. Social insecurities thereby reign, and people are often rendered disproportionately dependent on the opinions and judgments of others for economic and emotional survival. One may be virtually enslaved through what I call socially symbiotic bonds, understandably anxious about losing one's paycheck, or welfare payment, or medical benefits, or reputation, or lover, or child—yet still believe oneself to be quite free. As I suggested, even those predominant sadists whose sheer existence may not be at stake are still subordinately masochistic, to some extent caught within the same social psychological maze.

Perhaps I have placed too much stock in overly abstract concepts like *capitalism* and *patriarchy* to describe the way overlapping sadomasochistic propensities are created by class, gender, and racially divided aspects of social organization in the United States. But, at a more basic level, it is really this gaping specter of social insecurity that I have most wished to capture in the concretized instances scattered throughout the manuscript. These instances are drawn from the political as well as from the personal arenas of life because such symbiotic dependencies are experienced in both dimensions, public and private. I tried to unite the two through the conceptual intermediary of a sadomasochistic dynamic that can operate amidst the publicity of a workplace, within the privacy of a home, or both. Moreover, one cannot say that either sphere has precedence or "causes" sadomasochism in the other. Rather, I think the relationship works in two directions, back and forth, in dialectical fashion. Fears engendered by a sadomasochistically structured workplace often redound to intimate relationships between family members, between lovers, or between races: similarly, a sadomasochistically structured family often affects how one feels in a classroom or at a job. Throughout, I suspect, a dynamic may be set into motion wherein persons are often driven, dissatisfied, even frantic, to meet needs their society has denied and disowned. These needs may be invisible, relegated to a kind of sociological unconscious, even when they manifest themselves at or just below the surface.

It strikes me as worthwhile to have propounded what I hope is a suggestive thesis, and to have linked it with a critical diagnosis of U.S. society. So much for the commission side. Nevertheless, there are several comparative and historical issues on which I have not focused that future writing (my own or others') would do well to address. For one thing, if the United States is sadomasochistically oriented according to definitional criteria enumerated in part 1, are other societies more or less so? How would one know, and is this empirically verifiable? Empirically, sadomasochistic dynamics of the type I emphasize are often not admitted to be such by persons who do not perceive their own behavior to be sadistic or masochistic. It is therefore a difficult phenomenon to "prove," explaining why this work relies mostly on secondary sources and theoretical argumentation. Nonetheless, one could still try to assess the presence (or absence) of some of sadomasochism's more glaring incarnations in a particular society along very approximate empirical lines. For example, how much street and domestic violence exists in a society? How much sexual harassment and abuse? On the other hand, how much sexual freedom? Are there indeed social securities or community supports on which people can rely?

At a more theoretic level, comparative questions should be possible and not too difficult to pose based on the premises of this book. For instance, could a country that is democratically socialistic (or one that simply provides its members, as do Sweden and France, with a range of guaranteed benefits regarding health, childcare, and employment) be said to be less sadomasochistic than the United States model? Certainly, these insurances allow a greater balance to be forged between independence and dependence, and between individual and collective responsibility; in easing fundamental concerns about subsistence, the bonds of social symbiosis are likewise relaxed. In addition, beyond the public sphere, the existence of less repressive attitudes toward sexuality, sexual diversity, and personal intimacy affects the presence of compulsively sadomasochistic dynamics in a particular society. On the other hand, the provision of social security in the broadest sense is probably a necessary but not sufficient condition for the diminution of sadomasochistic dynamics. These dynamics might reappear in other forms and for other reasons in either the personal or the political realm or both. A case in point would be Soviet-style systems. Most Communist societies tended to reverse the trade-off between dependence and independence; the former dimension was culturally glorified, while the latter became the object of social disdain. Also, it remained the case in most Communist societies that one could neither challenge nor question social and sexual rules and regulations without great fear of reprisal, stigmatization, or other punishing consequences. By this crucial component of my definition, resultant societies are still sadomasochistically oriented to the extent that they perpetuate socially symbiotic dependencies.

But what about sadomasochism appearing more prominently at some time periods than at others within the _same_ society? In chapter 1, I began to address this historical question for the case of the United States though, again, a fuller approach needs development in future treatments of sadomasochism. My tentative suspicion is that sadomasochistic dynamics are intensified at times when social insecurities are also heightened. At such moments, traditional family values, often sexually repressive, may be reasserted by a conservative state because they have the appeal of the habitual and the familiar—as, of course, does the conservative government itself. (The relationship also feeds back in the opposite direction, as Wilhelm Reich pointed out in _The Mass Psychology of Fascism._ Sexually repressive family structures may themselves increase the likelihood of that conservative government's appeal.) People may feel that much more panicked about jobs and survival, turning more readily toward (apparently) reassuring authority figures who resuscitate nationalistic sentiment; incidents of hatred and bias may start to rise as angers and anxieties are displaced onto enemy others (as depicted in chapter 6). These general features coexisted with sadomasochistic imagery in, for example, late Weimar Germany and under the Nazi regime, also coinciding with a historical era of enormous economic and national self-doubt. It should be added that a number of similar conditions are present, disconcertingly so, in the case of the United States circa 1992.

But to contend that sadomasochism is exacerbated under certain historical conditions is not to imply that it is otherwise altogether absent. By no means have I intended to suggest that sadomasochism (as I use the term) is somehow a uniquely modern phenomenon, suddenly appearing for the first time in the United States in the 1980s and 1990s, or, for that matter, in Germany only in the 1920s and 1930s. On the contrary, the criteria I stated in chapter 1 apply to more societies, past and present, than not. One could therefore push the argument I have made to a conclusion parallel with Marx's famous assertion that all history is still the history of class societies. A social psychological translation of this statement might be that most societies have generated a compulsory form of sadomasochism to the degree that they have not been organized around the simultaneous acknowledgment of human dependence and independence, allowing both freedom and security to be experienced in both public and private life. (This point is elaborated at greater length in the book's conclusion.) For this to be different, one would have to slowly effect changes both within and without human consciousness, altering aspects of social structure as well as of social psychology. Unless serious attention is paid to dynamics that operate both internally and externally (at once psychologically and sociologically), prospects for transforming social structures may continue to be slim and utopian indeed.

This brings me to several last questions with which I would want a continuation of this book to begin. One is that of how particular individuals come to internalize sadomasochistic tendencies within a larger sadomasochistically oriented society. Even if social structures and mandates are agreed to produce generally sadomasochistic proclivities, this tendency will not affect all persons within that society equally or with the same intensity. Clearly, human beings are not determined by the social systems in which they are positioned but act as agents who mediate between the world they are given and the one they recreate. With sadomasochism, this means that those factors that influence how and if this proclivity is internalized need to be more specifically investigated. Which types of workplaces and work conditions exacerbate or offset the chances of sadomasochistic dynamics becoming operative? What psychic/sexual conditions within the family, or associated with one's educational exposure, increase this same likelihood, if any? Do community supports exist (say, the possibility of someone belonging to a union, a social movement or club, or a religious congregation), and might they sway how and whether sadomasochistic dynamics are played out? Such queries would broaden this book's approach even further in a direction at once theoretical and empirical.

Second, I would wish to inquire if something akin to the sadomasochistic dynamic of this book's description would not exist even in restructured societies. It is possible that the mad and maddening quest of this book's prototypical sadomasochist—a party obsessed with pursuit of satisfactions that evaporate the moment they arrive—is an *extreme and destructive form* of a more basic philosophical dilemma. For processes of Weberian-type routinization occur, after all, even if someone is *not* caught up in the socially sadomasochistic patterns of my definition. They occur because it is also a structural dilemma that one tends to become bored with a job or project one has repeated a thousand times; or seeks sexual novelty simply because the body of one's long-term partner cannot possibly remain a mystery over time; or tries to inject elements of newness into friendships or marriages ritualized simply because they are of extended duration. At root, each of these examples illustrates a human need for some kind of balance to be maintained between stasis and change in time, and between that which is familiar and unfamiliar over the course of our individual and historical lifetimes. An important theoretical dilemma thus becomes how we might best organize the social world to encompass not only the aforementioned need for simultaneous independence and dependence, but also this second requirement—that is, a desire for doses of both the new and the old, securities and bits of insecurities, to cohabit in our lives. How would the world look if it allowed us to have both the assurance of a job and the hope that this job will be interesting, changing, and diversified? Could the world ever manage to let us feel both secure in being loved and unafraid of loving experimentation? Once more, it is with these difficult problems that I would start anew were this book ever to come full circle.

In the meantime, and finally, the preceding chapters may be somewhat unfashionable from the perspective of some strands in current social theorizing. In particular, this book is not very "postmodern" to the extent that recent postmodern theories have stressed the futility and wrongheadedness of large-scale explanatory schemas. To write as though any one dynamic can elucidate significant aspects of a human condition, a postmodernist might say, is to ignore cross-cultural differences and to propound a falsely universalized narrative. Still, I believe it possible to do two things at once: to both assert the cross-cultural recurrence of certain patterns and yet to recognize how such patterns are expressed and channeled quite differently within differing social systems. In this respect, sadomasochistic dynamics are both generally distributed and extremely variable. But either to be afraid of making broad claims about society, on the one hand, or to ignore the facts of diversity, on the other, strikes me as an unfortunate trade-off. One risks losing vision, and a belief in transformative possibilities. (Even if unacknowledged, postmodern thought itself proffers wide claims and alternative visions.) And so in this book I attempted to do two things at once, to explore sadomasochism both from the perspective of a general social tendency and from the perspective of its very specific anchoring within U.S. society of the 1990s.

NOTES

INTRODUCTION. PERSONAL AND POLITICAL CRITERIA

1. See, for example, Pat Califia's discussion of sadomasochism in *Sapphistry: The Book of Lesbian Sexuality* (Tallahassee, Fla.: Naiad Press, 1988).

2. Interestingly enough, however, as I will argue in chapter 2, the sadist secretly desires some resistance, some fight, from the masochist. But this must only take place within limits controllable by the sadist and cannot be openly acknowledged. Otherwise, punishment is almost surely likely to ensue.

3. See Max Weber, *The Protestant Ethic and the Spirit of Capitalism* (New York: Charles Scribner's Sons, 1958).

4. For a more detailed exposition of this position, see, in particular, chapters 1 and 6 of Jessica Benjamin, *The Bonds of Love: Psychoanalysis, Feminism, and the Problem of Domination* (New York: Pantheon, 1988).

5. On blaming the victim, see Paula J. Caplan, *The Myth of Women's Masochism* (New York: Signet, 1987).

1. EXPLORING SADOMASOCHISM IN THE AMERICAN CONTEXT

1. See Theodor W. Adorno, *The Authoritarian Personality*, with Else Frenkel-Brunswik, Daniel J. Levinson, and R. Nevitt Sanford (New York: Norton, 1982).

2. See Erich Fromm, *Escape from Freedom* (New York: Holt, Rinehart and Winston, 1941), chap. 5, "Mechanisms of Escape," pp. 136–179.

3. Ibid., pp. 142, 174.

4. See preface and introduction to Robert N. Bellah, Richard Madsen, William M. Sullivan, Ann Swidler, and Steven M. Tipton, *Habits of the Heart* (New York: Harper & Row, 1985).

5. See R. Krafft-Ebing, *Psychopathia Sexualis* (New York: Rebman, 1900), and Sigmund Freud, *Three Essays on the Theory of Sexuality* (New York: Basic Books, 1962).

6. Freud, *Three Essays*.

7. Ibid.

8. Angela Carter, *The Sadeian Woman and the Ideology of Pornography* (Pantheon: New York, 1978), p. 28.

9. David Leavitt thoroughly described these disturbing developments in a *New York Times* article entitled "Fears that Haunt a Scrubbed America," *New York Times*, 19 August 1990, sec. 2, quoting the NEA's language. Also see *New York Times*, 24 August 1990, p. C16.

10. Ruth Sidel, *On Her Own: Growing up in the Shadow of the American Dream* (New York: Viking, 1990), p. 94.

11. Barbara Ehrenreich, *Remaking Love: The Feminization of Sex* (New York: Anchor Press/Doubleday, 1986), p. 119.

12. See the historical account by Ellen Willis in *The Sixties Without Apology* (Minneapolis: University of Minnesota Press, 1984) and Alice Echols, "Cultural Feminism: Feminist Capitalism and the Anti-Pornography Movement" (*Social Text* 7 [Spring and Summer 1983]: 34–53).

13. In *Sapphistry* and *Coming to Power* (Berkeley, Calif.: Samois, 1981) Pat Califia defines sadomasochism as "an erotic ritual that involves acting out fantasies in which one partner is sexually dominant and the other partner is sexually submissive. . . . The basic dynamic of sexual sadomasochism is an eroticized, consensual exchange of power—not violence or pain" (*Sapphistry*, p. 118). For Califia and other practitioners of S/M sex, sadomasochistic sexual interaction is equal and mutually consenting. Indeed, it is often thought that—exactly the opposite of the sadomasochistic dynamic I describe in chapter 1—it is the bottom rather than the top who calls the shots.

14. See Sherri Ortner, "Are Men to Culture as Women to Nature?" in *Women, Culture and Society*, ed. Michelle Zimbalist Rosaldo and Louise Lamphere (Stanford, Calif.: Stanford University Press, 1974).

15. Ibid.

16. See Karen Blaker, *Born to Please; Compliant Women/Controlling Men* (New York: St. Martin's Press, 1988); Susan Forward and Joan Torres, *Men Who Hate Women and the Women Who Love Them* (New York: Bantam Books, 1986); Kevin Leman, *The Pleasers: Women Who Can't Say No—and the Men Who Control Them* (New York: Bantam Doubleday Dell, 1987); Steven Naifeh and Gregory White Smith, *Why Can't Men Open Up?* (New York: Warner Books, 1984); Robin Norwood, *Women Who Love Too Much* (New York: Pocket Books, 1986) and *Letters from Women Who Love Too Much* (New York: Pocket Books, 1988); Brenda Schaeffer, *Is It Love or Is It Addiction? Falling into Healthy Love* (New York: Harper/Hazelden, 1987); and Peter Trachtenberg, *The Casanova Complex: Compulsive Lovers and Their Women* (New York: Poseidon Press, 1988).

17. See, for example, the use of "misogynistic" in the introduction to Forward and Torres, *Men Who Hate Women and the Women Who Love Them.*

18. Ibid., p. 10.

19. See comments I made in a review article entitled "Cinematic Confrontations with Feminism in the Age of Reagan," *New Politics* 1, 4 (Winter 1989): 216–220.

20. Georg Lukacs, "Reification and the Consciousness of the Proletariat," in *History and Class Consciousness* (Cambridge, Mass.: MIT Press, 1968), p. 89.

2. A BASIC DYNAMIC

1. Jenni Diski, *Nothing Natural* (London: Methuen, 1986), pp. 225–226.
2. Pauline Reage, *The Story of O* (New York: Ballantine Books, 1965), pp. 87–89.
3. Jessica Benjamin refers to this experience of "consuming" the other only to feel empty afterward in her "Master and Slave: Fantasies of Erotic Domination," in *Powers of Desire: The Politics of Sexuality,* ed. C. Stansell and S. Thompson (New York: Monthly Review Press, 1983).
4. Benjamin, *The Bonds of Love,* p. 58.
5. Ibid., pp. 58–59.
6. For this observation, I credit an interesting essay by Lila Karp and Renos Mandis entitled "Genderless Sexuality: A Male-Female Psychological Exploration of the Future of Sexual Relationships," in *Woman in the Year 2000,* ed. Maggie Tripp (New York: Arbor House, 1974).
7. Diski, *Nothing Natural,* p. 129.
8. Reage, *The Story of O,* p. 162.
9. Diski, *Nothing Natural,* pp. 85, 83, 226, 228.

3. EXISTENTIALISM AND PSYCHOANALYSIS

1. Benjamin, "Master and Slave," p. 283.
2. See George Bataille, *Death and Sensuality* (New York: Walker, 1962). Benjamin, "Master and Slave," pp. 285, 296.
3. See the section entitled "Lordship and Bondage" in G. W. F. Hegel, *The Phenomenology of Mind* (New York: Harper & Row, 1967), pp. 234–240.
4. Benjamin, *Bonds of Love,* p. 54.
5. Benjamin, "Master and Slave," p. 292.
6. See, for example, Margaret Mahler, *The Psychological Birth of the Human Infant: Symbiosis and Individuation* (New York: Basic Books, 1975); Suzanne Schad-Somers, *Sadomasochism: Etiology and Treatment* (New York: Human Sciences Press, 1982); and Esther Menaker, *Masochism and the Emergent Ego* (New York: Human Sciences Press, 1979).
7. Benjamin, *Bonds of Love,* p. 25.
8. Mahler, *Psychological Birth,* p. 42.
9. Ibid., p. 45. Note that Mahler uses the term *social symbiosis* to stress a matrix of "sociobiological dependence" in which the child responds to positive as well as negative aspects of its environment.
10. Nancy Chodorow, *The Reproduction of Mothering: Psychoanalysis and the Sociology of Gender* (Berkeley and Los Angeles, Calif.: University of California Press, 1978), p. 105, as well as the perspective presented throughout the same chapter, "Pre-oedipal Gender Differences."
11. Schad-Somers, *Sadomasochism,* p. 47.

12. Alma Bond, "Sadomasochistic Patterns in an 18-Month-Old Child," *International Journal of Psychoanalysis* 48 (1967): 597.
13. Ibid.
14. Freud, *Three Essays*, p. 24.
15. Ibid., pp. 58–59.
16. Ibid., pp. 23–24.
17. Ibid., p. 25.
18. Freud, "A Child is Being Beaten" in *Sexuality and the Psychology of Love* (New York: Norton, 1963), pp. 117–118.
19. Wilhelm Reich, *Character Analysis* (New York: Farrar, Straus and Giroux, 1988), p. 241.
20. See Freud, "The Economic Problem of Masochism," in the *Standard Edition of the Complete Psychological Works of Sigmund Freud*, ed. J. Strachey (London: Hogarth Press, 1964), 19:160.
21. Ibid., p. 169.

4. EMPLOYING CHAINS OF COMMAND

1. For figures, see the epilogue to the recently revised edition of Stanley Aronowitz's *False Promises* (Durham, N.C.: Duke University Press, 1991).
2. Richard Edwards, *Contested Terrain: The Transformation of the Workplace in the Twentieth Century* (New York: Basic Books, 1979), pp. 133–134.
3. Barbara Garson, *All the Livelong Day: The Meaning and Demeaning of Routine Work* (New York: Penguin Books, 1976), pp. 75–76.
4. Ibid., pp. 12–13.
5. Ibid.
6. Harry Braverman, *Labor and Monopoly Capital: The Degradation of Work in the Twentieth Century* (New York and London: Monthly Review Press, 1974), pp. 366–369, 296.
7. Arlie Russell Hochschild, *The Managed Heart: Commercialization of Human Feelings* (Berkeley and Los Angeles, Calif.: University of California Press, 1983), p. 25, in which Hochschild describes a training seminar at Delta Airlines.
8. Ibid., p. 11.
9. Judith Rollins, *Between Women: Domestics and Their Employers* (Philadelphia: Temple University Press, 1985), p. 162.
10. Michael Lewis, *Liar's Poker* (New York: Penguin Books, 1989), pp. 41–42, and review of Donald Trump's *Surviving at the Top*, *The New York Times Book Review*, 2 September 1990, p. 3.
11. See L. N. Newell, *Contemporary Industrial/Organizational Psychology* (St. Paul, Minn.: West Publishing, 1983).
12. Lewis, *Liar's Poker*, pp. 46–47, 43.
13. See Andrew J. Durbin, chapter 1 of *Survival in the Office* (New York: Mason/Charter, 1977).
14. Ibid., pp. 10–11, 19.

15. William A. Cohen and Nurit Cohen, *Top Executive Performance: 11 Keys to Success and Power* (New York: John Wiley & Sons, 1984), pp. 79–86.
16. Michael Burawoy, *Manufacturing Consent; Changes in the Labor Process under Monopoly Capitalism* (Chicago: University of Chicago Press, 1979), pp. 87–88.
17. Edwards, *Contested Terrain*, pp. 91–92.
18. Braverman, *Labor and Monopoly Capital*, pp. 104–106, excerpted from Frederick W. Taylor's *The Principles of Scientific Management.*
19. Edwards, *Contested Terrain*, p. 103.
20. Elton Mayo, *The Human Problems of an Industrial Civilization* (New York: Macmillan, 1933), pp. 73, 78.
21. Ibid., p. 78.

5. ENGENDERING SADOMASOCHISM

1. Freud specified three types of masochism, of which feminine masochism was the second, in "The Economic Problem of Masochism," *Standard Edition of the Complete Psychological Works of Sigmund Freud*, ed. J. Strachey (London: Hogarth Press, 1964), pp. 164–169.
2. See Karen Horney, "On the Genesis of the Castration Complex in Women" and "The Problem of Feminine Masochism," in *Feminine Psychology* (New York: W. W. Norton & Co., 1967). Juliet Mitchell, *Psychoanalysis and Feminism* (New York: Vintage Books, 1974), p. 131.
3. See Helene Deutsch, *The Psychology of Women* (New York: Grune & Stratton, 1944).
4. It strikes me as in bad faith that sociobiologists like Steven Goldberg, who argue on scientific grounds that patriarchy is inevitable, are not eager that traditional sexist arrangements between the sexes be radically altered. Their biological theses would only be falsifiable in a setting that had revolutionized gender relations and still found them to be unalterable. This would seem to be the perfect proof.
5. Cynthia Fuchs Epstein, *Deceptive Distinctions: Sex, Gender, and the Social Order* (New Haven, Conn: Yale University Press, 1988), p. 14.
6. Kate Millett, *Sexual Politics* (New York: Ballantine Books, 1969), pp. 33–34.
7. See, for instance, Arlie Russell Hochschild's account of the "leisure gap" in *The Second Shift* (New York: Viking, 1989). Her research reflects that women's association with domesticity has remained in place long after other aspects of their/our material situation have changed.
8. See Ortner, "Are Men to Culture."
9. See Norman Mailer, *The Prisoner of Sex* (Boston: Little Brown, 1971).
10. Simone de Beauvoir, *The Second Sex* (New York: Vintage, 1974), p. 303.
11. See my brief allusions in chapters 1 and 7 to the implications of this approach (shared with Beauvoir by Sartre, since both of their writings are traceable to a similar phenomenological orientation) as a theory of the possibly universal rather than socially based roots of sadomasochistic interaction.

12. Beauvoir, *The Second Sex,* p. 305.

13. Ibid., p. 305.

14. More specifically, I think here of men coming to associate power with control over women's bodies in a patriarchal setting. Thus, for example, the well-to-do male corporate executive or powerful politician often believes a benefit of his hard-won success to be access to attractive women.

15. Beauvoir, *The Second Sex,* pp. 307, 316.

16. Ibid., p. 328.

17. See chap. 2, n16.

18. Wendy Simonds, *Women Who Help Themselves: Readers of Self-Help Books* (New Brunswick, N.J.: Rutgers University Press, forthcoming).

19. See Norwood, *Women Who Love Too Much;* Schaeffer, *Is It Love?;* and Forward and Torres, *Men Who Hate Women.*

20. Norwood, *Women Who Love Too Much,* xiv. Blaker, *Born to Please,* p. 2. Schaeffer, *Is It Love?,* p. 5.

21. Forward and Torres, *Men Who Hate Women,* p. 43.

22. Ibid., pp. 46–47. Blaker, *Born to Please,* p. 7. Leman, *The Pleasers,* pp. 7–8.

23. Norwood, *Women Who Love Too Much,* pp. 31–34, 2–5. Blaker, *Born to Please,* p. 7.

24. Leman, *The Pleasers,* p. 8.

25. Lenore E. Walker, *Terrifying Love: Why Battered Women Kill and How Society Responds* (New York: Harper 1989), p. 17.

26. See, for example, Diana E. H. Russell, *Rape in Marriage* (New York: Macmillan, 1982); Lenore Walker, *The Battered Woman* (New York: Harper & Row, 1978); or David Finkelhor and Kersti Yllo, *License to Rape* (New York: Free Press, 1985).

27. A thorough account of how divorce often leads to a diminution in women's economic and social standing, and of husbands' frequently spiteful behavior, is given in Terry Arundell's *Mothers and Divorce: Legal, Economic, and Social Dilemmas* (Berkeley: University of California, 1986). See especially her chapters entitled "Experiences with the Law" and "Downward Mobility."

28. See Chodorow, *Reproduction of Mothering,* especially "Pre-oedipal Gender Differences," pp. 92–111, in which she discusses mother-daughter relationships, and p. 101 on separation.

29. As Chodorow tells us, this pushing out of the son probably takes place in the pre-oedipal period but is later reinforced in the oedipal phase when the tendency is sexualized. The son at that time may find himself unconsciously still tied to and resentful of the remaining dependency on the mother he cannot acknowledge, so that his sexuality may become eroticized in a sado-masochistic direction.

6. CREATING ENEMIES IN EVERYDAY LIFE

1. Edward Sagarin, *Deviants and Deviancy* (New York: Praeger, 1975), p. 372.

2. Kai T. Erikson, *Wayward Puritans: A Study in the Sociology of Deviance* (New York: John Wiley & Sons, 1966), p. 67.

3. Ibid., p. 64.

4. Jean-Paul Sartre, *Anti-Semite and Jew* (New York: Schocken Books, 1949), p. 28.

5. Ibid., pp. 48, 28, 54.

6. Ibid., p. 25.

7. Ibid., p. 28

8. Ibid., p. 44.

9. Ibid., p. 149.

10. See Deirdre Bair, *Simone de Beauvoir: A Biography* (New York: Summit Books, 1990).

11. Sartre, *Anti-Semite and Jew*, pp. 45-47.

12. Frantz Fanon, *Black Skin, White Masks: The Experience of a Black Man in a White World* (New York: Grove Press, 1967), pp. 159, 177.

13. See, for instance, Bell Hooks's *Ain't I A Woman: Black Women and Feminism* (Boston: South End Press, 1981) and Angela Davis, *Women, Class, and Race* (New York: Random House, 1981).

14. Joel Kovel, *White Racism: A Psychohistory,* rev. ed. (New York: Columbia University Press, 1984), xliii.

15. Jonathan Rieder, *Canarsie: The Jews and Italians of Brooklyn Against Liberalism* (Cambridge, Mass.: Harvard University Press, 1985), p. 59.

16. See Lynn Chancer and David Forbes, "From Here to Panama: Face It, We're Addicted to Lies," *Village Voice*, 23 January 1990.

17. An excellent comparative critique of social versus biological attitudes toward crime in the United States is found in Elliot Currie's *Confronting Crime: An American Challenge* (New York: Pantheon, 1985).

18. Loic Wacquant, "Decivilisation et Diabolisation: La Transformation du Ghetto Noir Americain" (paper delivered at a conference on "L'Homme Atlantique," La Maison des Sciences de l'Homme, Paris, June 1991).

19. Kovel, *White Racism*, xi.

20. I am currently in the process of researching the differential application of such language to crime, having become interested in the racist use of wolf-pack language in the Central Park jogger case of 1989.

21. See, for instance, the perturbing account of the rise of such incidents on college campuses provided by Reginald Wilson in an article entitled "Racism on Campus," *New Politics*, 3(3) Spring 1991.

22. See Lynn S. Chancer, "New Bedford, Massachusetts, March 6, 1983–March 22, 1984: The 'Before and After' of a Group Rape," *Gender and Society* 1, 3 (September 1987): 239–60.

23. *New York Times*, 28 August 1989.

7. A THEORETICAL FINALE

1. I refer to Wilhelm Reich's description of nazism in *The Mass Psychology of Fascism* (New York: Farrar, Strauss and Giroux, 1970).

2. I refer here to the Weberian use of this term.

3. See not only Benjamin's *Bonds of Love* but Alice Miller's *The Drama of the Gifted Child* (New York: Basic Books, 1990). Also, the interpretation of Chodorow proposed in chapter 6 suggests this turnabout within familial relations.

4. See Donna Gaines, *Teenage Wasteland: Suburbia's Dead End Kids* (New York: Pantheon Books, 1991).

5. See an interesting analysis of this point by Julius Jacobson entitled "The Collapse of Totalitarianism," *New Politics* 2, 4 (Winter 1990): 137–156.

6. Adrienne Rich, "Compulsory Heterosexuality," *Signs: Journal of Women in Culture and Society* 5, 4 (Summer 1980): 631–660.

INDEX

academia, 5, 40, 111, 113, 130, 157, 194, 195, 211
acquired immune deficiency syndrome, 32
Adorno, Theodor, 15
AIDS. *See* acquired immune deficiency syndrome
Allen, Woody, 21, 106
All the Livelong Day (Garson), 101–102
Almodovar, Pedro, 21, 138, 144
American Management Association, 114
American Tragedy, An (Dreiser), 35, 36
Antinomians, 160, 161
"Anti-Semite and Jew" (Sartre), 160–165, 168
anti-Semitism, 91, 159; and class struggle, 165; dependency in, 161–162, 163, 167; and dominant and subordinate sadism and masochism, 161–162; hierarchy in, 161, 162–163; paradoxical attraction in, 167–168; and powerlessness, 160, 181, 196; and projection, 171; transformability of, 161, 163–164; triangulation in, 168, 172. *See also* prejudice

Arabs, 4, 178, 196
authoritarian personality, 15

Baby Boom, 31
Bad Influence, 21
Bair, Deirdre, 16
Balcony, The (Genet), 52
Barnard College: conference on sexuality at, 22–23, 24, 152, 211
Bataille, Georges, 69, 70
Beauvoir, Simone de, 131, 133–134, 135, 136, 145, 166; and patriarchy, 138, 140; and universal roots of sadomasochism, 219*n11*; and woman as mother, 150; and women as "second sex," 7, 27, 159
Beijing: 1989 student demonstration, 5–6, 204
Being and Nothingness (Sartre), 41
Benjamin, Jessica, 51, 81, 134, 189, 200; analysis of characters in *The Story of O*, 53; on problem of recognition, 69–70, 71–72, 75–76, 138, 169; on separation-individuation, 190–191
Berliner, Bernard, 75

Berman, Marshall, 34
Between Women: Domestics and Their Employees (Rollins), 104–105
Beyond the Pleasure Principle (Freud), 87
Black Skin, White Masks (Fanon), 168
Blaker, Karen, 140, 145. *See also Born to Please: Compliant Women/Controlling Men*
Blue Steel, 21
Blue Velvet, 21
Bolton, Robert and Dorothy, 114
Bond, Alma, 79
Bonds of Love (Benjamin), 7, 53, 71–72, 190–191
Born to Please: Compliant Women/Controlling Men (Blaker), 29, 140–141, 145
Braverman, Harry, 103, 118, 121
Buddhism, 72
Burawoy, Michael, 114–115, 116, 119
bureaucracy, 16, 106; and sadomasochism, 99–101, 123
Bush, George, 17, 21, 180

Califia, Pat, 25, 216*n13*
Calvinists. *See* Weber, and Protestantism
Canarsie (Rieder), 172–173
Capital, Das (Marx), 34
capitalism, 26, 155, 184; approval with the mode of disapproval in, 114, 115–117, 118, 119, 121; and bureaucracies (*see* bureaucracy); conditions set in, 96; and control, 117, 118, 120 (*see also* scientific management; Hawthorne experiments); and dependency, 95, 101, 108, 112, 116, 117, 118, 122, 123, 138–139, 204; and disapproval in the mode of approval, 110, 112–113, 119; and discontent, 106–108, 109, 163, 194; and Freudian theory, 103; and gender, 95, 108; independence in, 111–112, 113, 138–139, 203; and the "making out" game, 115–116, 117; Marx's theory of, 101, 103, 106, 107, 109, 114–115, 123; and masochism, 109; and object relations theory, 102–103; and power, 101, 108, 109, 114, 117, 122, 163; and racism, 174, 179; rebellion in, 114–115, 117–118, 123; resiliency of, 123; resistance required in, 110–114; and sadism, 109–110, 112, 114, 116, 118, 203; and sadomasochism, 16, 32–34, 35–38, 39–40, 94–97, 100, 102, 109, 111–112, 120, 121, 122, 126, 158, 165, 212 (*see also* sadism, and capitalism); and symbiosis, 94, 106, 117, 119, 122; transformability in, 123–124; in United States, 122, 202, 213–214; versus commu-

nism, 202–203; and welfare, 117–118. *See also* work and the workplace
Carter, Angela, 19
Casanova Complex: Compulsive Lovers and Their Women (Trachtenberg), 142
Ceaucescu, Nicolae, 4–5
Character Structure (Reich), 86
child abuse, 17, 24, 126
"Child is Being Beaten, A" (Freud), 84–86, 193
Chodorow, Nancy, 78–79, 134, 137, 147–153, 154, 191, 220*n29*
Civilization and Its Discontents (Freud), 213
Clyde (*American Tragedy*), 35–36
Cohen, William A. and Nurit, 113
colonization, 4–5
Coming to Power (Califia), 216*n13*
Commander (*Story of O*), 52, 54, 100
communism and Communists, 5, 6, 121, 165, 197; dependency in, 203; independence devalued in, 202, 204; and masochism, 203; as other, 159, 171; punishment under, 203–204; and rebellion, 203–204; and sadomasochism, 202–205, 212; and social symbiosis, 203; versus capitalism, 202–203, 204–205
Confronting Crime: An American Challenge (Currie), 221*n11*
Contested Terrain (Edwards), 117
Cook, The Thief, The Wife and Her Lover, The, 21, 157
crime: in the family, 17; and hate incidents, 181–183, 196; needed by society, 159–160, 170; organized, and capitalism, 96–97, 122; role reversal in, 164; and sadistic racism, 180–183, 221*n14*; and sadomasochism, 179; in United States, 160, 175, 176–177, 178, 180, 221*n11*
Crimes and Misdemeanors, 21
Currie, Elliot, 221*n11*

Darwinism, 180
Davis, Angela, 169
Death and Sensuality (Bataille), 70
Death of a Salesman (Miller), 35, 106
de Beauvoir, Simone. *See* Beauvoir, Simone de
deCrecy, Odette (*Remembrance of Things Past*), 7, 9, 60–61, 142, 144
DePalma, Brian, 21
Deutsch, Helene, 128
Dickens, Charles, 39
discrimination. *See* prejudice
Diski, Jenny, 44
Do the Right Thing, 173
Dreiser, Theodore, 35
Dukakis, Michael, 180

Durbin, Andrew, 113
Durkheim, Émile, 18, 161, 174, 188; on crime, 159, 160, 176, 181; on postindustrial individual, 16, 82, 200

Eastwood, Clint, 21
Echols, Alice, 23
"Economic Problem of Masochism, The" (Freud), 87, 219n1
Edwards, Richard, 100, 117, 119
Ehrenreich, Barbara, 22, 24, 32
employment. *See* work and the workplace
Epstein, Cynthia Fuchs, 128, 153
Erickson, Kai, 160, 174, 181
Escape from Freedom (Fromm), 16
existentialism: and capitalism, 107–108; and problem of recognition, 69, 70–75, 78, 109; and transformability of sadomasochism, 4

Fair Labor Standards Act, 100
family, 11, 12, 32, 93, 148, 150, 152; and alternative paradigm, 207–208, 210; and crime, 17; dependence and independence in, 92, 116, 191; and patriarchy, 30, 91, 151 (*see also* patriarchy); politicizing, 211; sadomasochism in, 18, 40, 91, 134, 184, 191, 193, 194, 211; and social symbiosis, 92
Fanon, Frantz, 168, 170
fascism, 15, 178
Fatal Attraction, 21, 31
Favorite Son, 21
Feliciano, Gina, 183
feminist movement and feminists, 146, 182, 210; black, 169; men's reactions to, 54; and parenting, 153; and patriarchy, 27, 30–31; and sadomasochism, 22–23, 24, 205, 211; and sexuality, 127. *See also* feminist theory
feminist theory, 12, 26, 129, 208. *See also* feminist movement and feminists
Fitzgerald, F. Scott, 35
Fortune 500, 110
Forward, Susan, 29, 30, 140, 141, 145. *See also Men Who Hate Women and the Women Who Love Them*
Foucault, Michel, 26
Frankfurt School, 15, 208
Freudian theory, 11, 91, 134, 189–190; and anger, 193; and capitalism, 103; criticism of, 127; on feminine masochism, 127; on roots of sadomasochism, 82–88; on sexual and aggressive drives, 70, 75, 127, 192; theories on the unconscious, 70, 137;

and transformability of sadomasochism, 4. *See also* Freud, Sigmund
Freud, Sigmund, 19, 41, 59, 71–72, 127, 128, 133, 193, 213, 219n1. *See also* Freudian theory
Friedan, Betty, 131
Fromm, Erich, 24, 32, 70, 82, 200, 208; on sadomasochism, 15, 16, 17, 18, 40, 139, 201

Gaines, Donna, 200
Garson, Barbara, 101–103, 119
Gatsby, Jay (*The Great Gatsby*), 35–36
gays, 21–22, 197
gender, 32, 54, 155, 219n4; and capitalism, 95, 108; and equality, 95, 143, 184; and patriarchy, 27–28, 33, 207; and sadomasochism (*see* gender and sadomasochism); and socialization, 58, 134, 138, 153; studies of, 130, 219n7; in United States, 30–31
gender and sadomasochism, 45, 83, 85, 125–127, 149–150, 154, 155, 220n14; biological basis for, 127–129; and patriarchy, 27; social basis for, 126, 127, 132–136, 219n11 (*see also* men, socialization of; women, socialization of). *See also* men, and sadism; patriarchy, and sadomasochism; women, and masochism
Genet, Jean, 52
Germany, 174, 208–209
Goldberg, Steven, 219n4
Gorbachev, Mikhail, 205
Great Gatsby, The (Fitzgerald), 35, 36
Greenaway, Peter, 21, 157
Gulf War, 175, 176, 178, 196

Habits of the Heart (Bellah et al.), 17
Harvard Business School, 119
Hawkins, Yusef, 181, 183
Hawthorne experiments, 119–121
Hegel, George Wilhelm Friedrich, 74, 189; on master-slave dialectic, 63, 66, 69, 71; on problem of recognition, 11, 25, 71–72, 138, 169, 202
Helena Rubenstein, 102
heterosexuality, 126, 127, 136, 148, 149
Hill, Anita, 95
History and Class Consciousness (Lukacs), 34
Hitler, Adolf, 162
Hochschild, Arlie, 35, 103–104, 105, 113, 219n7
homophobia, 154, 165, 166, 184, 196, 210; and anger, 24–25, 38, 91; and the other, 155; projection in, 170, 171
Hooks, Bell, 169
Horney, Karen, 127

*Human Problems of an Industrial Civiliza-
tion* (Mayo), 120
Hundred and Twenty Days at Sodom, The
(Sade), 19
Hussein, Saddam, 176, 196

imperialism, 24
industrial psychology, 115, 119, 121, 174
Industrial Revolution, 38
Inquisition, 159
Instincts and Their Vicissitudes (Freud), 83
Internal Affairs, 21
Iraqis, 176, 178
Israelis, 166, 197

Japan, 17, 174, 206
Jews, 4, 161, 162, 164, 165, 171, 172
Joshua (*Nothing Natural*), 46, 50, 60, 64
Juliette (Sade), 44, 47
Justine (Sade), 19

Kant, Immanuel, 37
Karp, Lila, 54
Katz, Jack, 164, 178
Kemp, Jack, 178
Klein, Calvin, 21, 22
Kovel, Joel, 168, 169, 179, 181
Krafft-Ebing, 19, 84
Ku Klux Klan, 197

Lacan, Jacques, 135, 192
Lasch, Christopher, 37, 200
Lee, Spike, 173
Leman, Kevin, 141, 144
lesbians, 22, 197
*Les Liaisons Dangereuses. See Liaisons Dan-
gereuses, Les*
Letters from Women Who Love Too Much
(Norwood), 29, 140
Lewis, Michael, 105, 110, 195
Liaisons Dangereuses, Les (Laclos), 49,
144–145, 192
Liar's Poker (Lewis), 105
Loman, Willie (*Death of a Salesman*), 35–
36, 106
Love Addiction (Bireda), 29
Lukacs, Georg, 34
Lynch, David, 21, 22

McCarthy era, 159
Mahler, Margaret, 79, 134, 137; theories
of, 75–78, 80, 81, 190, 217*n9*
Mailer, Norman, 131
Managed Heart, The (Hochschild), 103–
104
Mandis, Renos, 54
Manufacturing Consent (Burawoy), 114–
115

Maoism, 202
Mapplethorpe, Robert, 20, 22
Marchiano, George, 22
Marxist theory, 12, 33–35, 38, 207; and
capitalism, 101, 103, 106, 107, 109,
114, 115, 123. *See also* Marx, Karl
Marx, Karl, 33, 34, 35, 38, 96, 102, 123,
184. *See also* Marxist theory
masculinity, 78–79, 108, 126, 133, 134,
142, 153
masochism: and capitalism, 109; and
communism, 203; dominant, 90–92,
101, 107, 109, 123, 150, 151, 152, 164,
169, 177, 179, 195; feminine, 127,
219*n1*; and men, 126, 151, 154; moral,
87–88; and object relations theory, 79,
80–82; and prejudice, 156; subordinate, 90, 111, 150, 151, 162, 163, 169,
213; and women (*see* women, and
masochism); and the worker, 101, 107,
108, 109, 113, 114, 115–116, 118, 121,
122–123, 151, 214. *See also* masochist;
sadomasochism
Masochism and Modern Man (Reik), 83
masochist, 57–67; anger of, 61, 107,
192, 198, 204; and approval within the
mode of disapproval, 65–66, 114,
115–117, 118, 144, 189; attitude toward self of, 57–59, 65; dependency
of, 49, 58, 59, 81, 92, 122, 137, 190
(*see also* sadomasochism, and dependency); good and bad, 172;
independence of, 62, 65, 67, 78, 137,
139, 170, 190, 192, 204 (*see also* masochist, power of); as opposite of sadist,
57, 58; pleasure of, 59–60, 63, 64;
power of, 56, 59, 60, 63, 66, 67 (*see
also* masochist, independence of); resistance of, 56, 63–64, 65; and
Weber's Protestant, 107, 108, 109,
151, 214. *See also* masochism; sadomasochism
Massachusetts Bay Colony, 160, 174
Mass Psychology of Fascism, The (Reich),
86, 171
Mayo, Elton, 119, 120, 174
Mead, George Herbert, 12, 37, 194
men: dependence of, 138, 141, 143, 145,
154; independence of, 143–144, 153;
and masochism, 126, 151, 154; and
projects of culture, 130–131; and sadism, 125, 127, 129, 134–135, 137,
139, 140, 141, 142, 143, 145, 147,
149–151, 153, 220*n29* (*see also* gender
and sadomasochism); socialization of,
126, 132–133, 138, 220*n14* (*see also*
gender and sadomasochism)
Menaker, Esther, 75
Men Who Hate Women and the Women Who

Love Them (Torres), 17–18, 29, 140, 141
Miller, Alice, 191
Miller, Arthur, 35, 106
Millett, Kate, 129, 130, 131, 132, 140
Mind, Self and Society (Mead), 12, 37
Mitchell, Juliet, 85, 127
moral masochism. *See* masochism, moral

National Endowment for the Arts (NEA), 20
nazism, 15, 21, 40, 161, 162, 171, 174, 178, 188
NEA. *See* National Endowment for the Arts
Negro, 168. *See also* racism
New York Post, 180
New York Times, 95, 105, 178
Newton, Helmut, 22
Nicaragua, 171
Nietzsche, Friedrich Wilhelm, 163
9-1/2 Weeks (McNeill), 21, 44, 46, 47, 51, 53, 54–55, 65; film version of, 21, 53
Norwood, Robin, 29, 30, 140–141, 145. *See also Women Who Love Too Much*
Nothing Natural (Diski), 44, 46, 47, 50, 54–55, 60, 64

O (*The Story of O*), 46, 74; and masochism, 57, 58, 59, 62; and the paradox of sadomasochism, 65; and sadist's dependence, 48, 58; and sadist's need for resistance, 53; and sadomasochism's transformability, 45, 62, 91, 152
object relations theory, 133; and capitalism, 102–103; and problem of recognition, 70, 72; and sadomasochism, 4, 190–192, 193; and symbiosis, 75–82, 92, 134, 137, 217n9
oppression, 165, 166–167; and resistance, 173–174. *See also* prejudice
Ortner, Sherri, 27, 130–131

Palestinians, 166, 197
Panamanians, 176
patriarchy, 29, 62, 91, 131, 134, 155, 207, 219n4, 220n14; definition of, 26–27; good woman/bad woman in, 142–143, 169, 172; hierarchy in, 129–130, 131, 138, 139, 143, 153; men linked to projects of culture in, 130–131; and paradoxical longings of sadist and masochist, 131–132, 138; and parenting, 153, 191; and problem of recognition, 143; and punishment, 131; and sadomasochism, 16, 27–28, 30, 32–33, 34, 35, 126, 129, 146–147, 150–151, 153–154, 212; sexuality in, 58; in United States, 202; woman as

other in, 183–184; women linked to nature in, 130–131
People's Express Airline, 122
perestroika, 17
Persian Gulf, 17. *See also* Gulf War
Phenomenology of Spirit (Hegel), 63
Pleasers: Women Who Can't Say No and the Men Who Control Them (Leman), 140, 141
Polaroid Corporation, 100
pornography, 20, 23
Powers of Desire (Benjamin), 69
prejudice, 155; dependency in, 167; effectiveness of, 171–172; hierarchical dichtomy in, 167; increased during conservative times, 171; and otherness, 158–159; and paradoxical attraction in, 170; problem of recognition in, 170; projection in, 169–170, 171; and role reversal, 157–158, 164; and sadomasochism, 156–158, 161, 174. *See also* anti-Semitism; homophobia; oppression; racism; sexism
Pretty Woman, 136
Principles of Scientific Management (Taylor), 118–119
Prisoner of Sex (Mailer), 131
"Problem of Masochism, The" (Freud), 127
Protestant Ethic and the Spirit of Capitalism (Weber), 107
Protestantism, Weberian. *See* Weber, and Protestantism
Proust, Marcel, 7, 9, 60, 144
Psychology of Women (Deutsch), 128
Psychopathia Sexualis (Krafft-Ebing), 19
Public Enemy, 194
Puritans, 161, 176

Quakers, 160, 161
Quayle, Dan, 21–22

Rachel (*Nothing Natural*), 46, 50, 54–55, 60, 64
racism, 154, 161, 165, 188, 210, 211; and capitalism, 174, 179; forms of, 179, 181; and otherness, 155; paradoxical attraction in, 167, 168; and powerlessness, 38, 91; projection in, 169–170, 171; and sadism, 24, 166, 196; and sexism, 169; transformability of, 168–169, 178; triangulation in, 172–173; in United States, 176, 178; between women, 195. *See also* oppression; prejudice
Rambo, 21
rape, 17, 25–26, 126, 145, 169; Central Park jogger case, 183, 221n14; fantasies of, 58; New Bedford case, 182

Reagan, Ronald, 17, 171, 176
Reage, Pauline, 23, 44, 58, 119, 151
Reich, Wilhelm, 86–87, 168, 171, 174, 188, 193, 208–209
Reichian theory, 4, 11, 188
Reik, Theodore, 83
René (*The Story of O*), 46, 52, 53, 57, 58, 62, 65, 74, 151
Reproduction of Mothering, The (Chodorow), 78–79, 147–153, 191
revolution, 4, 5
Rich, Adrienne, 207
Rich, Matty, 184
Rieder, Jonathan, 172–173
Rollins, Judith, 104–105, 195
Rules of Sociological Method (Durkheim), 159
Rumania, 4–5

Sacher-Masoch, Leopold von, 19, 20, 44, 84
Sade, Marquis de, 19–20, 44, 84, 168
Sadeian Woman, The (Carter), 19
sadism: and capitalism, 108–110, 112, 114, 116, 118, 122, 123, 203; dominant, 90–92, 101, 123, 150, 151, 162, 163, 164, 169, 182, 195; and male aggressivity, 75, 127; and men (*see* men, and sadism); and object relations theory, 78–79, 80, 81–82; and power, 110, 114, 139; and prejudice, 156; and socialization, 126; subordinate, 90, 91, 107, 150, 152, 169, 177, 180, 182, 195, 196. *See also* sadist
sadist: and anger, 192; dependency of, 48–49, 51, 55–57, 58, 59–60, 61, 62, 63, 65, 78, 80, 81, 92, 112, 122, 133, 134, 137, 139, 145–146, 167, 190, 192, 204 (*see also* sadomasochism, and dependency); and disapproval in the mode of approval, 56, 65, 110, 112–113; and domination, 46–48; independence of, 190; resistance craved by, 50, 56, 106, 110–111, 114; and sexuality, 47; and Weber's Protestant, 107, 151. *See also* sadism
sadomasochism: in all of us, 165–167, 184, 188, 213; and anger, 165; characteristics of, 55–56, 97; conditions and limits in, 5, 6, 96, 117, 215*n*2; and conscious awareness, 213; criteria for, 3–6; and dependency, 3, 69, 74, 189, 195, 196, 197 (*see also* masochist, dependency of; sadist, dependency of); and the economy, 39–40; effectiveness of, 171–172; and gender, 27, 45, 53, 54, 83; hierarchical division in, 46, 55–56, 97, 129, 130, 172, 189; in historical context, 4–5, 16, 30, 31, 32, 39, 41;
and individualistic psychotherapy, 208–209; interest of modern society in, 10, 20, 26, 30, 39 (*see also* sexual sadomasochism, cultural interest in); literature of, 17–18, 28–30, 31, 140–142, 200 (*see also* sexual sadomasochism, literature of); paradoxes of, 56, 139, 189, 204 (*see also* sexual sadomasochism, paradoxes of); and personal/political transformation, 205–214; postmodern, 179–180, 181, 182; and power, 31, 38, 106, 139, 146; and problem of recognition, 65, 70–74, 78, 143, 169, 170, 189, 197, 202; and punishment, 5–6, 131, 145 (*see also* sexual sadomasochism, and punishment); and rebellion, 144, 196 (*see also* masochist, resistance of); roots of, 3, 15, 18, 26, 82–88, 132–133, 138, 192, 197, 211 (*see also* gender and sadomasochism; object relations theory); and sex (*see* sexual sadomasochism); and sexual repression, 193–194; and society, 2, 4–5, 15, 17–18, 43 (*see also* social sadomasochism; United States); symbiosis in (*see* symbiosis); systems of, 184–185; the term, 9–10, 19; transformability of, 4, 36, 38–39, 52, 129, 134, 147, 161, 163, 165, 178, 190, 193, 194, 195, 213 (*see also* sexual sadomasochism, role reversal in); as transhistorical and universal, 41, 211–212; triangulation in, 168, 172; as unconscious to individuals or groups, 163, 190; in United States (*see* United States, sadomasochism in); and the workplace (*see* capitalism; work and the workplace). *See also* masochism; masochist; sadism; sadist; sexual sadomasochism; social sadomasochism
sadomasochistic sex. *See* sexual sadomasochism
sadomasochistic society. *See* social sadomasochism
Sagarin, Edward, 159, 160
Salomon Brothers, 105, 110
SAMOIS, 23, 45, 62, 152
Sandinistas, 171, 176
Sapphistry (Califia), 216*n13*
Sartre, Jean-Paul, 69, 134, 174, 189; on anti-Semitism, 160–165, 167, 168, 171, 172, 181; on sadomasochism, 41, 219*n11*; treatment of women by, 166
Schad-Somers, Suzanne, 75, 79–80
Schaeffer, Brenda, 140, 141
scientific management, 118–119, 121
Second Sex, The (Beauvoir), 7, 131–136
Second Shift, The (Hochschild), 219*n7*
Seductions of Crime, The (Katz), 164

Severin (*Venus in Furs*), 45, 46, 47, 48, 51, 60, 61, 91, 127
sexism, 24, 133, 161, 165, 183; and projection, 171; and racism, 169. *See also* patriarchy; prejudice
Sex-Pol (Reich), 86
sexual harassment, 95, 126
Sexual Politics (Millett), 129–130
sexual sadomasochism, 1, 5, 10, 30, 40–42, 43, 69, 97, 187–188, 200, 201; as challenge to or parody of social sadomasochism, 2–3, 25–26; characteristics of, 49, 55–56; cultural interest in, 19–24, 32; films on, 21; gender in, 45, 53; literature of, 44–46, 47, 50, 51–52, 53, 54–55, 57, 58, 60–62, 65, 74, 91, 119, 127; as an ongoing process, 49–50, 52–53, 54, 56, 63, 65–66; paradoxes of, 49, 50, 51, 56, 59, 62–63, 65, 66, 116; patterns of, appearing in nonsexual relationships, 53–54; and power, 44, 45–49, 50, 55–56, 57, 61–62, 63, 65, 67, 91, 216n13; and punishment, 47, 48, 50–51, 54, 56, 58; role of sexually repressive society in, 47; role reversal in, 50–52, 61–62, 63, 78, 83–84, 90, 168; sexual import of, 47; symbiosis, in, 48, 50, 56, 92, 217n9; and television, 21–22; termination of dynamic in, 54–55, 56, 65, 67, 116–117. *See also* masochism; masochist; sadism; sadist
sexuality, 43–44, 127, 211; and repressiveness, 47, 212
Sidel, Ruth, 21
social sadomasochism, 12, 18, 24, 26, 32, 41, 70, 212; case studies of, 197, 202–205; causes of, 198; and dependency, 198–199, 200–201; hierarchy in, 201; and individual sadomasochism, 191, 194–195; and new paradigms necessary, 205–208, 210–211; and punishment, 199–200; and rebellion, 196, 197; symbiosis in, 200; transformability of, 193, 195, 197, 203; in United States, 198, 202
South Africa, 173, 174, 197
Soviet Union, 17, 205
Stalinism, 4–5, 195, 202, 203
Stallone, Sylvester, 21
Stephen, Sir (*Story of O*), 52, 53, 54, 57, 58, 62, 65, 74, 91, 151
Story of O, The (Reage), 23, 44, 47, 48, 51, 53, 54, 62, 119; role reversal in, 52, 151, 152. *See also* O
Straight Out of Brooklyn, 184–185
Survival in the Office (Durbin), 113
Surviving at the Top (Trump), 105

Swann, Charles (*Remembrance of Things Past*), 7, 9, 60–61
symbiosis, 182; and capitalism, 94, 105, 117, 119, 122; and object relations theory, 76–78, 81–82, 134, 190, 217n9; in sadomasochism, 48, 50, 56, 92, 189, 197, 200, 217n9; social, 39, 92, 106, 117, 119, 122, 138, 203, 217n9; women and, 137, 149, 150, 151, 152

Taylor, Frederick, 118. *See also* scientific management
Taylorism. *See* scientific management
Terrifying Love (Walker), 145
Thomas, Clarence, 95
Three Essays on Sexuality (Freud), 19, 83, 85, 127
Tie Me Up, Tie Me Down, 21, 138
Top Executive Performance: 11 Keys to Success and Power (Cohen and Cohen), 113–114
Torres, Joan, 29, 140, 141, 145
Trump, Donald, 105
Turner, Frederick, 174
Twin Peaks, 22

United States, 16–17; capitalism in, 32, 122, 202, 213–214; conservativism in, 32, 197, 213–214; crime in, 160, 175, 176–177, 178, 180, 221n11; as culture of narcissism, 37, 200; effects of feminist movement in, 30–31; ideology of, versus communism, 202–203; individualism in, 112, 191, 198, 199, 200, 201; media coverage and sadomasochism in, 178–180, 181, 182–183, 196, 221n14; new paradigms necessary, 206–208; otherness in, 174–178; as patriarchal society, 202 (*see also* patriarchy); prejudice in, 156, 171, 176; racism in, 176, 178; rape of black women in, 169; recession in, 96, 175; sadomasochism in, 10, 126, 158, 198–199, 200, 201, 202 (*see also* social sadomasochism); sadomasochistic sex in, 20–21; seventeenth century, 174; war on drugs in, 176, 178; War on Poverty in, 181; and welfare capitalism, 121

Vance, Carol, 23
Venus in Furs (Sacher-Masoch), 19, 44, 46, 47, 57, 60, 62; role reversal in, 45, 51–52, 91, 127
Vietnam and Vietnamese, 17, 175, 178

Wacquant, Loic, 177, 181
Walker, Lenore, 145, 146
Wall Street, 96, 105

Wanda (*Venus in Furs*), 45, 46, 47, 51–
   52, 57, 60, 91, 142
WAP. *See* Women Against Pornography
Weber, Max, 12, 99, 100, 101, 106, 129;
   and Protestantism, 7, 107, 108, 109,
   151, 171, 194, 214
Weimar Republic, 16, 21, 40, 174, 178
Western Electric Company, 119, 121
White Racism: A Psychohistory (Kovel), 169,
   179
Why Can't Men Open Up? (Naifeh and
   Smith), 29, 142
Wild at Heart (Lynch), 21
Wild Orchid, 21
Willis, Ellen, 23
witchcraft, 159, 160, 161
women, 30, 121, 197; battered, 145–146,
   196; dependence of, 27, 137–138,
   140, 141, 142, 145, 153; and domesticity, 130–131, 219n7; and feminist
   movement, 31 (*see also* feminist movement and feminists; feminist theory);
   independence of, 137–138, 142, 143–
   144, 145, 153; individuation of, 149,
   151–152, 190–191; and masochism,
   28, 29, 58, 125, 127, 128, 129, 135–
   137, 139, 140–141, 143, 146, 147,
   150, 219n4 (*see also* gender and sadomasochism); and mothering, 147–153,
   191; and nature, 130–131; and rac-

ism, 195; and sadism, 126–127, 195;
   and sadomasochism, 3, 33; sexuality
   of, 23, 58; socialization of, 126, 132–
   133, 137, 138 (*see also* gender and
   sadomasochism); and symbiosis, 137,
   149, 150, 151, 152
Women Against Pornography, 23
*Women on the Verge of a Nervous Break-
   down*, 144
Women Who Love Too Much (Norwood),
   18, 28, 31, 140
work and the workplace, 2, 11, 12, 40;
   and alternative paradigm, 207; and
   changes in labor composition, 103; dependency in, 32, 60, 92, 94, 95, 103–
   104, 105, 106, 116, 117, 142; and
   emotional labor, 103–104, 105; and
   independence, 142; and powerlessness, 38; and sadomasochism, 1, 18,
   24–25, 33, 93–94, 104, 105–106, 113,
   114, 115–116, 155, 156, 157, 158,
   211; split between good and bad, 142–
   143; symbiosis in, 105, 117. *See also*
   capitalism
Working Girl, 136

xenophobia, 24

Zelig, 106